India's Silicon Plateau

Development of Information and Communication Technology in Bangalore

India's Silicon Plateau

Development of Information and Communication Technology in Bangalore

R.C. Mascarenhas
The University of Melbourne
Melbourne
Australia

Orient BlackSwan

Contents

List of Tables

ORIENT BLACKSWAN PRIVATE LIMITED

Registered Office
3-6-752 Himayatnagar, Hyderabad 500 029 (A.P.), India
e-mail: centraloffice@orientblackswan.com

Other Offices
Bangalore, Bhopal, Bhubaneshwar, Chennai,
Ernakulam, Guwahati, Hyderabad, Jaipur, Kolkata,
Lucknow, Mumbai, New Delhi, Patna

First Published 2010

ISBN 978 81 250 3708 8

Typeset by
Le Studio Graphique, Gurgaon 122 001
in Arno Pro 11/13

Printed at
Aegean Offset Printers
Greater Noida, India

Published by
Orient Blackswan Private Limited
1/24 Asaf Ali Road
New Delhi 110 002
e-mail: delhi@orientblackswan.com

Introduction

In adopting an import-substitution industrial development strategy in its early post-Independence phase, India's central government channelled scarce resources towards basic industries resulting in the creation of a science and technology (S&T) infrastructure and several elite institutions of higher education. In implementing that strategy, it appeared to favour the Mysore region (incorporated into Karnataka with the reorganisation of states on a linguistic basis), already known for its educational and industrial development prior to independence, as a suitable location for several defence related industries such as aerospace, machine tools, electronics and telecommunication equipment. In the area of information and communication technology (ICT), however, growth was both gradual and uneven although policy formulation had started as early as the 1960s. Following liberalisation in the 1990s, that impressive institutional base, apart from producing advanced manufacturing capability, helped to fuel the explosion in computer software in certain regions. While the aim of a development strategy in a pluralist democracy like India is to promote the national economy as a whole, it is possible for certain areas, owing to resource endowments and historical advantages, to benefit more from such a strategy than others. The climate of the 1990s enabled those states that were industrially advanced to utilise the opportunity offered by the central government to explore new avenues such as ICT and move further ahead.

A highly complex society steeped in tradition, India is also held as a model of a democratic political system which adopted state intervention to develop the foundation of what has turned out to be a knowledge economy. The Nehruvian model of development, which started India on the path to leapfrogging its way to a predicted position as the next knowledge super power (*New Scientist* 2005), has not escaped criticism from those who believe that India should have adopted the East Asian open market model. As I see it, analysts in their comparisons have adopted a narrow concept of development, largely economic. While economic growth is the objective of Third World (TW) development evidenced by the constant focus on Gross Domestic Product (GDP), that concept has gradually changed to incorporate quality of life indicators influenced by the writings of Denis Goulet, Albert Hirschman and Amartya Sen. Taking a leaf out of their work, I view development as the transformation of a country from being a victim of circumstances to a stage where it can develop capability to manipulate its physical and social environment and thus assume some control of circumstances.

Political and administrative institutions may be central to the effective formulation and implementation of development policies, but their impact cannot be delinked from societal forces, where social embeddedness and social capital play an equally important role in response to programmes of development. In my critique of development studies, I question analysts who ignore a range of political and social factors which are basic to true development. Essentially, TW countries are more socially embedded than others, suggesting that behaviour and institutions are constrained by ongoing social relations. A recurring problem with studies in development is the adoption of a narrowly economic perspective which highlights some aspects at the neglect of others. To overcome such a narrow focus I adopt a more broad-based political economy approach, focusing on the development and capability of political and administrative institutions. It helps to explain why Bangalore, and why India, have had this measure of success when regions in many wealthier, better educated countries have failed to develop a competitive industry that is at the heart of the third industrial revolution.

To understand the importance of the interrelationships between the economy and society, I emphasize the need to direct attention to political, historical and institutional factors hitherto neglected in development studies. The political economy approach that I adopt attempts to overcome this lacuna by acknowledging the crucial role of the state in development. The state plays different roles in relation to the market. Essentially, these are complementary, not adversarial, and vary at different stages of development from country to country. However, their implementation in India through a regime of controls has allowed the bureaucracy extraordinary power without technical competence. Despite being viewed by advocates of liberalisation as an irritant to the functioning of markets, state intervention is crucial in TW countries, where markets are unwilling to invest in infrastructure. While governments fund universities and research institutes and offer promising opportunities through incentives, societies ought to develop institutional capability in order to generate new techniques and technological skills and adapt others so that they are relevant to their unique needs. India's deliberate policy of import substitution and its S&T infrastructure provided a strong indigenous foundation by bringing together universities, business and government. This 'triple helix', as Cooke (2002) termed it, together with the norms of reciprocity and trust, characterise social capital which can be developed at a local level to provide a solid foundation for growth.

To understand the national–local (central–state) link in the working of the triple helix, I examine the role of the Department of Electronics (DOE, 1970) and Electronics Commission (EC, 1971) in the development of information technology (IT). Apart from their positive enabling role, their firmness led to the exit of IBM in 1978, providing an unexpected boost to the domestic software industry. Within this policy environment, the state government (Karnataka) established KEONICS and Electronics City at Bangalore to encourage entrepreneurs in IT. Such timely intervention by the state government and its close working relationship with the National Association of Software Companies (NASSCOM) and research institutions such as the Indian Institute of Science (IISc) played a significant role in promoting Bangalore as the software capital of India. Further support came from the Science and Technology Parks of India (STPI) set up in 1989 which provided satellite communication and other facilities for software exporting companies. Apart from its science and technology infrastructure, Bangalore's attraction to both investors and professionals includes its quality of life, its cosmopolitan character, its openness and its climate. With rapid growth that image has suffered as the city copes with the demands for improved infrastructure, housing and education and other civic services/facilities.

The process of agglomeration of high technology in certain areas is akin to Marshall's industrial districts (1919), areas with a concentration of certain specialized products. Their revival in Germany and Italy, with the decline of mass production, led Piore and Sabel (1984) to term this the Second Industrial Divide, following Marshall's identification of industrial districts in the nineteenth century. While those industrial districts thrived on natural resources, the ones studied by Piore and Sabel are based on scientific knowledge and government support. The continuation of that phenomenon of agglomeration in the twenty-first century despite technological advances in transport and telecommunication and mobility of labour is an important aspect of this study.

ICT is categorised as a general purpose technology (GPT), an enabling or transforming technology rather like steam and electricity (Hubner 2005). Its influence on modern economies has been both dramatic and volatile leading analysts to label it the 'new economy'. An outcome of the new economy is the significance of complementary institutions like technology parks and elite universities that are present in high technology areas, demonstrating that economic growth stems from technological and institutional changes generated by government, universities and S&T parks.

While the foundations of the modern ICT sector in India were laid primarily by the government through the development of infrastructure and incentives, it then adopted policies to promote the private sector. Thus, in the 1990s, both the public and private sectors became involved in contributing to the dramatic growth of ICT. Investment in this technology tends to be concentrated in certain areas, and to aggravate inter-regional and intra-regional inequalities. If development is intended to alleviate inequality, in the case of ICT, however, one notes a growing digital divide. A major challenge facing countries is that key resources like scientific and creative knowledge are concentrated in certain areas, causing imbalances in the distribution of economic opportunity. Admittedly, a development model based on modern science and technology has failed to provide basic entitlements like universal primary education, health, clean drinking water and housing. Although it offers opportunities to many, the new economy can, apart from causing new inequities in the developing world, exacerbate the existing situation leading to the altogether new but aptly termed 'digital divide'. The task of reaching out to the disadvantaged, which is a huge challenge for policy makers in India, is explored in this study (Chapter 6).

To explain why the Bangalore region has retained its importance in the 'new economy', I draw a distinction in this study between codified knowledge, which is in the form of designs and blueprints and is easily transferable, and tacit knowledge, which is identified with specific individuals and is, therefore, difficult to transfer. This distinction between types of knowledge helps to understand how regions continue to prosper despite the growing pressure of globalisation. Bangalore's concentration of high-tech industries demonstrates that codified knowledge can be transferred globally with ease in comparison to tacit knowledge which, because of its sticky properties, requires spatial proximity.

In my study of Bangalore's emergence as the 'Silicon Plateau' (Saxenian 2002), I adopt a historical approach for tracing its development. A crucial factor here was the establishment of the IISc in 1911 at Bangalore and a university at Mysore where the education of scientists and engineers received high priority. Mysore's industrial development and other innovations in education and health placed that state ahead of other areas in the country offering a clue as to why it is now a leader in software technology (Chapter 7).

While examining the historical foundations, I take a look at the post-Independence growth of aeronautical and aerospace industries, major public investments in industries such as machine tools, telecommunication equipment, electronics for defence purposes and the establishment of a host of central government institutes such as the National Aeronautical Laboratory, Central Machine Tool Institute, Indian Space Research Organisation (ISRO), Institute for Avionics, Centre for the Development of Telematics (C-DOT), and the Centre for Development of Advanced Computers (C-DAC) (Chapters 2, 3 and 7), all of which have contributed to the growth of ICT. In the 1970s, Bangalore was home to thousands of skilled workers and technicians housed in colonies equipped with schools, hospitals, clubs and other facilities. In all probability, today's engineering graduates from this area are descendants of the workers and technicians of the 1970s. As Marshall would have said, technology is in the air in this region.

While recognising that liberalisation opened the Indian economy to foreign private investment in ICT, the fact that Bangalore became the focus of their investment is due, in large measure, to its network of S&T institutions, from which emerged highly trained human power, and its cosmopolitan character and tolerance towards outsiders, features that one associates with Mysore during the reign of the Wadeyars in the early twentieth century (Chapters 7 and 8). When one attempts to study why a particular area is successful in comparison with other areas within a country, one has to, apart from endowments (physical and economic), extend one's analysis to history and culture. Is there a unique 'Mysore culture' which explains the openness and cosmopolitan character of the state? In those early days, Mysore encouraged an open culture to attract qualified people to teach at the university, invited experts to develop its indigenous resources and sent bright young Mysoreans away on scholarships for further education. For purposes of this study, that was the first aspect, the laying of foundations for a modern industrial state; the second aspect is the post-Independence period (1950–80) when public sector industries were in the forefront of engineering design and innovation, thus creating both domain knowledge and engineering talent. Being the premier centre of that knowledge, Bangalore became the leader in IT in the 1990s, the third aspect to this study.

Open cultures generally benefit from external stimuli in the form of new technology and innovations, and such openness, has, owing to global competition, become more important in the case of high-technology industries. Similar to California, the economic strength of Bangalore is partly a result of a certain kind of 'social openness' allowing a permanent influx of human capital from outside and its successful integration. Such regions thrive on their social and technological diversity and heterogeneity. Bangalore's success is summed up in the three Ts: technology, talent and tolerance (Florida 2005). In this new global-local environment, Indian expatriates, once part of the Indian brain drain after establishing themselves abroad, have become the catalysts at 'Silicon Plateau'. In recent years, Bangalore has become the favoured destination with about 200 multinational development centres providing opportunities for expatriate Indians keen to return home. That process of development should offer deep insights to policy makers elsewhere.

As a political economist, I have, in this study, emphasised policy learning, timing in policy and policy sequencing as vital to understanding the development of ICT in India. In tracing its policy, I have become convinced that 'the critical thing to understand is not where the seed comes from, but what makes the soil fertile' (Kingdon 1984).

Why Study This Region

To this study, I bring my long-standing interest in technology and industrial development, as well as my personal association as a third-generation Mysorean. During 2003–2005, I undertook three visits to the field for research and data collection. For historical aspects of the old Mysore State, I found Hayavadana Rao's *Mysore Gazetteer* (1929 edition) an outstanding source. Two recent studies, James Heitzman (2004) and Janaki Nair (2005) offer information specific to Bangalore. Other historical sources were located at the Bangalore Public Library and the Mysore University Library. If there is one name that stands out in the history of the state, it is that of Bharat Ratna Sir M. Visvesvaraya. I was fortunate to establish contact with his niece, Mrs S. Krishnamurthy, who kindly permitted access to material in her possession. My thanks to her. My insight into old Mysore was further enhanced through conversations with Nitoor Srinivas Rao, since deceased, former Chief Justice of the Mysore High Court and India's first Vigilance Commissioner who, despite advancing years, generously spent time with me.

In 2003, I was fortunate to be based at Dhvanyaloka, Mysore, a residence for scholars set up by Professor C. D. Narasimhaiah, now no more, whom I had known since my university days. While it offered the right environment for me to recollect my formative years in that city, I also had several interesting discussions with him during that visit. I spent long hours with Dr T. S. Satyan, a renowned photojournalist (who passed away on 13 December 2009), exchanging views on old Mysore. During subsequent visits, I stayed at the Administrative Training Institute which provides excellent facilities for visitors including a good library. I am grateful to these institutions for allowing me access to their facilities.

While historical aspects are vital to understanding the present, the links are not always easily visible. To understand recent developments, I discussed aspects of this work with officials from Bharat Electronics (BEL), Indian Telecommunication Industries (ITI), C-DOT, Indian Institute of Information Technology (IIIT) and the IISc. During my visit in 2004, I had the opportunity to interview Dr Srikantan, who had worked for Electronics Corporation of India Limited (ECIL) in its early days and pioneered the development of the first computer in India in the 1960s. Interviews were also held with people at KEONICS, who had set up Electronics City in Bangalore, and the staff at the STPI. While visits to the field have been extremely useful, I have also relied extensively on published research on information technology. In this connection I must acknowledge the work of Ananda Parthasarathy of *The Hindu* whose coverage of new developments in IT has been of great assistance.

In the rest of this study I intend to elaborate on some of the issues raised in the introduction. Following is a schematic presentation of the chapters covering the study.

In Chapter 1, I explore the theoretical framework based on studies of development while focusing on the role of state intervention. I discuss the approaches I adopt, in particular the comparative political economy of institutions. I also review the work of other social scientists in the area.

Following Independence, the Government of India launched a major programme of scientific and industrial development under the leadership of Prime Minister Jawaharlal Nehru, which is covered in Chapters 2 and 3. While Chapter 2 analyses policies in S&T, Chapter 3 examines the role of the state in industrial and technological development.

Chapter 4 evaluates India's policy in computer technology starting with the mid-1960s, a policy that was heavily geared towards a self-reliant industrial strategy where the state played a dominant role in promoting computer hardware. It discusses the important role played by public undertakings such as BEL, Computer Maintenance Corporation (CMC) and ECIL set up between the 1950s and 1970s.

Chapter 5 examines the influence of policies enacted specifically for the development of ICT, as well as other policies that have had an indirect impact on the development of related technologies. These include the establishment of C-DOT, liberalisation of the telecommunication policy, advancement in space technology and special benefits for the export of software, setting up of science and technology parks and encouragement of foreign private investment.

Chapter 6 is an evaluation of the response of the software industry to liberalization in terms of the growth of the industry in the 1990s. A key issue here is whether Bangalore could have responded to liberalization without the pool of qualified manpower and the infrastructure that had been built up as a result of earlier policies of both the state and central governments. Areas discussed in detail are the use of ICT in business and government, why the software industry became export-oriented, overcoming the digital divide and the backlash caused by the growth of outsourcing.

Chapter 7 provides a historical background focusing on cultural, educational, industrial and political development from the early years of the twentieth century to independence in 1947 when the erstwhile princely state of Mysore was integrated with the rest of India. In 1956 the state was enlarged incorporating contiguous Kannada speaking regions, and in 1973 it was re-named Karnataka. Our study is confined to the areas under the old Mysore state, more particularly Bangalore, its industrial heartland.

Chapter 8 discusses the emergence of Bangalore as the software capital of India and identifies some of the distinctive characteristics that have attracted investment from domestic and multinational sources. It also looks at the role of the state government in that process and examines the different institutions that have supported the development. I will try to explain why the boom in IT has occurred in Bangalore and not elsewhere. In Chapter 9, the conclusion, I attempt a summary of the study.

I acknowledge my association as a Principal Fellow in the Department of Political Science, The University of Melbourne, which provides me with access to library and office facilities. In principle I do not seek any funds for my research; I meet my travel and other costs personally. My main support in undertaking this study is my wife Iris, who, apart from accompanying me on my fieldwork, brings to my work her meticulous editing. I would also like to acknowledge the encouragement I receive from my daughters, Antara (who co-authored a conference paper with me in 2005) and Arati, and my son-in-law, Steve. My sincere thanks to them.

I must express my sincere thanks for the painstaking effort put in by the reviewer in reading through the manuscript and making helpful suggestions. As a result, the manuscript has undergone some structural changes. I found Janaki Nair's (2005) study of Bangalore, referred to by the reviewer, useful in that it provides a different perspective from usual urban studies and offers a better insight into the problems of a fast changing city.

For the final shape of this study special thanks are due to Suranjan Roy of Orient Blackswan who brought to the task his special skills of editing and constantly reminded me of the need to keep in mind the reader's perspective.

List of Abbreviations

ADA	Aeronautical Development Agency
AEC	Atomic Energy Commission
AICTE	All India Council of Technical Education
ALH	Advanced Light Helicopter
APDP	Accelerated Power Development Programme
AVATAR	Any Where Any Time Advance Reservation
BALCO	Bharat Aluminium Company Ltd.
BARC	Bhabha Atomic Research Centre
BATF	Bangalore Agenda Task Force
BEL	Bharat Electronics Limited
BITES	Board for Information Technology Standards
BOSS	Burn-Out Stress Syndrome
BOT	Build, Operate and Transfer
BOW	Bharat on Wheels
BPCL	Bharat Petroleum Corporation Ltd.
BPO	Business Process Outsourcing
BSNL	Bharat Sanchar Nigam Ltd.
BT	Biotechnology
CAG	Comptroller and Auditor General
CBI	Central Bureau of Investigation
C-DAC	Centre for Development of Advanced Computers
CDMA	Code Division Multiple Access
C-DOT	Centre for the Development of Telematics
CEDT	Centre for Electronic Development and Technology (of IISc)
CET	Common Entrance Test
CGI	Computer Graphics Imaging
CIVIC	Citizens Voluntary Initiative for the City
CLIK	Consortium of Electronic Industries in Karnataka
CLIP	Clinical Information Processing Platform
CMC	Computer Maintenance Corporation

CMM	Capability Maturity Model
CMTI	Central Mechanical Training Institute
CNC	Computerised Numerically Controlled Machines
CPU	Central Processing Unit
CRL	Computational Research Lab
CSC	Common Service Centres
CSO	Central Statistical Organisation
CSIR	Council of Scientific and Industrial Research
DARE	Defence Avionics Research Establishment
DOE	Department of Electronics
DOS	Department of Space
DOT	Department of Telecommunication
DRDO	Defence Research and Development Organisation
DSP	Digital signal processing software
DTH	Direct-to-home (broadcasting)
EC	Electronics Commission
ECIL	Electronics Corporation of India Ltd.
ERNET	Education and Research Network
ERP	Enterprise Resource Planning
ESC	Electronics and Software export promotion Council
ETT	Electronics Trade and Technology Group
EVM	Electronic Voting Machines
FBR	Fast Breeder Reactor
FCV	Flue-cured Virginia Tobacco
FERA	Foreign Exchange Regulation Act
FICCI	Federation of Indian Chambers of Commerce and Industry
FPD	Flat Panel Industry
FW	First World
GDM	Global Delivery Model
GDP	Gross Domestic Product
GNP	Gross National Product
GIR	Geographic Indication Registry
GIS	Geographic Information System
GNSS	Global Navigation Satellite System
GPS	Global Positioning System
GPT	General Purpose Technology
GSG	Global Software Group
GSMC	Global Service Management Centre

GTRE	Gas Turbine Research Establishment
HAL	Hindustan Aeronautics Limited
HCDC	High-speed data communication
HCL	Hindustan Computers Limited
HMT	Hindustan Machine Tools
HPCL	Hindustan Petroleum Corporation Ltd.
HTL	Hindustan Teleprinters Limited
IAF	Indian Air Force
IARI	Indian Agricultural Research Institute
ICAR	Indian Council of Agricultural Research
ICICI	Industrial Credit and Investment Corporation of India
ICNDT	International Committee for Non-Destructive Testing
ICT	Information and Computer Technology
IGCAR	Indira Gandhi Centre for Atomic Research
IIDC	Intel India Design Centre
IIHT	Indian Institute of Hardware Technology
IIIT	Indian Institute of Information Technology
IISc	Indian Institute of Science
IIT	Indian Institute of Technology
ILI	Infosys Leadership Institute
iMFAST	Integra Micro Financial Applications Secure Terminal
INVITE	Initiative to Nurture a Vibrant IT Ecosystem
IPPs	Independent power producer
IRCTC	Indian Railways Catering and Tourism Corporation
ISRO	Indian Space Research Organisation
IT	Information Technology
ITES	Information Technology Enabled Services
ITES	Integrated Train Enquiry System
ITI	Indian Telephone Industries
ITI	Indian Telecommunication Industries
ITC	Indian Tobacco Company
ITP	International Technology Park
ITPL	International Technology Park Limited
KEONICS	Karnataka Electronics Development Corporation
KPO	Knowledge Process Outsourcing
LCA	Light Combat Aircraft
LSP	Local Service Provider

MAIT	Manufacturers' Association of Information Technology
MEMS	Micro electromechanical sensors
MNC	Multinational Corporation
MPP	Massive parallel processing
MSD	Mental Stress Disease
MSSRF	M. S. Swaminathan Research Foundation
MTNL	Mahanagar Telephone Nigam Limited
NADA	National Aeronautical Development Agency
NASDAQ	National Association of Security Dealers Automated Quotations
NASSCOM	National Association of Software Companies
NCDCT	National Centre for Software Development in Computing Technology
NCST	National Committee on Science and Technology
NDDB	National Dairy Development Board
NDE	Non-destructive Evaluation
NEGAP	National E-Governance Action Plan
NGN	Next GenerationNetworks
NIC	National Informatics Centre
NICNET	National Informatics Center Network
NIIT	National Institute of Information Technology
NIXI	National Internet Exchange of India
NKC	National Knowledge Commission
NMITLI	National Millennium Indian Technology Initiative
NOC	Networks Operations Centre
NPOL	National Physical Oceanographic Laboratory
NSERF	National Science and Engineering Research Foundation
NTTF	Nettur Technical Training Foundation
ODC	Offshore Development Centre
OOS	Occupational Overuse Syndrome
OSI	Optimal Solutions Integration Inc
PCO	Public call offices
PFBR	Prototype Fast Breeder Reactor
POTS	Plain Old Telephone Services
PSI	Processor System Incorporated
PSP	Procurement Solutions Provider
PTIC	Public Tele-Information Centre

PURA	Providing Urban Facilities in Rural Areas
PWR	pressurised water reactor
R & D	Research and Development
RCI	Rehabilitation Council Of India
RD&E	Research, development and engineering
RFID	Radio Frequency Identification
RISC	Reduced instruction set chip
RUP	Rational Unified Process
SAC-PM	Science Advisory Committee to the Prime Minister
S & T	Science and technology
SCL	Semiconductor Complex Limited
SCM	Supply Chain Management
SDPA	Software Development Promotion Agency
SEB	State Electricity Board
SEI	Software Engineering Institute
SEZ	Special Economic Zone
SPV	Solar photovoltaic cell
SRE	Space capsule Recovery Experiment
STD	Subscriber Trunk Dialling
STPI	Science and Technology Park(s) of India
STQC	Standardisation, Testing and Quality Certification,
TDC	Technical Development Council
TDICI	Technology Development and Information Company of India
TEA	Tirupur Exporters Association
TERI	The Energy Research Institute
TECSOK	Technical Consultancy Services Organisation of Karnataka
TI	Texas Instruments
TIFAC	Technology Information and Forecasting Assessment Council
TIFR	Tata Institute of Fundamental Research
TNC	Trans-national corporation
TRAI	Telecom Regulatory Authority of India
TSP	Technological Services Provider
TW	Third World
UIDAI	Unique Identification Authority of India
VC	Venture Capital
VKC	Village Knowledge Centre

VPT	Village Public Telephones
VSNL	Videsh Sanchar Nigam Ltd.
VSAT	Very Small Aperture Terminals
WAN	(satellite-based) wide area networks
WSIS	World Summit on the Information Society

1

A Conceptual Framework

A Review of Issues

1.1 Introduction

Recent developments in information and communication technologies (ICT) have been dramatic, giving rise to the 'new economy', identified with the post-1995 acceleration in the rate of technical change and the development of the Internet. Frequent references to India as the next knowledge superpower are a recognition of developments in ICT, which I attribute to the Indian government's emphasis on promoting science, technology and higher education. This explosion in IT is not, however, to be equated with knowledge. While information is often confused with the knowledge required to develop economic or business strategies, knowledge actually relates to the ability of individuals and organisations to analyse a problem in the light of advances in the field of science. The success of countries in the new economy depends on their capacity to produce and use knowledge. Therefore, the emphasis is on individual knowledge workers, whose work in the 'new economy', although intensely personal, being related to ideas and knowledge, rather than products or services, is also dependent on a viable work environment.

In this context, Foray (2004) reminds us of the responsibility of experts and politicians to understand the importance of the public dimension of knowledge-based economies. As competitive markets are not suited to the job of producing and distributing knowledge, she claims that there is a clear economic rationale for public intervention so that a country can develop its capacity to create new knowledge and ideas. Accordingly, knowledge economies are characterised by the ability to create new knowledge. Describing the IT explosion as the Connectivity Revolution, Hinds (2003) writes, 'Its output is not visible; it gets embedded in the products of other activities: in the shape of their design; in the improved coordination of their production and marketing; in the reduced cost of their production; in the accelerated rate of innovation in all areas of science' (6). It therefore defies the prospect enjoyed by economists and business alike: quantification. Notwithstanding the comment of Solow that computers are seen everywhere except in statistics, there is no doubt that the impact of IT on the economy has resulted in the creation and growth of new industries (software) allowing for productivity gains, cost minimisation and encouragement to adopt new organisation models (Foray 2004).

Investment in IT in itself is not enough; progress lies essentially in the capacity that people acquire to manage extremely complex tasks from afar. Globalisation associated with the movement of funds, goods and services and the speed at which such transactions occur have virtually eliminated territorial borders and, in the context of global pressures and increasing influence of new technology, we are witness to a new dynamism in the economy. This dynamism is the result of greater openness of economies, arising out of ICT followed by deregulation and privatisation—a process when manufacturing enterprises base their operations in various locations to exploit comparative advantages. According to Cooke and Piccagula (2006), 'Regions have become key intersectors of different knowledge systems with global and local reach that requires superior policy guidance to that of the past for optimising both economic innovation and social integration' (16). In this context, the nation state which took the initiative to develop ICT and subsequently promoted the liberalisation of the economy is, in the view of some critics, becoming less important as an economic entity. In a global economy, 'nation states' have become unnatural units, while 'region states', based on economically functional rather than political boundaries, are the right size and scale to tap into the economy (Sugden and Wilson 2003, 16).

While regions may have an advantage, funds necessary for the development of high technology are likely to come from national governments which also retain the promotional and regulatory role. I argue, in this and other studies, that public institutions and policies, central and state, have played and will continue to play a vital role in promoting economic and political development (Mascarenhas 1999).

A crucial argument to support the emergence of regional or local development is the ease or difficulty in creating and disseminating knowledge fundamental to the functioning of the new economy. To comprehend that, we recognise that the knowledge that is transferred globally is codified knowledge, which, with ICT, has become cheaper and easier to transfer. The opposite occurs with tacit knowledge which, because of its sticky properties, requires spatial proximity for its creation and dissemination. Therefore, the proliferation of new economy strategies has not entailed the death of the significance of distance. On the contrary, it has contributed to the formation of new industrial clusters especially in high technology industries (Brunner in Hubner 2005, 153). The diminishing role of the nation state in a global economy forces governments to search for new ways and means to pursue their policy goals.

To understand the origin of current globalisation as distinct from old globalisation (cross border trade), Hinds links the connectivity revolution with the production process where enterprises can split operations on the basis of cost and efficiency. With this new ability to coordinate complex tasks from afar, production can be located according to the level of complexity, taking into consideration low to high value added production. The real impact of ICT lies in using the microprocessor and embedded software (in cars, appliances, machine tools, etc.) to enhance worker capability. Global companies have been quick to use the opportunity to locate their operations using this capability for horizontal coordination. All these innovations contributing to the connectivity revolution have resulted in an economy where knowledge and coordination have become sources of wealth (Hinds 2003, 13).

Governments in both the first (FW) and third worlds (TW) have selectively removed barriers to the entry of knowledge and capital in the 1980s and allowed areas with resources and skills to seek capital and markets beyond their immediate surroundings. Increasing mobility of skills and information as well as the fragmentation of production has encouraged local areas to offer incentives, eliminating the old core-periphery distinction identified with capitalist development (Saxenian 2006). Crucial to the post-liberalisation era of economic development, particularly in TW countries, is the impact of high technology, where skills and knowledge have acquired greater significance, giving areas such as Mysore (now Karnataka) in India, which were already advanced in technical education, a distinct advantage when compared to other areas (discussed in Chapter 7). Apart from the historical advantage gained prior to independence in 1947, Mysore state, it must be said, was fortunate, perhaps because of location or other reasons, to receive central government support in the form of major investments in public undertakings and in the establishment of national institutes in scientific and technological research.

Discussions on the new economy question the role of the nation state suggesting its replacement with networked forms of governance. Exploring this anomaly which involves an emphasis on local interconnectivity in an economy where global forces have triumphed, Cooke (2002) offers a clue. It lies in the emergence of a network model of development which is responsive, innovative and flexible and aided by proximity when compared to the hierarchical corporation of the Fordist-type. Scott and Storper (1992) characterise the post-1970s decline of Fordist mass production and the revival of flexible production on the one hand and globalisation of economic flows on the other as a contemporary puzzle (4). Accordingly, they see the world economy as a mosaic of specialised productive regions which are interdependent, presenting a double–faced view of economic development in a global context. To understand this puzzle, the authors employ the insights of the regulationist school of capitalist development as well as historical and institutional ideas from evolutionary economics (4–5).

That state institutions and policies have played an important role in promoting ICT development is widely acknowledged (Hinds 2003, Foray 2004 and Brunner in Hubner 2005). In the case of Mysore, decisions implemented during the 1950s and 1960s created a sound technological (knowledge) base, boosting its pre-Independence head start, explaining why Bangalore (part of the old Mysore state) has come to be known as Asia's Silicon Plateau. Although the nation state has become less significant with globalisation, in the case of IT in India, a state can progress to a limited extent only, because it has to rely to a great extent on the central government which can allocate resources and regulate services particularly telecommunication (see Chapters 2 and 3) This aspect is not restricted to India alone, although its federal system is geared towards giving the central government a greater role. Kogut (2003) notes that: '...this coincidence of the Internet and globalisation poses deep challenges to the historical institutional models that govern the exploitation of technologies and innovations within nations.... The Internet technology was global, but its economic and business development was molded in the context of prevailing national institutions' (2). The federal government by permitting duty-free import of computers helped Bangalore to 'leverage the technological strength of its Indian Institute of Science and invest in a digital network with a satellite port to the world' and thus 'created a dynamics by which Indian entrepreneurs and engineers found an institutional island within the regulated industry of a developing country' (454).

To understand the political and socio-economic inter-relationship in the development of IT in India, I adopt a comparative political economy approach which offers a broader perspective than that observed in current studies of IT which are deterministic. Boyer (2004) questions the deterministic argument by looking at ICT as a set of generic technologies which can be applied to a wide range of business activities and yet do not constitute a radical innovation capable of increasing productivity and profits across entire economies. As a general purpose technology (GPT), the ICT impact is less certain and takes time to adapt. The 'Solow Puzzle', which centres on why computer growth does not show in statistics, is understandable when one appreciates that companies need time to develop appropriate business models and the supporting infrastructure required by new technologies (see Chapter 6). Viewed from this perspective, ICT is no different from other GPTs that needed long periods of social learning to deliver expected results (Hubner 2005). ICT in India has taken several decades to develop with the government playing a vital role culminating in the convergence of computers and communication technology after the deregulation of telecommunication in 1994. While ICT offers tremendous potential for the transformation of the economy and society, its impact at this stage is unevenly spread across India and in parts of the world. This concern has naturally influenced the focus of my study.

Following this introduction, I explore various conceptual approaches to assist us to understand local development. In Section 1.2, I discuss the characteristics of the 'new economy'. In Section 1.3, I discuss modern institutionalist and evolutionary economists' approach to technological change centred around path dependency and lock-in. In Section 1.4, I examine agglomeration and in Section 1.5, I analyse the decline of Fordism and the emergence of flexible specialization where I introduce the Marshallian concept of Industrial Districts as central to the theory of local development. In Section 1.6, I discuss the puzzle of globalization as consistent with local development. Section 1.7 sums up the chapter.

1.2 The Knowledge or New Economy

The new techno-economic changes centred around IT with their impact on every aspect of behaviour throughout the economy and society have come to be identified as the knowledge economy or new economy (Foray 2004, Hubner 2005). Less easily defined but more easily distinguishable from the old economy because of the rapid pace of technological change, the new economy is characterised by the use of knowledge which helps to create new knowledge. It is characterised by innovation, a level of openness and tolerance, quality manpower willing to take risk, a high level of trust, the use of stock options as incentives, open access to encourage people with ideas to work in physical proximity and a vibrant entrepreneurship which brings together scientists and engineers with venture capitalists. Added to this is the vital role of government in funding universities, research institutes and the promotion of promising opportunities through a variety of incentives. This 'triple helix' is held together, as it were, by its social capital—'the expression of norms of reciprocity and trust between individuals and organisations that are embedded in a system of cooperation and ... belong, usually to a particular locality' (Cooke 2002, 11).

There are some reservations when one moves from the 'hard' factors which refer to technology, organisation and market forces, to 'soft' ones that are socio-cultural and institutional and difficult to quantify. Within the triple helix, separation between hard and soft factors is not easily done as one has to recognise the need to understand the inter-relationship between the three in policy settings. While the development of norms of trust and reciprocity are necessary for the generation of interactive actions, one must be aware of the prospect of inflexibility arising from the 'weakness of strong ties' (Granovettor 1985). Cooke (2002) highlights the inflexibility of the Swiss watch industry which was locked into its springs and jewels only to be outsmarted by the Japanese who pioneered the use of quartz to develop electronic watches.

Problems of inflexibility arising from lock-in are less common in the new economy, because of the reliance on social capital which is more extensive and intensive. It is extensive in that it reaches out to a 'wide spectrum of stakeholders, including basic research science as the knowledge capital which is the source of raw value at one pole and venture capital at the other...' It is intensive because 'many participants are rootless recent arrivals, who seek out economic communities within which to swiftly build economic and social relationships' (Cooke 2002, 109). Being an intangible and relational concept, social capital differs from physical, financial and human capital. The deliberate and planned approach that can be adopted in developing other forms of capital cannot be relied on in the case of social capital as trust and reciprocity are indirect outcomes of social relations and not 'primordial cultures and institutional dispositions' (Coenen and Asheim in Cooke and Piccaluga 2006, 93). As planned development of social capital is difficult, it is better to 'focus on collective learning and innovation processes in the triple-helix allowing social capital to be built along the way' (ibid.).

The new economy offers abundant opportunity arising, firstly, from the speed of reaction and creativity, and secondly, from the opportunity to operate in networks based on alliance and cooperation where size of operations is irrelevant. While Cooke (2002) claims that the 'new economy' creates imbalances in the distribution of economic opportunity, Hinds (2003), on the contrary, asserts that 'connectivity and its associated globalisation open more opportunities for the small companies in both developed and developing countries than for multinationals' (17). Further, he claims that 'connectivity has created the best opportunity that TW countries ever had to catch up with developed countries' (ibid., 19). However, there is the other major challenge to contend with: the concentration of key resources in certain areas which causes imbalances in the distribution of economic opportunity (Cooke 2000).

Preer (1992) and Scott (1993) refer to this phenomenon of the interaction of science and technology at a specific location resulting in new products and processes as the creation of 'technopolises'. Characterised by entrepreneurship and a large pool of scientific and technical manpower, the emergence of such technopolises is the result of dramatic developments in IT and related fields. At the core of each technopolis is an institution that creates new knowledge. 'The university or knowledge center functioning as a growth pole is a relatively new phenomenon and perhaps the most distinctive feature of the technopolis' (Preer 1992, 58).

Proximity to knowledge centres, the available pool of technical resources, venture capital and informal information flows carry the cumulative reinforcing effects of agglomeration. Such factors, typical of high-tech regions, encourage economies of agglomeration resulting from interactive factor costs and supportive public policies. 'Because of the geographical proximity of producers to one another, the velocity of circulating capital through the system is accelerated and this increases the advantages of agglomeration' (Scott 1993, 25). Agglomeration then is a process where there is a 'disposition of certain kinds of industries to concentrate locationally'. However, Saxenian (1994) considers such externalities to be insufficient to explain differences in performance between regions. She prefers to use the concept of industrial system or Herrigel's (1995) regional industrial order to understand how firms respond to changing markets and developing technologies. Such regional industrial orders are characterised by spatial proximity of industrial firms which rely on specialised information or skills or rapidly changing innovations. Production in a localised or specialised area occurs when there are certain characteristics identified with a technopolis.

A technopolis then is a new kind of regional economic development centred around knowledge, identified as high-technology. Each technopolis has a core technology or technologies, such as aerospace, semi-conductors, software, electronic equipment, bio-technology, etc. Certain agglomeration advantages develop in such a specialised technopolis when supplier and service firms emerge to provide services to a growing industry (Preer 1992). As the industry develops, downstream markets join the cluster and that growth gets reinforced by the attraction of specialized labour. Once that happens, 'local educational and research institutions collaborate with industry to develop programmes to meet the needs of industry. Universities thus develop national and international reputations for excellence in a specialized field of the region'.

By the late 1970s, studies of high technology regions in the US such as Silicon Valley (California) and Route 128 (Massachusetts) established the close association of such growth to the research universities of Stanford and MIT, respectively. Other contributory factors were an established infrastructure, a favourable climate and the prospects for a good life that attract high quality professionals. Such studies emphasized the importance of science-based organisations for the development of new technologies. Cooke's triple helix (2002) is evident in Mysore state in the early twentieth century when the research carried out by the IISc resulted in the successful extraction of sandal oil while the Sericulture Institute worked to promote Mysore silk. The factories set up by the government for the manufacture of these products earned Mysore an international reputation as the region's prized export earners, only to be overtaken by software in the 1980s (see Chapter 7).

1.3 Institutionalist and Evolutionary Economics Approaches to Technological Change

In this study, I adopt an inter-disciplinary approach, incorporating work in the comparative political economy of institutions in both industrialised and industrialising economies. In adopting such an approach, I recognise the vital role played by the state. Having earlier emphasised the relative capacity of societal institutions to manipulate their economic, physical and social environment (Mascarenhas 1999), I stress the need for the state to play an active role in promoting political and economic development by creating such institutions through active state intervention. If the purpose of development is to transform less developed societies by promoting industrialisation through the adoption of S&T, that process is dependent on the relative role of the state in the economy, whether it is limited to enforcing contracts and property rights or extended to a more active role in promoting industrial development. In the case of developing economies particularly, where the capacity of the private sector is limited, it is up to the government to develop appropriate policies of state intervention (ibid., 52).

The effectiveness of the state in promoting the growth and development of the economy, both private and public, rests on appropriate institutions. Institutions are set up by societies to establish order and this takes the form of rules and regulations for its citizens enforced by government. The term 'developing economies' conveys the idea that certain countries are in the process of evolving or building appropriate political and economic institutions to ensure stability and thus facilitate social and economic growth. However the very routines, customs, traditions and culture that contribute to social stability can become obstacles to economic change and may be transformed only in the event of a major upheaval.

Institutionalism is now seen as a useful framework for the analysis of socio-economic and political systems, arising from dissatisfaction with both neoclassical and Marxist analyses and greater reliance on contextually-based explanations in the social sciences (Barnes and

Gertler 1999, 9). Differences in economic and political institutions provide answers to variations among nations in their policies and economic performance (Mascarenhas 1996). In his comparative institutional evaluation of policies adopted by India, Brazil and South Korea to promote informatics capacity, Evans (1995) noted that these countries relied on the institutional resources available. 'Each had distinctive traditions of intervention, distinctive relations with the private sector, and distinctive organizational capacities' (105).

In studies of comparative national systems of capitalism (Mascarenhas 2002), the focus is on the impact that institutional advantages have on the performance of their economies. Economic growth in the medium term is governed by the ingenious coupling of technological and institutional changes and not, as mainstream economists claim, on technological progress exclusively (Hubner 2005). These studies focus on state versus market mechanisms of economic coordination and distinguish them as liberal or state-centred. Kogut (2003) asserts that it may be necessary to distinguish between the best configuration of institutions and practices, and attempts to explain 'the variety of institutional configurations that support particular innovations and productive capabilities' (45). Such an approach helps to explain regional variations wherein certain infrastructural factors promote certain technological developments (Herrigel 1996, Mascarenhas 2002).

The institutionalist approach draws from several strands or variants which have originated from 'technological choice and its consequences' (Barnes and Gertler 1999, 10) and is identified with evolutionary economists who adopt two ideas: 'path dependency' and 'lock-in'. Path dependency accepts 'that past decisions about technology will shape future ones, thus establishing a trajectory of development' (ibid., 11) whereas lock-in occurs when a decision about technology becomes irreversible, driven to that position by a strong positive feedback that has reinforced that initial choice. Once a technological advantage emerges, factors such as 'externalities, spillovers and untraded interdependencies render that advantage more advantageous over time' (ibid.).

Generally, we tend to be path-dependent because 'technologies are products of interdependent choices and interdependency means uncertainty, since we cannot determine exactly what others, upon whom our choices are dependent, will do' (Storper in Barnes and Gertler 1999, 37). Citing the practice of driving on a particular side of the road or the use of the querty keyboard even in the days of PCs, Storper explains that 'there are reasons why producers follow certain pathways'. Industry is characterised by technological spillovers, i.e., manufacturers build on each other's skills and knowledge. Firms then become open to external influences or decisions made outside their boundaries. In terms of sustaining local development, one has to acknowledge that innovative capabilities are generated through local communities that share a certain base of knowledge.

In the context of their complex social and historical backgrounds, it is difficult to proclaim the superiority of either market or state as the coordination mechanism (Nelson 2005). Hence the need to adopt a comparative historical approach to studies of development to counter the limitations of the economist's approach to development studies based on the rationality assumption which is useful for a limited range of issues in microtheory, but not to help us understand the process of economic change. It is through a process of development that a country can create the institutional variety to cope with complex activities.

Both path dependency and lock-in have been used by analysts of development to explain the sustained performance of high technology regions. The increasing emphasis on regions as centres of innovation and growth has led evolutionary economists (Nelson and Winter 1982) to contribute to institutional approaches by combining the importance of embeddedness with the geographical information necessary for success. Embeddedness of these industrial sectors is necessarily geographical; place and space enter into the very constitution of the industry (Barnes and Gettler 1999, 15). Granovettor's (1985) concept of social embeddedness also helps to highlight negative effects of lock-in like the inflexibility illustrated by Swiss watchmakers, adhering to time-bound methods, who were outmanoeuvred by the Japanese with their pioneering use of quartz-based electronics. The Swiss had become 'locked-in' to jewels and springs because of the 'weakness of strong ties' (Granovettor). Relationships based on the 'strength of weak ties' (Cooke 2000, 79) are easier when attempting to overcome lock-in. Regions can break away from the path by adopting new technology which offers new perspectives and institutional structures, thus giving less favoured regions the opportunity to depart from established development paths (Gertler in Fuchs and Shapira 2005).

1.4 Economic Agglomeration

Economists and other social scientists rely on the concept of external economies where producers share the costs of common external resources such as services, infrastructure and skilled labour pools. 'When these factors of production are geographically concentrated, firms gain the additional benefits of spatial proximity, or "economies of agglomeration"' (Saxenian 1994). Proximate location of firms encourages innovation, helps firms to sieze opportunities faster, to produce at lower costs and to respond quicker to market changes. Agglomeration economies thus accrue from access to workers with specialised skills and from intermediate inputs and services and technological spillovers. In his study of the behaviour of firms in a particular industry choosing to locate in certain areas where they can reap the benefits arising from proximity, McKendrick (in Kenney and Florida 2004) divides their operations into technological and operational. Based on his research on the disk drive industry in the United States, he concludes that a maturing industry appears to have separate locational requirements for its technological and operational aspects making it organise itself into a distinct geographic configuration (146). McKendrick is critical of theoretical models of agglomeration that fail to distinguish innovation from manufacturing and believes that 'there is little reason to think that the agglomerative forces enhancing innovation and those making operations more efficient are the same' (ibid., 147).

The phenomenon of industries locating and developing in proximity to each other and benefiting from externalities was recognised by Marshall (1919) who named them industrial districts. The industrial district, a nineteenth century form of industrial organisation which was overtaken by mass standardised production, has once again emerged as a form of flexible specialisation in response to the decline of mass production. Academic interest in them has been revived by Piore and Sabel's 1984 classic *The Second Industrial Divide,* followed by studies in regional development in Germany (Herrigel 1996), Italy (Beccatini 2002) and the US (Saxenian 1994). Such shifts in systems of production are marked by growing uncertainty in political and economic relations. Factors basic to the uncertainty, according to Wolfe (in Barnes and Gertler 1999), are the emergence of new IT, the phenomenon of globalisation which is increasing linkages and interdependence and the decline of Fordist methods of mass production. Apart from their impact on roles and relationships of governance at global, national and local levels of the economy and society, such changes have propelled the region into greater prominence. Such research interest has remained steady across the industrialised world since the 1980s, particularly in Italy and Germany (Beccatini 2002, Herrigel 1996) where small and medium sized enterprises have succeeded in surviving the pressures of large-scale mass production. It has grown further, with the focus of attention moving to Silicon Valley which has become a sort of model for the rest of the world (Saxenian 1994, 2006).

In an age dominated by global forces, it is intriguing to explore this interest in regions or areas. How and why does this trend continue in the face of globalisation? A possible explanation is that regional networks are innovative, responsive and flexible when compared to hierarchical corporations of the Fordist-type. Basically it is a fundamental shift from a centralised, vertically integrated model of business and government towards a more decentralised, horizontal and networked regional model. It offers the additional advantage of proximity. In the case of India, the partial shift in power from the centre to the states occurred after the liberalisation of the 1990s which was essentially a response of the governments at the national level to globalisation.

Exploring policy-related lines of reasoning and action relating to local or regional development in a knowledge economy, Cooke and Piccaluga (2006) conclude that the increasing variety of regional development policies arising from regions become key intersections of different knowledge systems with local and global reach and require superior policy guidance to optimise economic innovation and social integration. Accordingly, a regional economy is concerned with the production, distribution and consumption of goods and services in a particular geographical region while regional development involves the cultural, economic and social enrichment of a region and its people.

To explain why regions such as Silicon Valley and India's Silicon Plateau continue to attract resources and skills in a global economy, I adopt Polanyi's (1958) distinction between codified and tacit knowledge. Polanyi drew a distinction between codified (know that) and tacit (know how) knowledge based on the oft-quoted saying 'we can know more than we can tell'. Tacit knowledge resides in people, institutions or routines and is difficult to transport, memorise, recombine and learn. Given its sticky character, it is costly to transfer from one site to another in a usable form (Foray 2004). However, such difficulties can be overcome when the number of people possessing tacit knowledge is high. Besides, access to information that is less easily available (tacit) depends on developing complementary assets to develop and access such knowledge. In the case of developing countries, their development has to be largely through state intervention (Mascarenhas 1999). Accordingly, codified knowledge is easily transferred in the form of designs and blueprints and is therefore easily replicable. Tacit knowledge that remains with the individual can only be transferred through face-to-face interaction and is time consuming.

Indigenous sources of knowledge are generally compatible with existing local institutions. With liberalisation being advocated as 'one best way', any decision to adopt competitive approaches must take into consideration the ability of existing institutions to adapt to such policies. Likewise, policy makers must take into consideration the institutional capacity for absorption of new learning, particularly when existing tacit knowledge acts as an obstacle. The local level is thus critical to the transfer of tacit knowledge. While it encourages learning through interaction because of spatial proximity of actors, a common culture is shared by firms which facilitates social learning and becomes of critical advantage to firms operating in such networks. Similar arguments are raised in the adoption of innovative technology. The growth of IT has led to an upsurge in knowledge-intensive activities which have a distinct effect on economies.

1.5 Emergence of Flexible Specialisation

In *Comparative Political Economy of Industrial Capitalism* (2002), I critique the decline of the Fordist model of standardised mass production and categorise the post-Fordist phenomenon of flexible specialisation as alternative capitalism. Referring to it as the '*Second Industrial Divide*', Piore and Sabel (1984) predicted the emergence of a network of small firms in the form of industrial districts similar to the nineteenth-century industrial districts that existed prior to the first industrial divide (Mascarenhas 2002, 114).

According to Marshall (1919), 'When an industry has thus chosen a locality for itself, it is likely to stay there for long: so great are the advantages which people following the same skilled trade get from near neighbourhood to one another. The mysteries of the trade become no mysteries; but are as it were in the air, and children learn many of them unconsciously. Good work is rightly appreciated; inventions and improvements in machinery, in processes and in general organization of the business have their merits promptly discussed; if one man starts a new idea it is taken up by others and combined with suggestions of their own, and thus becomes the sources of further new ideas' (152–3).

Like the institutionalists, other social scientists have rediscovered the region by studying the industrial districts of Italy, Silicon Valley and Route 128, among others. When attempting to explain why localisation persists despite forces of dis-agglomeration, the oft-quoted 'mysteries in the air' is cited. According to Marshall, the knowledge and skills associated with guilds in nineteenth-century industrial districts remained in the territory tending to cluster or localise because of the constant market for skill. 'Therefore this sense of "mystery" takes us beyond ideas or information and starts to put some limits on where knowledge will flow and where it won't. Knowledge of the sort that is valuable in the Valley doesn't spread easily unless people are engaged in the skill, craft, or practices to which the knowledge applies' (Brown and Diguid in Chong-Moon Lee 2000, 22).

The concentration of favourable factors in an area such as natural resources, skilled labour and a salubrious climate encourages newcomers into that area while the very existence of firms in the same industry located in that area proves attractive for other firms. The self-augmenting process that occurs through these mechanisms helps to explain why so many multinational companies since the mid-1980s followed Texas Instruments in setting up development centres at Bangalore. By 2000, their number had exceeded 230. Depending on their ability to attract local talent, such centres contributed their R&D skills to develop a particular component for a new product. In the totality of functioning of global firms, their respective contributions towards a product are not generally identified, and the use of terms like 'cluster' or 'industrial district' in the literature does not explain this phenomenon as operations become increasingly dispersed globally.

In a knowledge-based economy, there is intensive interaction at the economic and technological levels bringing pressure on existing arrangements that have to be continuously reassessed. For the state, then, the focus needs to be on three areas: (1) entrepreneurial stimuli and investment coordination, (2) creative destruction management—solving problems associated with structural change, and (3) institution-building and bridging which involves shaping both regulatory and developmental policy frameworks and building cooperative organisational capabilities (Burlamaqui 2000).

The disposition of certain types of industries to concentrate in specialised areas leads to locational agglomeration like Marshallian industrial districts which were, in effect, geographical clusters of production activities. Such industrial districts facilitate job search and job matching because they are often surrounded by housing facilities for their workforce. Combined with availability of qualified people, a set of incentives included in government policies, and the existence of a network of institutions, such clusters can generate new knowledge and encourage new investments. Prospective investors and professionals rank different locales according to such qualities. Attributing the creation of successful industrial districts to a favourable environment, Marshall concluded: 'the secrets of the industry are in the air'.

1.6 Globalisation and Growth of High-Technology Regions

Small innovative firms continue to perform well in certain high-technology areas despite growing global forces because advances in ICT enable them to split operations according to cost and complexity and to coordinate them from afar. (Ann Markusen, 98–124 in Barnes and Gertler 1999, Hinds 2003). The work of Gourevitch et al. (2000) in the hard disk drive industry records two types of agglomeration, each playing a distinctive functional role. For example, Silicon Valley has a concentration of research, design, development and marketing, while component manufacture and assembly take place in other agglomerations like Singapore and South East Asia (310). On the basis of this study, the authors claim that 'the geographical disaggregation of the value chain has important implications for arguments about proximity and clustering in explaining location. These two kinds of clusters resulted from the interactive factor costs, supportive public policy, and agglomeration economies' (313).

Hinds (2003) points out that the separation of high value production, which is located in the United States where such skills abound, from the lower value production, which has been farmed out to the less skilled and lower-wage countries, is essentially a response to competition from East Asian economies. A case in point is Motorola which chose this two-track strategy to overcome competition and move towards a global outlook. While the coordinating of activities from afar has been facilitated by improved communication, that process has been completed only because of the technological leap that has lifted the productivity of local American production. A crucial factor therein is the development of the microprocessor and the small computer which have speeded up production. All of this has been possible because of the new technology which is a feature of the current trend in globalisation and is 'primarily a phenomenon of production rather than one of trade' (ibid.).

Following batteries, integrated circuits and memory, the flat panel industry (FPD) is the fourth essential hardware ingredient in the digital era. The high investments required for large-scale manufacture of FPDs are dependent on joint efforts among companies from several countries. 'The FPD industry was the first new manufacturing industry to fully emerge in a global economy defined by trade in knowledge rather than trade in physical products' (Murtha et al. 2001, 3). The FPD industry had to rely on knowledge creation which was tacit and not easily codified. 'The ability to share and recombine tacit knowledge, as well as explicit knowledge that remains verbal but not otherwise codified, depends in part on direct observation, interpersonal interaction, and demonstration, which in turn depends on proximity to events and other people.... Successful FPD companies recognised this in formulating plans to start up new production lines. Companies generally assigned many of the same engineers and operators as those who started up previous lines to 'wake up' new lines, especially when the lines incorporated new generation technology'. Proximity in itself is insufficient according to the authors as organisational processes are needed to recombine both tacit and explicit knowledge (ibid., 36).

Scott and Storper (1992) observe that there is a strong association with particular industrial agglomerations in the international division of labour. In any one of these, part or semi-assemblies are made in a local industrial network and supplied to plants in other locations and agglomerations. Such 'roundaboutness' can be both functional and spatial (15), their sustenance being dependent on appropriate institutional-regulatory structures being in place. These structures, generally referred to as technological-institutional systems, are viewed by regulationists as a regime of accumulation and a mode of social regulation (Mascarenhas 2002). Due to a variety of internal and external factors, such regimes of accumulation are sometimes confronted by a crisis which, like the decline of Fordist mass production, can only be handled by restructuring. The flexible production system that emerged from that transition in regimes gave the high-tech sector an opportunity to break away from the old mass production and to establish itself in new industrial spaces. In such places, 'a new dynamic of growth and local agglomeration was set in motion, creating poles of attraction for new high technology firms'. While such growth poles create specialised technological regions, there is a need to overcome uneven development resulting from globalisation and open markets.

Despite disagreement over the role of nations in a global economy, there is a clear acknowledgement on the local dimension to globalisation, prompting Sugden and Wilson (2003, 15–16) to suggest that localities should be used 'as important units of analysis', particularly because the sources of knowledge, viz., schools, colleges and universities, are locally based and because people communicate and learn by living in geographical proximity (ibid., 16). Illustrative of the above is the increase in the number of multinational companies setting up development centres in the area of IT in Bangalore.

In noting the importance of the locality as a unit of analysis in a globalised economy, there is a tendency to equate the new industrial district, a product of flexible production, with clusters. High-technology industries such as computers in Silicon Valley and Route 128 are characterised by technological dynamism and their commercial success. Coinciding with the decline of mass production, these firms rejected the post-war integrated model of manufacture of all components within the firm. Instead they created a network of sources for the supply of parts for the manufacture of computers such as the central processing unit (CPU) which includes a microprocessor and logic chips, an operating system and applications software, information storage products (disk drive, memory chips) input-output devices, power supplies and communication devices or networks to link computers. This feature of creating a network of suppliers in preference to in-house manufacture has to do with the need for flexibility for products with short life cycles. In other words, the design and manufacture of computers cannot be accomplished by a single firm; a variety of specialist firms need to collaborate. The close cooperation between the manufacturing firm and its principal suppliers that has become essential in the high technology competitive environment differs from the 'arm's-length relations of mass production systems in which suppliers manufactured parts according to specifications and competed against one another to lower price, and in which portions of production were subcontracted as a buffer against fluctuations in market demand, output and labor supply' (Saxenian in Kenney 2000, 148). This process of disintegrated manufacture typical of high-technology industries with high levels of collaboration and cooperation is a departure from conventional business practices.

On the basis of the above, one can question Porter's (1990) analysis of clusters, where the emphasis is given to competition and rivalry between firms because it distorts the view of trust and underplays the cooperative aspect of economic coordination in favour of competition (Cooke in Barnes and Gertler 1999). Further, Porter's illustration of the Dutch cut flower industry comes in for further criticism at the hands of Cooke, who considers it an inappropriate choice owing to its unique characteristics (59).

Using social embeddedness or social capital as a base, Evans (1995) developed the concept of synergy or network between public and private organisations. This synergy or complementarity is a network of ties that connects citizens and public officials across the public and private divide. In other words, networks which transgress the boundary between the public and private spheres are valuable social capital defined by Wolfe (in Barnes and Gertler 1999) as 'various features of the social organization of a region, such as the presence of shared norms and trust that facilitate coordination and cooperation among individuals, firms and sectors for their mutual advantage' (132).

The term 'social capital' has attracted multiple interpretations. In trying to understand the role of social capital in the functioning of Silicon Valley, Cohen and Fields (in Kenney 2000) distinguish it from Putnam's (1992) 'networks of civic engagement' (191). Claiming that it is 'vastly different', the authors state that social capital in the case of Silicon Valley 'can be understood in terms of collaborative partnerships that emerged in the valley owing to the pursuit by economic and institutional actors of objectives related specifically to innovation and competitiveness' (192). The networks of social capital in Silicon Valley involve interactions among institutions and instruments, such as the research universities, venture capital firms, business networks, labour markets, etc. Cooke (2002) extends the use of social capital in economic development to explore the role of civic entrepreneurs whom he sees as catalysts in the creation of local economy and community relationships, a view confirmed by Cohen and Fields (in Kenney 2000), who feel that the discussions centred around differences between regional economies have resulted in the resurfacing of Marshallian ideas in the social capital literature (198).

1.7 Conclusion

In this conceptual framework which offers a review of the literature on local development and related fields, I have sought, for analytical purposes, to break the chapter into distinct areas. However, I am aware of a significant overlap which cannot be easily overcome and realise that this is the price one pays for adopting an inter-disciplinary approach. It does however raise some important issues that will occupy us in subsequent chapters of this study. Having indicated in the introduction that I am exploring the development of IT in one area, Bangalore in Karnataka State, India, this conceptual chapter brings together work from comparative political economy, institutionalist and evolutionary economics and development studies.

This introduction to the study of local industrial development builds on the foundation of Marshall's industrial district. In doing that, it looks into two other areas covered in my analyses, the first being new industrial districts and the other, post-Fordist flexible specialisation. On this broad canvas of local development, a significant role is accorded to the underlying theme of the Marshallian industrial district which played such an important role in the first industrial divide and was revived in the second industrial divide heralding the emergence of flexible specialisation and the decline of Fordism. In the study of technology and industrial development in the 'new economy', Marshall emerges as a dominant figure, overshadowing both Smith and Keynes.

India has already achieved a remarkable level of development in the ICT sector. Considering its design-intensive human resources and the strength of its political and economic institutions, it would be appropriate for its leaders to adopt some strategic directions to utilise these advantages.

2

Science and Technology Policy

2.1 Introduction

Since achieving independence in 1947, India has, in its quest for development, given priority to the promotion of science and technology (S&T). A key part of this thrust is the establishment of S&T institutions to undertake basic and applied research so as to acquire greater self-reliance and develop indigenous sources of technology. Starting virtually from scratch India has, in a period of six decades, acquired a solid science and technology foundation. This includes the Atomic Energy Commission (AEC), Tata Institute of Fundamental Research (TIFR), Indian Space Research Organisation (ISRO), IISc, various national laboratories in different fields of fundamental and applied science and over two hundred universities. The existence of such a large S&T infrastructure has attracted several research and development (R&D) laboratories of high-tech international companies which employ qualified and capable Indians to carry out industrial and technological research. Research is generally distinguished either as pure or applied. Pure or fundamental research, as carried out by Bohr for example, aims at producing knowledge which gives a fundamental understanding of the laws of nature or society. Applied research, as carried out by Pasteur, say, aims at producing knowledge which can be used to solve practical problems. While such analytical distinctions are possible in theory, in real life situations, as in bio-technology, such distinctions become blurred. Discussing Pasteur's Quadrant, Stokes (1997) asserted that there is considerable overlap between the pure and applied, as Pasteur worked practically and theoretically at the same time. This dichotomy between basic and applied is indistinguishable in the real world because basic science being fundamental exploration of nature has potential application in practical contexts.

Appreciating the co-evolution of S&T, Nelson (2005) asserts that 'most modern scientific research, including research done at universities, is in fields in which practical application is central in the definition of a field. Not surprisingly, these are fields on which efforts to advance technology mostly draw' (238). The interaction of the two, basic (curiosity driven) research and applied (mission oriented) research, through the building of bridges between ivory tower and society, is crucial to the future of science and the health of society at large (Sonnet 2002).

Kuznets points out that the growth of scientific and technological knowledge follows distinctive patterns. 'In attempting to trace these patterns, Kuznets distinguishes between (a) a scientific discovery, an addition to knowledge, (b) an invention, the application of existing knowledge to a useful end, (c) an innovation, the first industrial use of an invention, (d) an improvement, a minor application, and finally (e) the spread of an innovation, usually accompanied by improvements' (Musson 1972, 15).

To achieve the objective of self-reliance and encourage indigenous sources of technology, the Indian government established a set of institutions to create and transfer knowledge essential to economic and social development. The result is the world's largest network of public sector research centres which was intended to offer a bridge between knowledge and industry. However, that interaction or bridge has been evident only since the 1990s, largely due to the pursuit by these institutions of research in fundamental or basic science without regard to its social applications.

In the next section of this chapter, I discuss the efforts of the Indian government over the years to establish an S&T infrastructure in order to promote industrial development. In Section 2.3, I analyse the S&T policies which set the objectives and goals that such institutions were expected to promote. Section 2.4 discusses priorities and policy directions for S&T. Section 2.5 notes how quality research can quite often get overlooked due to lack of support when located in large universities. Section 2.6 examines the sources for training S&T personnel and Section 2.7 concludes the discussion.

2.2 The Institutional Infrastructure for Development of Science and Technology

Even prior to gaining Independence, there was the recognition within the leadership of the national movement that economic growth, while having less to do with the extent of resources depended essentially on the capacity to create knowledge and ideas, with vital roles being reserved for education, training, research and development. India's first Prime Minister, Pandit Jawaharlal Nehru, took personal interest in the development of S&T by encouraging the establishment of a multi-level set of institutions. Between 1948 and 1958, several national laboratories under the Council of Scientific and Industrial Research (CSIR) were set up. In 1958, Parliament passed the Scientific Policy Resolution (SPR) drafted by Nehru with the assistance of Dr Homi J. Bhabha who headed the AEC. The intent of the policy resolution was to secure for its citizens all the benefits that can accrue from the acquisition and application of scientific knowledge. Since the enunciation of that policy, India has developed a substantial infrastructure of institutions and capabilities in a variety of scientific and technological fields (See Bhargava and Chakrabarti 2003). While India's S&T institutions enjoy considerable political support, being primarily tax-payer funded, they are also constrained by aspects of accountability and political responsibility. High-profile institutions such as the AEC, ISRO and Defence Research and Development Organization (DRDO) operate as independent entities enjoying direct access to the Prime Minister or Defence Minister. By contrast, the forty-one laboratories under the CSIR have become increasingly difficult to administer. India's gigantic S&T establishment involves enormous investment and is administered through a range of complex agencies (Bhargava and Chakrabarti 2003). With national laboratories undertaking targeted research and universities undertaking both teaching and research, funding, evaluation and monitoring become a very complex task.

Owing to circumstances therefore, India's S&T establishment is predominantly a public sector venture. With the exception of a few private colleges, most education and training is publicly funded. Even the IISc, which was set up at the initiative of the Tatas, is now predominantly funded by government. In recognition of its outstanding contribution to teaching and research, the Government of India allocated a special grant of Rs 100 crores to IISc in the 2004 budget. Knowledge, being a public good, offers little incentive for the market, and Foray (2004) considers it a daunting task for the market to set a price on knowledge. Recognising the complex nature of knowledge production, most countries adopt direct government intervention by providing budget grants, offering subsidies or regulating the producers (Foray 2004). Researchers working in the open university culture receive grants to carry out research and are expected to do some teaching in return.

This differs from research in a national laboratory where researchers carry out only targeted research, with no teaching commitments. Both, however, fall under the category of publicly-funded research.

Either due to lack of foresight or resource constraints, the government, in laying the foundations of an S&T infrastructure, failed to establish links between universities and the national laboratories. What has transpired now is a 'two-box' disease (Parthasarathi, *The Hindu*, 19 October 2005) where some institutes are treated as 'islands of excellence' and receive generous financial support, while universities are neglected on grounds that they lack creative ability. The system clearly is in need of reform (Parthasarathi, *New Scientist*, 19 February 2005).

Exploring diverse institutional mechanisms to foster scientific initiative, Foray advocates the concept of 'reputational capital' which is compatible with a 'collegiate reputational award system based upon accepted claims to priority'. This, she considers, is 'a remarkable device since it allows for the creation of private assets, a form of intellectual property, resulting from the very act of foregoing exclusive ownership of the knowledge concerned....In this sense, the priority rule is a highly effective device that offers nonmarket incentives to the production of public goods' (Foray 2004, 174). To look for practical outcomes in the allocation of resources for scientific research is a mistake, according to Nelson (2005). On the contrary, he suggests that scientists should work on problems where the chances of serendipity are the greatest, and the choice of what to explore should be left to them. Were government or market to intrude into the allocation of scientific resources, such intrusion would only serve to kill the goose that lays the golden egg.

2.3 Development of Science and Technology Policy

The institutional structure for the development of S&T policy in India can be viewed from three levels. The first is the national level where the overall needs and problems are considered by the Planning Commission in consultation with the National Committee on Science and Technology (NCST), set up in 1971 to overcome some of the negative aspects so widely discussed within the scientific community. The second involves agencies like CSIR and similar agencies in the central government which review various research plans submitted by the constituent laboratories and assess them against national guidelines. At the third level are the various laboratories which formulate research projects based on priorities established by the second-level agencies (see Bhargava and Chakrabarti 2003).

The complexity of such a gigantic structure for the development of S&T policy has raised concerns about efficient overall administration. 'The report on the implementation of the scientific policy resolution during 1958–68 revealed an increase in expenditure on R&D from 0.21 per cent to 0.43 per cent of the GNP, strengthening of facilities for R&D in scientific institutions and establishment of new institutes, laboratories, centres and stations under scientific agencies and departments, thus creating employment opportunities' (Mohan Bhatia, *The Hindu*, 9 November 1993). During that period too, there was a fourfold increase in enrolments at postgraduate courses in S&T and an increase in the number of scholarships and fellowships offered. The NCST issued a policy document titled 'An Approach to Science and Technology Plan' which listed several objectives: meeting minimum needs, achieving technological self-reliance and maximising the utilisation of existing S&T resources.

A study carried out by the New Delhi-based National Institute of Scientific Technology and Development Studies (Bhatia, *Deccan Herald*, 14 May 2003) revealed that a public scientific establishment is not commonly regarded as a conducive environment for creative research and suffers from a high attrition rate. Being predominantly public (government), its internal structure and operational procedures reflect a governmental culture which acts as a constraint on young scientists. This problem of brain drain, which has afflicted India since the 1980s has, in recent years, become worse. According to surveys, about 85 per cent of Indian science and engineering doctoral degree holders from American universities are keen to stay on in the USA while 45 per cent have definite plans of residing there permanently. (National Science Foundation 1998, cited in Mani 2003, 24). That situation has to be gauged from the growing number going overseas, estimated at over forty thousand annually. Indians top the list of foreign-born scientists and engineers in the United States, which, according to Mani, has both costs as well as benefits. While it affects the quality and quantity of S&T personnel, such costs are compensated by increased remittances, investment inflows from expatriate Indians, 'not least, national pride that India is seen as one of the world's prime sources of computing know-how' (Mani 2003, 24). The earnings from the Indian diaspora estimated at $300 billion, equivalent to thrice the annual

Indian GDP, have prompted the Indian government to offer incentives like dual citizenship to attract their skills and investment towards India's development. In his first address to the Indian Science Congress as Prime Minister, Dr Manmohan Singh promised to rid scientific institutions of bureaucratic tyranny and to create career opportunities for scientists so as to retain talent at home. In pursuance of that quest, he announced the formation of a Science Advisory Council with C. N. R. Rao as chairperson (*The Hindu*, 4 January 2005). Following the Indian Science Congress, the Prime Minister announced his plan for a National Knowledge Commission (*The Hindu*, 13 January, 2005) with Sam Pitroda as Chairperson. It is fitting that in the 'knowledge century' India has had a rocket scientist as President and an economist as Prime Minister, who together have provided an excellent role model for Indian youth. Launching the Commission, Prime Minister Manmohan Singh hailed this as an opportunity for a 'second wave of institution building where the youth of the country will be an asset if the nation invests in their capabilities. Denied this investment, it (the youth) will become a social and economic liability'.

The interest shown by Manmohan Singh in transforming the S&T framework was translated into increased budget allocations to various S&T departments in the 2004–05 annual budget. In addition to the ad hoc announcement of a grant of Rs 100 crores to IISc, the total allocated to the departments of Science and Technology, Scientific and Industrial Research, Biotechnology and Ocean Development registered an increase of 28 per cent. This is almost twelve years after the last significant increase.

With the acceptance in principle of the proposal of the Science Advisory Committee to the Prime Minister (SAC-PM) to set up a National Science and Engineering Research Foundation (NSERF) on US lines, there is optimism regarding substantial increases in science funding and possibly an entirely new mechanism for its direction (*The Hindu*, 25 May 2005), replacing the current one which is too bureaucratic. NSERF could receive Rs 1000 crores annually from the government and would be free to accept funding from industry and other sources. Endorsing its establishment, Professor C. N. R. Rao said that there should be 'one body overseeing the funding of scientific research, which could establish a funding policy and direct funding appropriately. The proposed foundation should also carry out scientific audits and monitor the country's scientific output' (ibid.). Such a foundation was to have been set up during the tenure of Rajiv Gandhi as Prime Minister. However, an unsuccessful election and certain unfortunate events intervened, precluding its establishment.

To overcome some of the negative effects so widely discussed within the scientific community, the government in 1983 issued a 'Technology Policy Statement' affirming its intentions to provide incentives for self-reliant inventors who use indigenous resources. However, Mani (2003) notes that subsequent to this statement there have been no 'major technological breakthroughs based on domestic R&D nor has the state created any institutional mechanism to effect such breakthroughs'. A notable exception is the effort being made towards developing advanced computing which, because of political difficulties, was forced to acquire commercial products. 'The establishment of the Centre for Advanced Computing (C-DAC) and the concurrent efforts at other national laboratories marked the beginning of high performance computing in the country' (Mani 2003, 13). The objectives stated in the 1983 statement for promoting indigenous technology through linkages between research institutes and industry were achieved by the Technology Information and Forecasting Assessment Council (TIFAC), which published several reports in different sectors under the 2020 Technology Vision. Apart from these efforts there has been insufficient encouragement towards implementing other goals of the 1983 statement.

In 1993, a new draft Technology Policy Statement was issued (*The Hindu*, 9 November 1993). Since then, there have been two more policy statements—one issued in 1993 and another in 2003. The aims of the 1993 policy statement were the promotion of indigenous technology in the context of the 1991 industrial policy statement and improvement in the quality of management of R&D institutions. 'Recognising the critical importance of innovative research, a far more prominent role for research, development and engineering (RD&E) is envisaged in the decade ahead' (*The Hindu*, 7 May 1993). The Government's intention is to encourage investment in R&D especially by industry and to work towards an increase from 0.9 per cent to 2 per cent of GNP. Identifying the absence of linkages with industry as a key weakness, government aimed to initiate a move from localised excellence to integrated excellence through the encouragement of greater collaboration between research institutes, universities and industry by funding linked projects (laboratories and universities), university and industry exchanges and greater mobility in general between those institutions and industry. The policy measures were intended to reduce dependence on government initiative and financing and promote greater cooperation between universities, laboratories and industry (Mani, 19). In May 2006, government announced a policy whereby thirty-nine laboratories under CSIR may forge alliances with industry for knowledge generation in new areas of S&T. Industry may set up incubation centres in CSIR laboratories and scientists are permitted to take up assignments in industry without any adverse effect on their careers (*The Hindu*, 23 May 2006). Although the 1993 draft paper was not adopted as policy, expenditure on R&D, according to the 2003 Science Policy Statement, increased minimally from 0.8 per cent in 2000 to 1.81 per cent of GNP in 2002 and was expected to increase further to 2 per cent by 2007 (*Nature*, vol. 421, 9 January 2003).

2.4 The Role of Leadership

In emphasising the importance of S&T in development, Kuznets points out that the most important capital for industrial development is not physical but human capital. For the development of human capital and its effective utilisation, good leadership is essential. In the Indian context, that quality of leadership appears to have generally developed at the top fostered through the role of maintaining the boundaries of the organisation from political and bureaucratic interference and building access to vital centres of power. Outstanding persons of that calibre were Homi J. Bhabha, Chairman of AEC, Vikram Sarabhai of ISRO, M. S. Thacker of CSIR, Dr Swaminathan of Indian Agricultural Research Institute (IARI), Dr Verghese Kurien of the National Dairy Development Board (NDDB), and, more recently, Sam Pitroda of the Knowledge Commission and Dr R. A. Mashelkar of CSIR.

However, to be successful, an organisation cannot rely solely on leadership at the top; it is essential to build future leaders. Bhargava and Chakrabarti (2003) credit the success of the space programmes undertaken by the Department of Space (DOS) to the leadership of eminent scientists like Sarabhai, Satish Dhawan, U.R. Rao and K. Kasturirangan. 'They have all been outstanding scientists, super-managers of men and resources, and visionaries with rare human qualities who have always appreciated and taken forward what has been done by their predecessors.... As the rules that bind the DOS are no different from those binding the other scientific departments and agencies of the Government, there is a lesson to learn from the DOS as to how a scientific department can run efficiently within the existing framework of Government rules' (39).

In his presidential address to the Indian Physics Association, Dr Abdul Kalam recalled how Sarabhai had nurtured young scientists in the 1960s. During his visits to Thiruvananthapuram, young scientists had the opportunity to discuss ideas with him. Proposals from Dr Gupta, Dr Amba Rao and Dr Abdul Kalam led to the emergence of the Guidance Laboratory, Advanced Dynamics Group and Reinforced Plastic Centre, respectively. It was 'these centres of excellence which incubated many advanced technology missions that fed critical inputs into the Indian Space Programme. Once the potential of young scientists is understood, organizational heads must invest in them boldly irrespective of their positions or age. If this philosophy is pursued with sincerity, research will flourish and youth will be encouraged to embrace science' (*The Hindu*, 9 April 2005).

The outcome of such emphasis on S&T is the design-intensive quality of human resources largely emerging from the Indian Institutes of Technology (IITs) and other elite institutions. The availability of such resources has drawn many MNCs to set up development centres in India. Although beneficial in many ways, their presence and the salaries they offer act as a disincentive for students to pursue higher studies and take up academic careers. The situation has been exacerbated by the growth of institutions rushing to cater to the growing demand for professional education. Such growth has resulted in a corresponding decline in the quality of student intake as well as that of teachers and will, in the long run, require a monumental effort to remedy. In an editorial titled 'Promoting Science', *The Hindu* cited the present system of science education as a critical weakness and recommended the matter be accorded the highest national priority (23 July 2004). In announcing the setting up of Science City in 2006, the Minister for Science and Technology noted the lack of interest in teaching. To overcome the shortage of science teachers in high school and pre-university colleges, it is intended to start a five-year BSc course in engineering colleges. A national conference titled 'Science then, today and tomorrow' held on 24 June 2007 (*The Hindu*, 10 June 2007) focused more on the future, compared to earlier conferences which had dwelt largely on the underutilisation of human resources within Indian science. While some commentators wonder whether Indian higher education can meet the challenge of a knowledge economy without broader support for research, there is also the need for a 'culture of research where knowledge will be created and not just consumed' (Konana, *The Hindu*, 6 December 2005).

2.5 Knowledge Transfer

To understand problems in knowledge transfer, one needs to distinguish between codified knowledge and tacit knowledge because of the difficulty of transferring such knowledge in the form of designs or instructions. The latter 'cannot be expressed outside the action of the person who has it' (Foray 2004, 71). The practice of apprentices working under master craftsmen is an example of such learning as it takes place in a face-to-face situation. Such transfer of knowledge is both time consuming and difficult when compared to codified knowledge which can be transcribed into designs or blueprints with relative ease (Teece 1981). A major contributory factor to success in knowledge economies is the close association between research universities, business and government, named the 'triple helix' by Cooke (2002). However, in India, with the exception of IISc, which has had extensive interaction with industry over the years, the link between the many institutions undertaking research in S&T and producers has been noticeably weak. Such interaction did begin in Mysore in the early years of the twentieth century when Sir M. Visvesvaraya requested the IISc's Department of Applied Chemistry to carry out research in the manufacture of soaps and the extraction of oil from sandalwood. The Sericulture Institute set up by the Mysore government at about the same time helped to improve the quality of silk and withstand competition from China and Japan. Today, Mysore sandalwood products and Mysore silks continue to contribute to the region's exports.

Unlike the CSIR which in the 1980s expressed uncertainty about government's interest in utilising its knowhow on silicon, the IISc has used its indigenous knowhow in the use of silicon to assist the establishment of a major chemical industry for the production of electronic grade silicon and other silicon-based materials. While contributing to the basic material for the electronics industry, the Institute has also participated in the designing of hardware and software systems to upgrade and modernise industrial operations at Indian Telephone Industries (ITI) and Hindustan Computers Limited (HCL) (Maddox and Rich 1984, 250–53). Unlike many of India's universities and national laboratories, IISc has, over several years, successfully combined teaching, research and innovation.

Lamenting the lack of demand on science by industry, R.A. Mashelkar, retired Director-General of CSIR, stated, 'The fact that science has to make economic and social sense has not dawned on a large number of our institutions'. To foster that interaction, he established the National Millennium Indian Technology Initiative (NMITLI), which funds collaborative projects between universities, government laboratories and companies. This has resulted in several new products: two new drugs to control TB and psoriasis and a software package called Bio-Suite (*New Scientist,* 19 February 2005, 41). Under this programme, CSIR has funded thirty-seven projects involving sixty-five industry partners and 175 R&D institutions with an outlay of Rs 270 crores. One of these projects involves Encore, a Bangalore–based company led by Vinay Deshpande, Ashok Jhunjunwala of IIT Chennai and N. Balakrishnan of IISc which received Rs 3 crores to develop a portable personal computer with all the basic features to be marketed at a cost of Rs 10,000 (*The Hindu,* 11 May 2005). Citing development as the crucial weakness of Indian S&T, Dr R. Chidambaram, Principal Scientific Advisor to the Government of India, initiated measures to enhance academia-industry interactions and technology delivery, hoping that it will result in the creation of national wealth, improvements in the quality of life especially of the rural population and the enhancement of national security (*The Hindu,* 20 June 2004).

The inconsistency between achievements in S&T and real-life situations has prompted the reputed journal *Nature* to characterise post-Independence Indian achievements as 'excellence in the midst of poverty' (Maddox and Rich 1984). Although India has made great strides in defence, space, electronic and computer technology and created a sophisticated S&T system producing trained personnel, overall these achievements appear uneven. Nonetheless, one witnesses growing confidence now emerging, especially with Indian achievements beginning to have a worldwide impact. What is conspicuous is the failure to develop technology suited to Indian conditions (see Chapter 3). An interesting case of adaptation between FW and TW, based on climate, was highlighted in the recent campaign for mass immunisation against polio undertaken as a part of the technology missions in India. For the vaccine to retain its potency, it needs to be stored below a certain temperature. Packed in ice, referred to as 'cold chain', the vaccine is transported across the nation. When received at the other end, however, it cannot be administered until it is determined whether it has retained its potency. The problem was solved by an enterprising group which added a coloured compound to the vaccine solution to act as an indicator. If the vaccine has retained its potency, the solution in the vial displays a particular colour. If not, the colour changes and the health worker will then discard the vial. The indicator itself is benign and does not affect the properties of the vaccine in any way—truly an ingenious solution to the problem (Balasubramaniam, *The Hindu Science and Technology Magazine*, 19 December 1996)! Another possibility now available is the Solar Chill, invented by Dr Shende, an Indian working for WHO, seen as a viable and eco-friendly solution, particularly for TW countries (*The Hindu*, 1 November 2006).

The above discussion raises a question: is there a distinct Indian S&T identity? Balasubramaniam equates the state of Indian S&T to the film '*Morning Raga*' in which three musicians from classical and semi-classical backgrounds offer fusion music. Following poor audience response at a restaurant performance, they seek an answer from the manager of the restaurant. 'He is candid in his response: "What is this music? You think you are white? You think you are black? Where is the you? Where is your music?"' Balasubramaniam links this with comments at a seminar in Bangalore by Raghavendra Gadagkar who appealed to Indian scientists to seek answers to our problems within the limits of our resources and desist from researching problems that US scientists work on because India cannot match their resources. Given our bio-diversity, there is enough scope to pursue research in India and to seek collaboration only if required. Such a strategy, according to him, would generate both recognition and confidence and also advance the climate for science in the country (*The Hindu*, 16 December 2004). People like Mashelkar (of CSIR) are needed to champion the cause of Indian science. 'In 1997, when a company was awarded a US patent for the wound healing powers of turmeric, Mashelkar fought the decision and won, arguing that the patent would "steal" India's traditional knowledge. India has since successfully challenged patents on neem and basmati rice' (*New Scientist*, 19 February 2005, 41).

Now known internationally as the Silicon Plateau, Bangalore is also becoming equally well known in the area of biotechnology (BT). Such success prompted Finance Minister P. Chidambaram to urge local people to make Bangalore 'India's true knowledge capital'. The city is already home to a large number of BT companies in clinical research, BT–pharma, BT–agri and IT–bio. Research now taking place in nanotechnology at the IISc will further boost its status as a centre for information, bio and nanotechnology. Plans were afoot to inaugurate, within Electronics City, the Bangalore Helix, a Biotechnology Park, which will house the Centre for Human Genetics, that would concentrate on research, and the Institute of Bioinformatics and Applied Biotechnology (IBAB), to train quality manpower in BT.

India's emergence as a major biotechnology player is built on a broad institutional foundation of national laboratories employing approximately fifteen thousand scientists, a range of college-level training institutes offering courses in biotechnology, bioinformatics and biological sciences, and several hundred medical colleges of varying standards. In the context of the ever-growing threat of HIV/AIDS and other diseases in the Third World, India's advances in producing low-priced vaccines through several drug companies offer hope for millions who otherwise cannot afford drugs manufactured by international companies. Some Indian companies have attempted to produce generic drugs, whose patents have expired. Other Indian scientists have returned from the US to launch new ventures. A case in point is Bharat Biotech, a unit at Hyderabad which produces Hepatitis B vaccine sold in developing countries for twenty-eight cents. Bio-Suite, the software package launched by Tata Consultancy Services, is the result of a collaborative venture between IISc and the Institute of Genomics and is designed 'to analyse DNA sequences to manipulate virtual molecules in three dimensions' (ibid.). In his positions as Director of the National Chemical Laboratory and later as head of CSIR, Dr Mashelkar urged Indian scientists to patent their discoveries. However, as a serious competitor on the global scene, Indian drug companies sometimes face legal threats from international companies. Novartis, for example, had filed a suit in the Chennai High Court, questioning the Indian Patent (Amendment) Act which disallows granting patents to medicines that are new forms of an existing drug rather than an innovation. Novartis's action was deplored by the Norwegian Minister for International Development and later by Médecins Sans Frontières (Doctors without Borders). In August 2007, the High Court rejected the drug company's challenge to patent law, which 'aid organisations declared... a victory for the rights of patients over patents' (*The Age*, 8 August 2007).

In pursuing a self-reliant S&T strategy, one observes a certain ambivalence deriving largely from Gandhian influence which persists even to this day, reflecting simultaneously the Gandhian concept of self-reliance and Nehru's concept of modern science and technology which transcended national boundaries (Bhatt 1980). This also reflects an underlying dilemma faced by countries which have experienced colonial domination: the acquisition of technology from other countries without once again undermining their own economic and political independence.

India is proud of its history as an ancient centre of culture and learning and its contribution to science since early times. While praising ancient Indian mathematicians like Aryabhata, Brahmagupta and Bhaskaracharya, President Abdul Kalam noted Albert Einstein's comment, 'We owe a lot to the Indians who taught us how to count, without which no worthwhile scientific discovery could have been made' (2002, 43–44). Greenspan (2004) writes, 'By far the most profound contribution that India has made to global culture ... is in giving the world the decimal number system. There is no doubt that the invention or discovery of zero is one of the most important innovations in the history of human culture' (144). (see Florida 2005, 255). Early Indian contributions to science, according to Sen (2005), were notable for two important aspects: their openness and interactivity, and their willingness to deviate from religious orthodoxy. He concludes, 'The constructive role of heterodoxy and of the courage to disagree is not any less pivotal in science than it is in the fostering of public reasoning and of constructing the roots of political democracy' (30). The intense public debate that has taken place over the Indo-US nuclear sharing issue, in which Indian scientists have taken a leading role, is further confirmation of India's healthy tradition of argumentative democratic participation.

2.6 Why Some Get Lost in the Wilderness

With India's numerous S&T institutions, the size and volume of scientific activity undertaken can often result in some research receiving greater publicity while other work goes unnoticed. It would be fair to say that the multi-level S&T infrastructure which includes national laboratories, research institutions and institutes of technology is supported predominantly by government and is not matched elsewhere. The enormous sum of Rs 11,494 crores set aside for this purpose in the 2002–03 budget met with some criticism with particular reference to the growing exodus of scientists and technologists who are trained at such institutes as well as the questionable performance of some organisations. Notable exceptions have been the AEC, ISRO and Indian Council of Agricultural Research (ICAR). 'The public perception of CSIR is varied. While a segment of Indian industry is indebted to CSIR for its help in its qualitative and quantitative development, another segment is disillusioned with the CSIR with respect to its reliability, trustworthiness, and utility of its applied and industrial research' (Bhargava and Chakrabarti 2003, 99).

One wonders how a nation's performance in S&T can be judged. The 2003 Science and Technology policy statement set a target of increased R&D investment from 0.8 per cent in 2000 to 2 per cent in 2006. While this may seem like an easy measure in comparison with other countries, evaluation is very difficult in a country of India's size and diversity. However, India has continued to invest in S&T, with much of the funding coming from government.

The reluctance of the private sector to invest in R&D on a substantial and sustained basis has slowed growth considerably. However, according to Ashok Parthasarathy (2003), 'Government initiatives in the development of human resources, fiscal and financial policies, the building of institutional capacities and the direct funding of R&D institutions and industry provide hope that such objectives will be increasingly achieved over the next decade. But the journey will not be easy' (*Nature*, vol. 422, March 2003, 17).

India has become an important player in strategic areas of technology despite attempts to curtail its growth. Such attempts originate from the United States which has withdrawn technological assistance in the development of super computers and exerted pressure on Russia to stop the transfer of technology in the area of space research. In a circular issued in October 2004, the US Commerce Department, through its Bureau of Industry and Security, placed seven subsidiaries of ISRO on the 'Entity List', automatically restricting open transactions of technology in certain areas of space research. These restrictions are in addition to those already in place in the area of atomic power plants and advanced computing (*The Hindu*, 1 October 2004). While geopolitical considerations cannot be ruled out particularly in strategic areas, one cannot overlook the positive effects that such embargoes have had in the area of atomic energy, space research, advanced computing and development of combat aircraft. In fact, Dr Kakodkar, Chairman of AEC, considers that such embargoes have been seen as a major challenge (*The Hindu*, 24 November 2004). To avoid the arm twisting which is inevitable, the Gas Turbine Research Establishment (GTRE) is developing Kaveri engines to replace the GE engines for Tejas (the indigenous Light Combat Aircraft) developed by the DRDO's Aeronautical Development Agency (ADA) (*Times of India*, 5 June 2004).

In the competitive globalised world of today where S&T have no national boundaries, it is becoming increasingly difficult to pursue science for science's sake. Further, in a country of India's size and population which functions as a robust democracy, it is difficult to justify the allocation of scarce resources to elite institutions. However, the excellent performance of IISc, TIFR, ISRO, C-DOT, C-DAC and the IITs clearly establish a case for a selective approach. We explore the implications of this option in this section.

Although smaller institutions tend to be looked upon as being elitist because of their increased funding and the talent they attract, it has to be admitted that they produce a higher quality of research in comparison with the national laboratories under the CSIR or the universities. A case in point is that of Professor Sivaramakrishna Chandrasekhar's liquid crystal team of twenty scientists which moved from Mysore University to the Raman Institute to avail themselves of better facilities. The Institute then liaised with a private company for the use of his latest liquid crystal display in the manufacture of watches (*Nature*, 1984, 590). Government agencies realised the significance of his work only after recognition had been received from a reputable scientific organisation in the US (ibid.). 'This institute is as vivid a proof as there could be that research of the highest class is alive and well in India. The necessary conditions seems to be that people of distinction should work in institutes which are small and generously endowed and that it should be possible for those with ideas freely to select those who work with them' (ibid.). What is certain is that if the liquid crystal team under Professor Chandrashekar had not had the opportunity to work in a well-known institute like the Raman Institute, its work would have been buried amid others. With the mushrooming of universities since the 1970s, genuine research, which could be usefully applied in the Indian context, receives inadequate or late recognition, if at all.

Some of India's established institutions in the area of S&T are small, better endowed and associated with scientists such as Bhabha, Sarabhai, Meghnad Saha, C. V. Raman and K. S. Krishnan. While work at such institutes is of a high order, their critics often question the relevance of their research to practical problems suggesting that they tend to be imitative. This depends entirely on the time frame that one adopts to judge the value of fundamental research.

The confidence that Maddox and Rich (1984) place in the future of India's S&T is reflected in the international recognition being accorded to Indian scientists. Dr Baldev Raj, Director, Indira Gandhi Centre for Atomic Research (IGCAR), received the 2004 award of the International Committee for Non-Destructive Testing (ICNDT). Awarded once every four years for contribution in non-destructive evaluation (NDE) S&T, it represents a comprehensive lifetime achievement award in recognition of a person's contribution to the field. Moreover, his student, Anish Kumar, received the Young Achiever award (2000–2004). Commenting on Kumar's achievement, Dr Raj felt that it was commendable in terms of existing facilities, which are not regarded as good enough for cutting-edge research. (*The Hindu,* 28 October 2004). IGCAR run by Baldev Raj is described by *New Scientist* as 'the temple of the future... a 500-mega watt, sodium-cooled fast breeder reactor, which generates not only electricity but plutonium too' (2005, 48). While countries like US, UK, France and Japan have been unsuccessful with commercial scale fast breeders, only Russia has run a fast breeder for any length of time. 'Yet India is determined to follow this apparently risky route as a key step towards long–term self–sufficiency in energy'. Located at Kalpakkam, IGCAR is the nerve centre of its programme and is staffed by 1200 scientists. 'Here is everything you would expect to see in a nuclear research centre....The vision these people are pursuing comes in three stages, each using a different type of reactor.... This is a colossal endeavour, but India should have the resources to carry it out. While the nuclear industry has been fighting for its life in the US and Europe, in India it has thrived' (ibid.).

Another advance in India's capability in nuclear research was the installation of a massive vessel at the Prototype Fast Breeder Reactor (PFBR) at Kalpakkam on 25 June 2008. The FBR, which will generate 500 MWe, will use plutonium-uranium oxide as fuel and liquid sodium as coolant. Its main vessel will be placed inside the safety vessel which will prevent the liquid sodium in the former from coming into contact with the reactor vault. Dr Kakodkar, Chairman of the AEC, described its launch as a 'milestone in the history of India's Fast Breeder Reactor (FBR)'.

An offshoot of the research undertaken at PFBR is the compact propulsion reactor, an exact prototype of the one installed to power India's nuclear submarine INS Arihant which was launched by Prime Minister Manmohan Singh in early August 2009. The new reactor technology will also be required for larger power programmes as it is based on pressurised water reactors (PWR). This achievement, according to Dr Kakodkar '... signifies both. We have a compact power plant for propulsion but we also have PWR technology which can be used for electricity production through the indigenous route in future' (ibid.). The indigenous route, he continued, is an achievement that '... one has to be proud of because it has been done here; it has been done by Indians and this is something which is not available for the asking whatever money you want to pay. There is no way to acquire that unless you do it yourself and not many countries have such a capability.' (The Hindu, 16 August 2009).

The Massachusetts Institute of Technology Review magazine included nine Indians in its list of a hundred top innovators under the age of thirty-five. This list included Srinidhi Vardarajan for building the third fastest computer at a cost of $5 million, Smruti Vidwans for her new approach in developing drugs to fight tuberculosis and Vikram Sheel Kumar, CEO, Dimagi, who founded an organisation in Boston to develop interactive software for motivating patients to manage chronic diseases such as diabetes and Aids. His systems are currently being used in rural India and South Africa (*The Hindu*, 9 November 2004).

Despite the reluctance of large public and private organisations to invest in R&D and innovative projects, India has still forged ahead in some areas like BT, pharmaceuticals and solar energy. Ashok Parthasarathy (2003) attributes this to sustained government support over several decades and the result of investment initiatives over the four previous years in the development of indigenous technologies. These areas for investment were chosen on different criteria: BT, for its impact on agriculture, health, industry and environment; vaccines which are needed as limited research is conducted on tropical diseases in Western countries; advanced batteries to promote photovoltaic-based power sources (solar energy), and microelectronics, atomic energy, space and defence technologies because they have been restricted by export controls. In addition government has offered a range of incentives to encourage the private sector to invest in R&D (Parthasarathy 2003, 17).

The selective or mission-oriented approach has proved successful, with success in high-technology areas such as space and super computers. Besides, it is becoming increasingly evident that India ought to rely on indigenous development in strategic areas in view of the fact that the United States in the recent past was openly preventing other countries such as Russia from selling technology to India (*The Hindu*, 25 August 1992). At the official naming ceremony of the Light Combat Aircraft (Tejas), the Indian Prime Minister categorised countries such as the USA as 'technology denial regimes' and pledged increased government support for indigenous development of defence armaments. Denial of technology, he said, had encouraged Indian scientists and technologists to respond splendidly to the challenge and develop world class technologies (*Deccan Herald*, 5 May 2003). While declaring open the supercomputing facility at C-DAC in Knowledge Park, Arun Shourie commended C-DAC for developing the super computer, the technology for which had been denied to India (*Asian Age*, 12 April 2003). 'PARAM Padma could be used in critical scientific and engineering fields such as computational atmospheric sciences, bioinformatics, computational structural mechanics, evolutionary computing, seismic data processing, etc.' (ibid.). Recalling the refusal of technology several years ago, Shourie asserted that 'technology denial should be taken as a blessing and a challenge' and urged the replication of the 'mission mode' approach initiated by Rajiv Gandhi which had helped C-DAC to blossom into a world-renowned institution (*Deccan Herald*, 2 April 2003). C-DAC has supplied over fifty supercomputers to domestic and export markets including countries like Russia, Germany, Canada and Singapore (Parthasarathi 2003, 18).

India's Department for Non-Conventional Energy Sources, set up in 1982, was the first such body, and, until 2003, the only government agency for renewable energy (Parthasarathi 2003, 17). By providing selective investments for advanced batteries, 'India now has 9 manufacturers of solar photovoltaic cells and 20 manufacturers of photovoltaic panels, with an installed production capacity of

20 MW per year. This is the fourth largest capacity in the world and by far the largest in a developing country. About 900,000 commercial photovoltaic systems have been designed, developed, manufactured and installed across the country to provide electrical energy that is desperately needed in rural, remote and industrial areas' (ibid.). The energy thus produced is used for water pumps for drinking and irrigation, street lighting, refrigerators for storing vaccines in rural health centres, warning systems at over 9,000 unmanned rail-road crossings, communication equipment, water desalination plants in desert settlements, anticorrosion protection systems for cross-country oil and gas pipelines and communication and control systems on offshore oil and gas platforms (ibid.).

As solar energy is being popularised, the need for hands-on expertise in installation techniques and operation and maintenance of solar energy systems has been recognised by The Energy Research Institute (TERI). TERI and four European institutions have joined to develop courses covering popular solar technologies relevant to Indian conditions (*The Hindu*, 4 March 2006).

2.7 Sources for Science and Technology Manpower

Although India's S&T manpower ranks among the largest in the world, there is a fear that the source of that manpower is declining, if not in numbers, certainly in quality with growing competition from other professions where career prospects seem brighter. In recognition of this, the 1993 Science and Technology statement offered specific programmes and incentives. In the case of engineering and technology however, the demand for places in elite institutions remains high. Typical of this are the IITs known for their highly selective entrance system with quality staff, most of whose graduates emigrate in search of better opportunities. '...Many in India shake their heads over what is happening, and agree with the academic who says that the IITs are India's most generous gift to the United States' (*Nature*, 1984, 593). In his review of *India in the Global Software Industry,* Anand Parthasarathy is critical of the much-hyped IIT product. 'These paragons and prima donnas provided a costly education, heavily subsidised by the Indian tax payer, think nothing of selling themselves to the highest bidder at annual campus recruitment drives and leave the country in droves every year' (*The Hindu*, 20 July 2004). Strangely, graduates of

IISc, established several decades before the IITs and reputed for its strength in both research and teaching in applied S&T, are in no rush to emigrate, if at all. One commentator thinks this is 'perhaps because those concerned have been given not merely a saleable education but a degree of engagement with the practice of science and technology in India' (Maddox and Rich 1984, 593). Two other contributing factors pointed out by authors of this report are the location of the Institute at Bangalore, which offers greater opportunities for its graduates and the good fortune the Institute has enjoyed in being led by a succession of directors renowned in their respective fields of research. An enduring and sustainable scientific structure cannot be built solely on the success of elite institutions. It has to be built on a wider base: a university system where a large number of students can receive high quality education.

As a TW country, India has made significant breakthroughs in the different fields of S&T. With the explosion in IT, Indians are well represented among entrepreneurs in Silicon Valley and hold senior technical and executive positions in international companies. Over the past decade, the IITs have together awarded 25,000 bachelor's degrees, 2,500 master's degrees, and 600 Ph.Ds. A survey of 6,000 IIT graduates revealed that they were employed in IT, manufacturing, consulting, education, telecom and financial services. Of the pre-1999 graduates, 57 per cent are departmental heads or in high positions, 39 per cent are vice-presidents of companies or in higher positions, and 19 per cent are CEOs or chairpersons of companies. Their reputation for excellence and leadership in the United States and Europe has led MNCs such as Microsoft ($400 m), Cisco ($200 m) and Intel ($100 m) to invest in India. In their turn, these graduates have made significant contributions to their alma mater (*The Hindu*, 13 February 2003). Critics view the IITs as good undergraduate schools administering a tight curriculum which demands hard work and perseverance. However, they appear to lack the research orientation that one commentator observed at the IISc. 'Lacking in national purpose, in social commitment, in focus and in creativity, IITs have only an aura conferred on them, as they were the brainchildren of Pandit Nehru. With the departure of Panditji, the vision was gone and only the aura remained. The aura was of the hope, which to a great extent has been belied' (Chary, *Deccan Herald*, 14 March 2003).

2.8 Conclusion

India's current rate of economic growth and its label as the next knowledge superpower is owed in part to its S&T infrastructure developed over the decades with predominantly government investment. Unlike developed economies, this sector had to be developed from scratch and constituted a genuine challenge in institution building. Believing 'that the world will ultimately be saved, if it is to be saved, by the method and approach of science' (Norman 1965, 357), Prime Minister Jawaharlal Nehru took a direct interest in promoting science in newly independent India. His association with Indian science and technology verged on the passionate, with his attendance at almost every opening session of the Indian Science Congress held annually during his tenure as Prime Minister. However, major breakthroughs in S&T in India need both strong leadership and political support. The Nehru-Bhabha association resulted in the foundation of the AEC with Sarabhai and his successors playing a crucial role in the development of space research. Likewise we have the association of C. Subramaniam with Dr Swaminathan and the Green Revolution and that of Indira Gandhi's support for Dr Kurien with the White Revolution (Mascarenhas 2004). Rajiv Gandhi's close association with Pitroda led to the dramatic transformation of telecommunication, which, in turn, has had a dramatic impact on the information technology boom.

In the case of IT, its main input, human resources, has emerged from the elite IITs. Steady migration of these graduates to the United States where opportunities are plentiful, and an appreciation of their experience and impact abroad, have led major multinationals to look towards India as a source of quality manpower. Latest reports indicate that there are close to 240 international companies which have set up operations in Bangalore alone. Many of these have established development centres using the engineering and technical skills available there. This trend has encouraged scores of IIT graduates, who were based in Silicon Valley, to return to India and set up as entrepreneurs in the IT sector.

Notwithstanding the criticism that much of the work done in Indian universities and national laboratories is too theoretical with little relevance to Indian problems, there are some notable exceptions like the AEC, ISRO, C-DAC and C-DOT which have made significant contributions. Likewise agricultural research and progress in dairy development have resulted in huge increases in food and milk production.

What one fails to recognise in a critique of Indian S&T is the diversity and size of the undertaking. In an effort to promote equitable distribution of resources under democratic compulsions, resources are often allocated to regions where a scientific ethos is lacking (Bhargava and Chakrabarti 2003). Further, when such institutions come under bureaucratic administration, more harm is caused through interference in appointments and in other ways. It must be said here that the brain drain in the 1960s and 1970s was caused partly by lack of opportunities for scientists to work without hindrance and with limited facilities. However, the success stories highlight the need for institutions to be of a manageable size and to be led by people with relevant knowledge, skills, foresight and determination.

3

State and Industrial Development

3.1 Introduction

The decision of the Indian Supreme Court in September 2003 upholding the plaintiff's claim that government disinvestment in Hindustan Petroleum and Bharat Petroleum would be unconstitutional highlights the complexities that can arise in the process of industrial development. In ruling that government may not use an executive order to disinvest an enterprise set up by an Act of Parliament, the court ordered the government to amend the statute by which these enterprises had been set up (*The Hindu,* 17 September 2003). Both enterprises had been established in the 1970s following the nationalization of MNCs which had refused to refine crude oil imported on rupee account from the Soviet Union. Earlier, in 1963, while promoting its policy of self-reliance in energy resources, the government had set up the Oil and Natural Gas Commission to compete with the international oil companies and to carry out explorations as well.

By the 1970s, Indian policy makers had adopted a policy of public ownership in vital sectors of the economy and this was applied to categories of industries listed in the industrial policy resolutions of 1948 and 1956. Existing enterprises in the private sector (both Indian and foreign) were largely allowed to function within the framework of rules, thus dispelling any notion that the government might be adopting an anti-private enterprise stance. Some companies like Hindustan Lever, ICI and Indian Tobacco were allowed to operate on condition that they increased their Indian equity holding and repatriated profits in accordance with the Foreign Exchange Regulation Act (FERA). In the late 1960s and early 1970s, government nationalised banks and insurance companies in order to spread the availability of capital. This process of indigenisation was not acceptable to all. Notable of these was IBM which was unwilling to accept greater Indian equity participation and withdrew its Indian operations in 1978 (Greico 1984).

Since then, one notices a distinct transformation in government policy and public attitude towards both industrial policy and the role of foreign private investment (Degnbol-Martinussen 2001). Government's attempt in 2000 to disinvest in the energy sector and the consequent challenge mounted against that attempt on grounds of constitutional propriety suggest that any serious study of India's policy of industrial development cannot ignore the political and institutional context (Mascarenhas 1999). Similarly, to understand the emergence of ICT in India, one needs to adopt a comparative institutional political economy perspective. Beginning with the launch of the Plans in the 1950s which marked the start of the state's guiding role, the next noticeable phase occurred in the late 1970s with the manufacture of computer hardware and this gradually extended into other areas from the mid-1980s until the economic liberalisation of the 1990s (Krueger 2002).

While economic liberalisation is the most obvious explanation for the burgeoning of ICT, one needs to give due credit to the role of the state prior to and following liberalisation. The state was instrumental not only in laying the foundations of the ICT sector (Evans 1995, Greico 1984) but also in developing the underlying infrastructure of telecommunication, transportation and energy development, in investing in higher education, S&T and in building up an extensive industrial public sector for the manufacture of steel, machine tools, telecommunication equipment, electronics, rolling stock, fertilizers and chemicals. Such extensive involvement in a range of technologies indirectly promoted a culture of modernisation which is vital to the sustenance of a high-tech sector such as ICT enabling it to compete internationally. Would economic liberalisation have achieved the dramatic industrial transformation of the 1990s without the economic, scientific, engineering and political foundations laid in the 1950s and 1960s and earlier?

This chapter focuses on the role of the state in the development of industry, complementing the analysis of S&T (Chapter 2). The intention is to offer a broader historical and analytical perspective to the development of ICT in India. It is divided into the following sections. In Section 3.2, we offer reasons for India's adoption of a system of state intervention to promote industrialisation. Section 3.3 explores the import substitution strategy adopted to achieve greater self-reliance, and Section 3.4 discusses public sector industrial undertakings. Section 3.5 analyses the economic liberalisation policy, its timing, importance of the foreign exchange crisis and its effects. Section 3.6 discusses efforts at disinvestment and its implications. The final section sums up the discussion.

3.2 Why State Intervention?

The argument offered by structuralists for state intervention in TW countries is the lack of an effective market that can act as an instrument of resource allocation. In its place the state has been called upon to play the role of entrepreneur by investing in the economy. In addition, it has regulated the private sector by requiring it to channelise investments through a system of licences issued by government agencies which have rationed scarce foreign exchange resources and maintained control through prices and various operations.

While India possessed a sizeable private sector particularly in consumer products such as food and textiles, it lacked both the capital and the organisational and managerial capability to operate industries such as steel, machine tools and fertilisers. Such industries were earmarked for public sector investment under various industrial policy resolutions (1948, 1956, 1971). The knowledge and technology for such industries had to be acquired through foreign collaborators who preferred to work with official rather than private agencies (Mascarenhas 1982).

The aspect that has irked critics of state involvement in Indian industry is not so much the role itself as the method employed i.e. the bureaucratic agencies which created a maze of rules and regulations that eventually acted as a hindrance rather than an aid to prospective investors. Such bureaucratic authority for purposes of 'rationing foreign exchange, restricting entry through licensing producers, and instituting tariffs or quantitative restrictions on imports are all ways of creating rents' (Evans 1995, 23). Not surprisingly, the entire machinery for policing resulted in limited growth. Bhagwati (1988) attributes the lack of growth to poor policies which gave power to politicians, bureaucrats and businessmen who together formed an 'iron triangle' and created a discouraging culture of don'ts i.e., controls as against encouraging a culture of do's that achieve growth. In other words, the difference in economic performance between countries is related to the quality of state intervention, one that encourages entrepreneurial behaviour against one which inhibits such behaviour (Mascarenhas 1999, 52). Such a restrictive system was a cause for concern to Rajiv Gandhi, who, on becoming Prime Minister attempted to remedy the situation and inject competitive vigour into an over-controlled, over-protected, over-priced market place (*The Economist*, 9 May 1987). However, his early efforts were described as merely 'rewriting the rules by which the Indian government regulates who makes how much of what and where.' (ibid.).

Such criticism of state intervention in India is probably viewed from the perspective of successful east Asian economies. In attributing east Asian success to open markets, the IMF and World Bank have overlooked the role of the state and other historical factors which have worked in their favour (Mascarenhas 1999). A crucial point of difference between East and South Asia is the varying political systems. Until the 1990s, the former was characterised by a bureaucratic-authoritarian system based on the exploitation of cheap non-unionised labour in a cohesive capitalist state (Kohli 2004). By contrast, the Indian political system is a highly pluralist and participative democracy, with free trade unions and a vibrant press in a heterogeneous society. Critics in the1980s made no allowance for the size of the Indian economy, its historical antecedents, its geopolitical dynamics or its complex socio-economic and political structure. The incorporation of the above factors requires the adoption of a broad-based comparative political economy perspective and the perception of the role of the state in a more comprehensive light (Mascarenhas 1999).

Evans (1995) characterises state structures very simply into two ideal types: the predatory and the developmental. While developmental states possess a type of 'corporate coherence' which gives them a certain kind of autonomy, they are not however insulated from society. 'To the contrary, they are embedded in a concrete set of social ties that binds the state to society and provides institutionalized channels for the continued negotiation and renegotiation of goals and policies' (12). A fine balance between autonomy and embeddedness is necessary as 'only when embeddedness and autonomy are joined together can a state be called developmental' (ibid.). Moving further, he acknowledges the existence of an 'apparently contradictory combination of corporate coherence and connectedness' which he terms 'embedded autonomy,' and which, according to him, 'provides the underlying structural basis for successful state involvement in industrial transformation' (ibid.). India, which exhibits partial and imperfect approximation of embedded autonomy, is, according to Evans, an intermediate case (1995, 13).

Although in agreement with some observers of East Asian economies who credit their success to the opening of their markets, Kohli attributes differing levels of industrialisation to the manner in which states use their power to promote economic growth. Based on a comparative analysis of four countries that vary from success to failure (Nigeria, Brazil, Korea and India), he argues 'that the way state power is organised and used has decisively influenced rates and patterns of industrialisation in the global periphery' (9). Characterising a modern state as one which exercises coercive control over a territory and where the public arena is both normatively and organisationally distinguishable from private interests, he identifies three types of states in the developing world: neo-patrimonial states, cohesive capitalist states and fragmented multi-class states. The first lacks a clear distinction in the exercise of authority; the second is the opposite of the first, possessing a competent bureaucracy and close alliance with producer and capitalist groups both aiming towards economic growth while the third falls somewhere between the two. While success or failure depends on how states use their power, states that succeed do so 'by mobilising resources, channelling them into priority areas, altering the socio-economic context within which firms operate, and even undertaking direct economic activities' (418). Policy discussions on development, he suggests, must 'abandon the state versus market dichotomy and need instead to focus on the various ways in which states and markets can work together to promote development' (423).

3.3 Strategic Approach to Industrial Development

Appropriate choice of technology and decision making involve the capacity of governments to decide on priorities and arrive at a development strategy. To do that, a country must identify different types of dependence which are then considered as targets of policy (Roemier 1981). These are:

- dependence on a single market for exports,
- technological dependence where a country relies on buying technology from outside,
- managerial and entrepreneurial dependence, and
- limited economic flexibility because of a narrow economic base.

Any strategy for industrial development must address these issues by adopting suitable types of industrial strategies. These include: import substitution, further processing of primary products, diversification of exports, the adoption of basic and heavy industry and small-scale labour-intensive strategy. While these options are matched against the type of dependency a country encounters, it is equally important to consider the overall context. This comprises the size of the economy, the type of resources—physical and human, its history and, of course, the political and administrative system in which an economy functions. While Roemier endorses the basic industry-cum-import substitution model for large countries like India, he warns against the inefficiencies associated with continued protection granted to domestic producers under political pressure. The main objective of India's concept of self-reliance was to reduce dependence through the adoption of import substitution and to invest in basic and heavy industry such as armaments, atomic energy, iron and steel, heavy engineering, chemicals and communication. Its industrialisation policy, clearly enunciated in the resolutions of 1948, 1956 and 1971 and in the planning documents, became the cornerstone of its strategy for economic independence, in pursuit of which three broad approaches were adopted (Mascarenhas 1982, 1999). The first was the development of an integrated industrial structure by investing in basic and heavy industry, which involved import of technology and know-how for a specific period for a particular industry. The second was the protection of the infant domestic industry, particularly in the consumer goods area, by adopting a strategy of import substitution. In adopting import substitution, it departed from the classic import substitution industrialisation which essentially places barriers on foreign competition in order to favour domestic enterprises. Instead of being favoured, domestic operators were throttled through the reservation of areas for the public and small-scale sectors and the adoption of licensing (Rodrik and Subramanian, *The Hindu*, 15 May 2004). The third was the encouragement of small-scale industry which helped to develop local skills and development and grew into an adjunct to the basic industry sector by supplying materials and components.

In implementing this mixed strategy, the government

- enunciated its industrial policy, clearly earmarking roles for both the private and public sectors in the economy,
- regulated private investment in these sectors through a system of industrial licensing,
- established control of foreign private investments through regulation, and

- allowed the import of technological know-how through collaboration, thus encouraging indigenous research and development (Mascarenhas 1982, 3–4).

3.3.1 An Import Substitution Development Strategy

In its early years of Independence, India adopted self-reliance as its objective of industrial development with the intention of reducing its dependence on developed countries. This implied a rejection of the open market or liberal market model that had been responsible for the growth of Western capitalist economies. India's planners had realised that the market model was inappropriate to address the problems facing a large developing country which had emerged from a long period of colonialism. In essence however, it was an expression of their desire to be independent of external forces in terms of capital, technology and expertise. This approach of 'selective dissociation' as opposed to complete dissociation was dominant in policymaking during 1950–1980 (Hveem 1983). Such a strategy called for the state to play an active role in industrial development by controlling the 'commanding heights' of the economy.

In advocating self-reliance, India, drawing from its historical experience, was confronted by conflicting pressures and consequently adopted two approaches: the communitarian approach which used local resources and indigenous technology and focused on rural and agricultural development, and the statist, which entailed modernising through large-scale industrial development. This resulted in tension which had its origins in the national movement for independence led by Mahatma Gandhi and Jawaharlal Nehru, whose ideas regarding India's future development were quite different. While the former represented the communitarian viewpoint, the latter promoted the statist viewpoint. Although the statist prevailed over the communitarian, the continued influence of the latter surfaces intermittently, revealing the underlying inconsistency. India's industrial development strategy is thus the product of a debate between the closed indigenous model advocated by Gandhi and the open S&T model advocated by Nehru. The latter has predominated in the form of institutions which have contributed to India's industrial and knowledge base and its ability to produce complete systems of design, process and manufacturing (Mascarenhas 1999). In answer to his own query as to why India, despite its advanced level of textile manufacturing, did not experience an industrial revolution, David Landes (1998) cites the reluctance of skilled Indian artisans to use instruments, iron and steel, or any type of substitute when hands are available in abundance. 'Such a leap would have entailed a shift from hand skills nurtured from childhood, linked to caste identity and division of labor by sex and age. It would also have required imagination outside the Indian cultural and intellectual experience' (229).

A large country dominated by agriculture which is still very traditional in parts, India has had to combat a variety of impediments and develop technology in its bid to modernise itself (Montgomery 1974). If a country is to seize the opportunities offered by technology, it must be confident enough to do so while retaining its unique identity. Dore (1989) cites the example of Japan which went through the process with 'teeth gritting humility'. However, the underlying conflict has, on occasion, surfaced when indigenous developments have been ignored. An example is the Swaraj tractor developed by the Central Mechanical Engineering Institute which was overlooked in favour of Hindustan Machine Tools' licence to manufacture the Czech Zetor tractor (Mascarenhas 1982, 60). The direction of India's industrial development strategy in terms of its linkages with the domestic and traditional sectors of the economy has been questioned by many. Bhatt (1980) questioned the excessive emphasis given to foreign technology at the expense of indigenous developments, citing the lack of support for developments like the biogas plant, baby food, the bamboo tube well and protein food extract (Bhatt 1980, Hveem 1983, and Mascarenhas 1982). Hveem summed up the strategy as a 'blurred xerox copy' (1983, 298–99).

Blame for rejection of indigenous developments like the bamboo tube well and biogas plants, seen as the 'peoples' technology', is attributed by Hanlon to the imitative elite (1977a, 467). 'In the present economic system, appropriate technologies exist and survive only by the grace and favour of the multinationals and big business houses. The issues are not technical, but social and political—about who controls the means of production and distribution' (1977, 469). This bias towards large players was encouraged by a regulatory framework which gave discretionary powers to bureaucrats who adopted a case–by–case approach, albeit marked by some inconsistency.

Indigenous development of technology has often been equated with traditional or appropriate technology. In the context of the current world economy, a strategy of selective dissociation and not complete dissociation is advocated if a country is to move towards greater self–reliance in S&T development. While the need to cling to tradition and reject Western technology is ever present in the Indian mind, the concept has been further reinforced by Gandhi's stance and his warning in 1909: 'Should India ever resolve to imitate England, it will be the ruin of the nation' (Elkins and Max Neef 1990, 5). While Gandhi and Nehru took different positions on India's industrial strategy, the present debate on the use of English for IT-enabled services has, according to Greenspan (2005), rekindled another version of that open or closed Indian mind. 'India's long history of colonialism reappears in various forms in the modern language of development' (24–26). Should a country of India's size, resources and cultural background ever attempt to isolate itself from international interactions, it would surely be an indication of insecure nationalism (Mascarenhas 1999, 145).

Distinguishing between confident nationalism on the one hand and insecure nationalism on the other, Dore (1989) pours scorn on alternative development strategies even expressing apprehension at 'the day when some ingenious blacksmith in Bihar (India) would produce a genuine third world alternative to the bicycle' (1673). In critiquing those visions of alternative technologies, one has to recognise marginal adaptations to local conditions. For example, automatic watches designed by Citizen for Japanese physical movements had to be adapted to the physical movements of Indians. Although technology is universal in that it does not have national boundaries, it still has to be adapted to local conditions like climate, soil, water, skills, needs and resources (Mascarenhas 1982).

Prominent among the several cases of adaptation of modern technology in India is the work of Sam Pitroda whose development of digital switching for rural telephone exchanges that could withstand overheating, operate in heavy monsoon conditions and be protected from dust led to a dramatic transformation in telecommunication services (Pitroda 1993, 66–79). Pitroda disputes those who equate appropriate technology with traditional low-level technology. 'Modern telecommunications and electronic information systems are appropriate technologies even in those regions of the world that still lack adequate water, food and power. The reason is simply that modern telecommunication is an indispensable aid to meeting basic needs' (66). Recognising that efficient telecommunications were essential to

India's development, he suggested the move from electromechanical to digital systems for switching and transmission, offering two important arguments in support: (1) that electromechanical switching was ill-suited to the Indian climate and to Indian conditions because it is more vulnerable to dust and therefore more likely to malfunction, and (2) apart from being more effective, digital switching would help to develop Indian electronics, software and related industries (70). Pitroda's aim was to modernise telecommunication technology which would in turn create the infrastructure to meet basic needs. To get his ideas across in the bureaucratic culture which controlled telecommunications in India, he sought the support of Rajiv Gandhi and this led to the creation of C-DOT, an autonomous design and engineering organisation for the development of digital switching systems (1993, 72, see Ashok Parthasarathy, *Nature*, vol. 422, 6 March 2003, 17).

The success of C-DOT in developing digital switching equipment and the emergence of enterprises to support the venture not only transformed the telecommunication system in India; it led to a major transformation in the use of technology to meet development needs. According to Parthasarathy (ibid.), 'Distinctive features of the technology include the use of the most powerful software available, a wide base of component suppliers to feed the assembly lines, and a "model" plant built just outside Bangalore. This plant was set up by the public sector company, Indian Telecommunication Industries, to produce and test pilot exchanges in the Telecom network under live operational conditions. High-quality technical documentation was generated to cover the engineering, manufacturing, testing, evaluation, installation and commissioning of the network, as well as training of operating and maintenance engineers'. Parthasarathy continues: 'By the end of March 2002, about half of the 37 million lines in the Indian telecom network had C-DOT switches. C-DOT licenses have secured significant orders and exported switches to about 12 developing countries against stiff competition from multinational companies. This has been possible because C-DOT switches are not only technologically state-of-the-art, but are also 30 per cent cheaper than those of its competitors' (ibid., 18).

Success in the telecommunication sector led Rajiv Gandhi as Prime Minister to launch Technology Missions to promote accessibility in relation to six basic needs: drinking water, immunisation, literacy, oilseeds, dairy production and telecommunications. Of the six, the area that has dramatically transformed India is accessibility and quality of both domestic and international telecommunication services. By offering opportunities for small entrepreneurs to own instruments equipped with small meters, India has popularised telephones, making them accessible to everyone at street corners in every city and town. Requiring very little capital investment, roadside public telephones now employ several millions, including women and the physically challenged (See Chapter 5 for changes in telecommunication policy).

In April 2002, the George brothers of Kochi received the award for excellence instituted by the Society of Indian Aerospace Technology and Indigenisation for their 'indigenous airborne antennae'. Having built antennae for Jaguar fighters, the advanced light helicopter (ALH) and Dorniers, their ancillary, Verdant Telemetry, had been approached by Hindustan Aeronautics Limited (HAL) and National Physical Oceanographic Laboratory (NPOL) to help build antennae that could be mounted on aircraft. The brothers claim that they have succeeded in achieving stringent international standards with locally available technology and materials, producing antennae at a fraction of the cost of importing them. 'We kept the costs low by inventing techniques for prototyping and innovating the composite material used for manufacturing antennae'. Referring to their unsuccessful efforts to borrow capital from banks, they say 'India has talent that can produce any stuff at minimum cost. What we only need is government support'. The support is needed mainly for linkages between various units so as to create a market atmosphere conducive for indigenisation. Such an environment did emerge when the United States and other Western countries applied sanctions after the Pokharan nuclear tests, but dissipated with the lifting of sanctions and the resumption of purchases from the West (Das, *The New Indian Express*, 25 April 2002, 7–8).

While technology denial by other countries has played a significant role in various aspects of S&T in India, there is enough evidence to support the claim that indigenous development of fighter aircraft for the Indian Air Force (IAF) has suffered because experts at the National Aeronautical Development Agency (NADA) have had to work to the demands of client agencies whose top brass, influenced by vested interests, has not shown its commitment in supporting indigenous designs. A typical case is that of the Light Combat Aircraft (LCA) for the IAF which took over two decades to develop because of the reluctance of the clients who had the final word on the type and potential of such an aircraft. Having progressed to an advanced stage of production, the IAF has set up an 'LCA Induction Team' based at Bangalore to oversee logistical problems when it begins operation in squadron service. NADA, which is responsible for the design and development of LCA, sees this as an attempt to minimise that disconnection between designers, technicians and pilots. (*The Hindu*, 3 December 2006).

There were a variety of factors that caused the delay in the development of the LCA, the main one being the replacement of the engine used for the Technology Demonstration Aircraft, the GE-404, that was being developed by Gas Turbine Research Establishment (GRTE). The new engine, the Kaveri, after twelve years of development work failed to meet its technical performance target factors that resulted in GRTE looking for a partner to co-develop an engine for the LCA. If, following collaboration, the Kaveri progresses to its performance level, it is expected to be fitted to the GE-404 and if, according to Parthasarathy and Puri (2008), the air-to-air missile system is included with necessary changes in design and required network capability, the LCA will be preferable both on the basis of cost and performance. In addition, an indigenous model which meets the criteria would, for strategic reasons, be far better than the Multi-Role Combat Aircraft (MRCA) now being considered by the IAF.

In sharing their frustrations, scientists and technologists involved in the development of the LCA expressed their dismay in March 2003 vis-à-vis an agency like ISRO which has complete control over its programme and has succeeded in developing a network of ancillary units with skills and expertise to contract out supplies in order to meet programme schedules. The widespread availability of telecommunication services in rural areas through the cheap and simple adaptation of technology is particularly significant when one notes the changes that have occurred in agriculture, especially the dairy sector, brought on by the 'green' and 'white' revolutions, respectively (Mascarenhas 1988, 1999). Once short of food because of its dependence on rainfall and low productivity owing to traditional farming methods, India with the adoption of a range of modernising techniques, along with improved seeds has been placed in a position where it can feed its 1000 million and have surplus to export. 'What accounts for India's agricultural turnaround? A decisive shift in public policy—or, put in another way, a change in the form of state intervention in the agricultural economy—is by now widely accepted to be the main reason' (Varshney 1989, 290). The frittering away of that achievement, during the term in office of the National Democratic Alliance, which was too urban-focused, leading to the neglect of agriculture, has caused a setback which will take some years for Indian agriculture to recover from and return to the prosperity associated with the success of the Green Revolution.

In the dairy sector, India, once the recipient of excess milk powder produced by European farmers on subsidies, has emerged as the largest dairy producer in the world by creating a massive cooperative sector using modern artificial insemination technology to improve cattle breeds, a network of village cooperatives to collect and market milk, the provision of veterinary services, feed processing plants, fodder growing farms and the establishment of a chain of cooling centres and dairy processing plants in urban areas. India's achievements in the agricultural and dairy sector are examples of the application of research and extension work undertaken at the central and state level Agricultural Research Institutes, the Agricultural Universities, the National Dairy Institute and NDDB. Success in such areas in India requires strong leadership. In agriculture, these changes swept in when C. Subramaniam was Minister of Agriculture in the 1960s and M. S. Swaminathan led the IARI. In the dairy sector, Dr Verghese Kurien almost singlehandedly engineered the white revolution while the telecommunication revolution was initiated by Rajiv Gandhi and Sam Pitroda in the 1980s (Varshney 1989, Mascarenhas 1988, 1999, 2004).

3.3.2 Public Sector Industrial Undertakings

By earmarking certain industries exclusively for the public sector, policymakers ensured that the latter would retain control of the 'commanding heights' of the economy, which would help it towards greater economic independence. Such an approach is understandable when viewed from a historical and political perspective. Enunciated within years of independence from colonial domination, the state as entrepreneur demarcated areas between public and private with the basic and heavy industry sector being assigned largely to public enterprises and the rest to the private sector. Apart from considerations such as national security, redistribution, complex technology and the development of the infrastructure, the areas that required considerable investment were set aside for the public sector. That such investment was to be in the public domain was pragmatic, considering the absence of required capital in the private sector. This was certainly the determining factor at least until the 1970s, a view subscribed to even by the private sector. Its continuation after the private sector had developed sufficient capability has, however, been questioned (Degnbol-Martinussen 2001, 94–5).

Between the 1950s and the 1970s, India set up enterprises in the public sector for the manufacture of aircraft, military hardware, steel plants, machine tools, fertilisers and chemicals, electronics and telephone equipment, mining, oil exploration and refining. Of these, some competed with private sector enterprises in areas such as iron and steel, chemicals and fertilisers, and machine tools. When the Indira Gandhi government in the 1970s sought to nationalise banks, insurance and oil companies, concern was expressed by the private sector. Degnbol-Martinussen (2001) comments, ... 'it thus appears that the development of the public sector can be understood essentially as a necessary supplement to the private, Indian controlled sector which, to some extent, implied supplanting or nationalising foreign controlled private enterprises' (100). Whether deserved or undeserved, the performance of public undertakings has come in for constant criticism. The Comptroller and Auditor General (CAG) noted with concern that 'a large group of PSUs ... are today beset with serious problems like slow growth, low productivity, inefficient management, poor project planning and unmanageable time and cost overruns in project implementation' (*Deccan Herald,* 28 April 2003). The very same issues have been raised over the years by the CAG without much effect. To be fair, one must acknowledge the handicaps or constraints that PSUs face in their operations. In my studies I have highlighted the importance of policy efficiency, focusing particularly on the importance of undertaking thorough analysis prior to the establishment of a public industrial undertaking. Subsequent performance of enterprises rests on decisions relating to technology, product mix, location, quality of raw material, proper project planning and implementation (Mascarenhas 1974).

Many public enterprises in the TW are products of a political and administrative system prevalent in newly independent countries which lack decision making capability while retaining suspicion of private capital, particularly foreign private capital. That their decision to establish public undertakings has been influenced in part by political reasoning rather than pure economic analysis suggests that they usually begin their operations with an inherent disadvantage. It helps to adopt categorisation of polities into command and demand types, suggested by Rudolph and Rudolph (1987). Such categorisation by combining both economic and political characteristics suggests that governments are governed by longer-term concerns in the command type and dictated by short-term considerations in the demand type. What is of concern, however, is the unequal access to political power in the demand polity leading to policies that benefit significant supporters of the regime and exclude larger sections of the society. This has led to popular characterisation of such states as 'intermediate regimes' which rely on the support of the rich peasantry and lower middle class to retain power. In return for support such governments adopt a policy of state entrepreneurship that provide access to jobs and scope for small-scale entrepreneurs to supply inputs to public enterprises. The outputs of such public enterprises are provided in the form of cheap inputs like power and water to industry and agriculture. The outputs from agriculture are procured by the state through assured prices and distributed to urban consumers through the public distribution system at subsidised prices. This, then, is a perfect model of a responsive demand polity adopting policies of a command polity in order to retain power. While this analysis fits the Indian situation in the pre-1970s perfectly, there has since been considerable change (Raj 1973, Mascarenhas 1999, 40–41).

Another factor to be considered is that the initial establishment of public enterprises is hindered by lack of experience and knowledge of operating business enterprises and this can become more of a burden if one acquires the wrong technology, poor product mix, or worse still, if they experience problems with technology suppliers. A number of such cases have involved incompetent policy decisions which have affected subsequent performance, with management rendered unable to extricate itself from decisions that it had not taken in the first place. Added to that is the fact that public enterprises are established to fulfil a variety of socio-economic and political objectives. Examples are the location of units such as the Hindustan Machine Tools (HMT) watch factory in Jammu and Kashmir or a unit of ITI in UP to generate employment in less developed areas. Likewise the building of industrial townships with elaborate housing, educational, health and recreational facilities adds to operational costs. Unless one incorporates such social responsibilities into their balance sheets, they are unlikely to erase the image of poor performance. (Mascarenhas 1974).

From Rs 29 crores in 1951, investment in 240 public sector enterprises in India rose to Rs 3,24,632 crores as of 2001–2002. Of this, the central government has contributed Rs 1,43,205 crores with the state governments contributing Rs 1,294 crores and banks and financial institutions Rs 1,42,047 crores. From what has been presented thus far, one has to realise the limitations of adopting the bottom line based on profit and loss accounts, which is the surest and easiest way to judge any business enterprise—public or private. When public enterprises are spawned through the political process or for a variety of non-economic reasons, it is certainly necessary to adopt a broad-based systems approach applying multiple criteria such as the one I have advocated (Mascarenhas 1974). Similar views were expressed by M. Natarajan of the DRDO in response to those who had criticised delays and cost-overruns of fighter planes, missiles and tanks. While acknowledging that the problems of defence production arise from a 'comfortable culture' of licence production and foreign purchases, he defended the need for indigenous research in defence which would otherwise fall into one of the 'triple traps—what is developed abroad may not suit local requirements, what is suitable may be denied and what is not denied could be unaffordable' (*The Hindu*, 15 November 2006). Agencies like DRDO are, according to Ramachandran, constantly under pressure from the sales pitches of foreign vendors, termed BBC (Best of Brochure Claims) by insiders, apparently emanating from a network of arms dealers, including ex-service personnel lobbying for business in a highly lucrative industry (*The Hindu*, 2 February 2007).

Noting that the ratio of pre-tax profit to the capital employed of central public sector undertakings rose from 3.5 per cent during 1990–93 to 8.0 per cent during 1995–98, Srinivasan cautions us against reaching hasty conclusions. 'This aggregate profitability measure is misleading, since the enterprises whose profits are aggregated include state oil and petroleum monopolies. In addition, at least for those enterprises that are competing with private enterprises, their post-tax return has to be compared with similar returns for their private counterparts' (in Krueger ed. 2001, 66–7).

While the above seems to confirm my reservation against adopting simplistic analyses to evaluate public sector undertakings in India, one cannot overlook the impact that such undertakings have had on specific areas like Bangalore where the central government thought it prudent to establish several public undertakings such as HMT, HAL, Indian

Telecommunication Industries, BEL, Central Industrial Laboratories and others. To that list one must add IISc, the National Aeronautical Laboratory and C-DOT. Together, these institutions employ about 200,000 scientists, engineers, technicians and skilled workers.

While increased financial and operational autonomy based on performance guidelines have acted as an incentive, there is also the challenge of competition from the private sector. In this context, Prime Minister Manmohan Singh, while addressing the gathering at the golden jubilee of the Administrative Staff College, Hyderabad, spoke of his government's desire to unlock the potential of PSUs (*The Hindu*, 6 December 2006). With increasing internal and external pressure towards privatisation, some reform of public enterprises could soon become a priority.

3.4 Economic Liberalisation

The edifice of the Indian industrial structure was, in the years after independence, built around a series of restrictions on entry of business and a range of bureaucratic controls on their operations. Characterised by a system that involved passing files from one bureaucrat to another, aptly described by Bardhan and Datta Chaudhuri as a 'multiple-veto-system' (*The Economist*, 21 January 1995), such a regime was operative for four decades in both the public and private sectors of the economy. Understandably, such attitudes had a stranglehold on the economy and affected its performance. Despite steady growth during the 1980s, the economy was faced with a major current account deficit running to $10 million annually with reserves down to weeks of imports. A major financial crisis in 1990 led to drastic changes with freedom and flexibility for investors to enter the market without being hampered by bureaucratic obstacles. Such an occurrence was fortuitous and arose from the premature resignation of the Chandrashekar-led coalition government, the unfortunate assassination of Rajiv Gandhi (who had favoured liberalisation during his term in office) while campaigning, and the coming to power of P. V. Narasimha Rao. Ably assisted by Dr Manmohan Singh, the architect of the reforms (who became Prime Minister in 2004), Rao introduced the package of reforms which, although formulated in the mid-1980s, had been held in abeyance owing to lack of political support or, more accurately, opposition in the Lok Sabha. However, when presented as an instrument of crisis management in 1991, acceptance was quicker (Degnbol-Martinussen

2001, 145). Following this crisis, the Finance Minister went beyond mere stabilisation measures and introduced further reform (Krueger ed. 2002).

Like most other reforms, the Indian package included short-term economic stabilisation followed by longer-term economic restructuring. The first target of stabilisation was the reduction of the fiscal deficit from 8.1 per cent of GDP in 1990–91 to 5.7 per cent in 1992–93. The rupee was devalued by 24 per cent; most exchange controls were removed; export subsidies were abolished and an import entitlement scheme for exporters was announced. Further, tariffs were reduced, restrictions on foreign private investment removed and a commitment made to divest investment in public industrial undertakings. The industrial licensing system was dismantled and areas hitherto closed to the private sector were now opened in areas such as telecommunication, air transport, electricity generation, roads and so on. Tax rates were also reduced for both companies and individuals.

The 1991 liberalisation is, according to one perceptive critic, not entirely attributable to the foreign exchange crisis. That push for reform came, writes Pederson (2000), from a 'new breed of Indian entrepreneurs'. Pederson further observes that 'the landscape of Indian industry has undergone a major change since the 1980s and the 1991 policies may be interpreted as a political reflection of these changes within the Indian society'. However, the timing was influenced by the Gulf war which created an oil crisis exposing India's vulnerability and reducing repatriation of savings from Indians working in the Gulf (Pederson 2000).

The outcome of such wide-ranging reforms has not been as dramatic as expected. It could be, as Degnbol-Martinussen suggests, that the institutional arrangements in India have not adapted to the requirements of liberalisation (154). 'The new bodies set up mostly reflected the preoccupation with control rather than genuine priority to the promoting and facilitating roles envisaged for the bureaucracy in the new policy framework. With few exceptions, government officials have received no training in how to perform in their new roles' (171). Describing liberalisation of the 1990s as a pro-business drift because of its limited range and its reflection of existing political forces in the country, Kohli (2004) claims that 'India's state is still heavily interventionist and the Indian economy is still relatively closed to external goods, finance and investors' (285).

After a period of political and policy stalemate following liberalisation, the Indian economy picked up in early 2000 with significant success in industry and agriculture and showed a period of consistent growth in GDP. Such steady growth and a healthy current account surplus enabled the Indian economy to absorb fluctuation in oil prices and to cope with natural disasters without external help. The rate of GDP growth increased from 4 per cent in 2002–03 to 8.2 per cent in 2003–04, 7.5 per cent in 2004–05 and 9 per cent in 2005–06 while the estimate for 2006–07, released by the Central Statistical Organisation (CSO), was 9.2 per cent. CSO's revised estimate of growth in national income was 9.4 per cent for 2006–07. While both manufacturing and services showed continuing growth, agriculture recorded a lower growth of 2.7 per cent as compared to 6 per cent the previous year (*The Hindu*, 2 June 2007).

TABLE 3-1 India's Rate of GDP Growth (per cent)

Year	*Rate*
2000–2001	5.5
2001–2002	5.0
2002–2003	4.1
2003–2004	8.2
2004–2005	7.5
2005–2006	9.0
2006–2007	9.4

Source: Economic Survey (Annual).

The rapid growth of the Indian economy is attributed to vastly improved financial intermediation following liberalisation and constitutes the strength of the Indian economy as noted by Rodrik and Subramaniam (2004). In advocating further liberalisation to promote India's growth towards a knowledge economy, Dahlman and Utz (2005) of the World Bank were particularly impressed with its macroeconomic stability, its dynamic private sector, institutions that support a free market economy, a well-developed financial sector and a rich cultural base that generates a wealth of ideas (ix). Other observers have noted India's favourable demographic dividend where approximately 450 million are under twenty years of age and its high savings rate as significant factors in future growth.

Attributed to structural changes in the economy, this growth has remained steady across all sectors of the economy, such as IT, automotive, pharmaceuticals, basic metals and minerals, banking and textiles. Indian manufacturing has, according to a recent study, emerged as a major player. Out of a total of 129 sectors studied, twenty-nine reported an excellent growth rate of over 20 per cent, thirty-five reported growth rates of 10–20 per cent while forty-nine registered modest growth of 0–10 per cent. Only nineteen sectors registered negative growth (*The Hindu*, 7 June 2004). While providing a boost to the overall growth of the economy, such a performance has had an impact on manufacturing exports. Dr Chidambaram, Chief Scientific Advisor, pointed out that independent of the automotive, petroleum, IT hardware, drugs and pharmaceutical sectors where academic–industry relations are strong, India's performance in the atomic energy, space, and IT software sectors have been at par with the developed world with Indian steel makers being rated among the world's best[1] (*The Hindu,* 9 May 2005). So it was no surprise when Tata Steel bought Britain's Corus 'which includes the steelmaking remnants of the old imperial power. Nor is Tata alone: younger Indian companies such as Infosys and Wipro are storming international markets. Meanwhile, the world's business people and investors queue up to lavish money on India's talented engineers and computer scientists' (*The Economist,* 2–9 February 2007, 9).

India's capacity for innovation combined with its earlier policy of indigenisation had forced Indian industry to initiate local technical capability and manufacturing. This environment encouraged the emergence of entrepreneurs who developed products sophisticated enough to be exported to industrialised countries, e.g. supply of radiator caps by Sunderam Fasteners to General Motors. Following Sunderam Fasteners' success, India was chosen as a link in the global supply chain of Toyota, Cummins, Hyundai, and Renault and, in 2003, became a favoured supplier of automotive components (*The Hindu,* 15 September 2003). In 2003, Tata Motors and MG Rover launched Indica, an Indian car marketed as City Rover UK. The World Bank views the Indian auto industry as having benefited with liberalisation. Apart from the 20,000 cars exported in 2004 and sold under MG Rover brand, prices fell by 8 per cent to 10 per cent because of competition (Dahlman and Utz 2005, 35). India's Scorpios are reportedly doing well in Europe, as is the electric-operated Rewa in the US (*The Hindu,* 9 May 2005).

A major breakthrough in automobile manufacturing was the launch of Tata's Nano in January 2008 estimated to cost around Rs 120,000. Concerned at seeing whole families travelling on two-wheelers, Ratan

Tata saw the need to offer the Indian public an affordable car that would be safer to travel in. Its launch has heralded India as 'a natural home for frugal engineering' and a low cost manufacturing centre, particularly for small automobiles (The Hindu, 11 January 2008). For those concerned about congestion and environmental impact of additional cars on the road, Ratan Tata claims that Nano has 'lower pollution levels than two-wheelers'. With India's reputation in the manufacturing of components, Nano has further highlighted the capabilities of India's low cost automotive manufacturing ecosystem. (Ramnath Subbu, 'Nano offers scope for cost-effective Component Hub', The Hindu, 29 March 2009).

With the rate of growth in the automobile industry, India is facing a shortage of skilled manpower. To meet the demands of the automobile and ancillary industries and the infrastructure sector, a VTU-Bosch Rexroth Centre of Competence in Automation Technology is to be situated at Mysore to impart training and education in a range of disciplines in high-end engineering and technology. State-of-the-art laboratories are to be set up with fourteen subject experts to be trained as its resource persons. As a fast growing economy with a growing market for cars, this will in the not too distant future constitute one of the key sectors in the economy (*The Hindu*, 17 November 2006).

With dramatic changes taking place in manufacturing, it probably surprises observers to note that India, until recently castigated for its shoddy quality and considered a laggard in manufacturing, could now be a showcase for a manufacturing revolution. Writing about the Moser Baer factory for manufacturing CDs and DVDs, Overdorf writes that the value of India's manufactured exports rose from about $37 billion in 2002 to above $54 billion in 2004, and it could rise to $4300 billion by 2015. India has an advantage over China here, with its talent pool of chemists, designers and engineers (Jason Overdorf, 'Future Factories', *Newsweek*, 7 March 2005, 38).

The success of the automotive industry, especially in small cars, has led the government in the 2006 budget to declare that it will attempt to make India a global manufacturing hub for other sectors (*The Hindu*, 11 March 2006). To sustain the levels of growth that India is now witnessing, huge quantities of raw materials like coal, iron ore and bauxite are required. However, such resources are located in Orissa, Jharkhand and Chattisgarh where local political and social conditions have changed from the days when the steel plants were constructed at Rourkela, Bhilai and Bokaro. Those areas with large deposits of mineral resources are populated by tribals who survive on forest land. Unlike the 1950s and 1960s when material incentives were sufficient to allow access to mine those areas, the situation has changed today. While local hostility to mining is easier to mobilise with the growth of political activism, environmental legislation acts as an additional hurdle, delaying the process for planned mining projects. While the massive projects of the 1960s under public sector control were seen as beneficial to the locals, the current prospectors, predominantly large private companies, are met with suspicion and hostility (Sachitanand, *The Hindu*, 13 March, 2006).

While ICT and manufacturing have performed beyond expectations, it is essential that small and medium-sized enterprises in towns and rural areas receive some of that largesse if the fruits of economic liberalisation are to benefit the common man. A case in point is Falna, a town in Rajasthan, where Karl Chen, owner of Taiwanese firm Futex, working with local manufacturers of umbrella parts, expresses his preference for Indian employees, whom he considers more intelligent than the Chinese. While a Chinese employee will do exactly what he is told, the Indian is likely to look for a short cut, which may not be so good in the short run because it could affect quality, but will eventually be beneficial because of the innovation that can occur. Falna with its population of 17,000 is also the home of Falna Television, owned and operated by Abdul Rahman, a 70-year-old self-taught manufacturer of satellite dishes. Starting with the manufacture of transistor radios, he moved towards satellite dishes and now produces 2,000 satellite dishes annually with a workforce of fifty people. Another Falna success story features Jagtar Singh, a former bus conductor, who now owns a fleet of 135 buses (India: A Survey, *The Economist*, 21 January 1995, 14–15).

India's current growth is apparently being sustained by new markets in towns and rural areas. Life Insurance Corporation sells more than 50 per cent of its policies in rural areas; 50 per cent of BSNL'S mobile connections are in small towns and villages and there are twice the number of Kisan credit cards in rural than urban India (Ajay Khanna, *The Hindu*, 27 February 2006). One cannot overlook the fact that today's dynamic private sector is riding on the shoulders of a modern industrial public sector including telecommunication equipment, electronics, space and communication technology and the quality of its human resources which are a product of public sector investment in higher education and S&T infrastructure (see Chapter 2). Even today, the IT sector depends heavily on state support, e.g. Electronics City, KEONICS, ISRO, STPI, etc.

GDP growth is expected to rise and perhaps touch 8 to 10 per cent in subsequent years and if such growth rates are to be sustained, attention will have to be given to the development of infrastructure. *The Economist* calculates that economic growth of 6 per cent requires an extra 9 per cent of power capacity a year requiring investment of $12 billion over the next twelve years. A major problem with electricity generation in India is that it is under the control of the states which, influenced by electoral calculations, sell power for less than it costs to produce (21 January 1995). Although private foreign capital sees power generation and distribution in India as an attractive investment, the experience of the Maharashtra state government and foreign investors with the Dhabol power plant has been a bitter one with ongoing legal disputes (*India Today*, 22 May 2000, 22 January 2001).

Apart from the dismal experience with foreign private investment in the power sector, the uncertainty of minimum return on investment owing to a complicated pricing and distribution system explains the lack of interest. To encourage more investment and to improve the State Electricity Boards (SEBs), the central government has decided to invest Rs 34,000 crores in an Accelerated Power Development Programme (APDP) to be implemented during 2001–2012. The focus will be on improving the commercial viability of SEBs by adopting the Karnataka model which mandates independent power producers (IPPs) to sell power to the SEBs with a Power Regulatory Authority and to revise power tariffs in phases (Das, *Deccan Herald*, 11 December 2000). For its eleventh plan (2007–12), India is targeting a 10 per cent growth with the Planning Commission and Power Ministry projecting an ambitious goal of 66,463 MW of power generation.

With India's growing population and pace of growth, the search for non-conventional sources of energy is inevitable. Government initiative and support have enabled great strides in the field of renewable energy through the setting up of wind, solar, biomass and small hydro power stations whose output together amounts to 5.5 per cent of installed capacity of grid-connected electricity. Currently, India's grid connected capacity of wind power is larger than the grid connected capacity of nuclear power. India's eight wind turbine manufacturers can meet demands at short notice, making windpower potential limitless (Ashok

Parthasarathy, *The Hindu*, 17 August 2005). In the area of solar energy, India had 'designed, developed, manufactured, installed in the field, and maintained around one million solar photovoltaic cell (SPV) systems by the end of March 2005, the largest in any country' (ibid.). Central Electronics Limited and BEL, both public sector undertakings, are the leading manufacturers of SPVs. Solar energy is currently used in rural homes, street lighting and traffic lights, to pump water for drinking and irrigation, for community TV sets, rural telephone exchanges, satellite communication terminals and to power the electronics on offshore oil production platforms. It plays a vital role in vaccine storage refrigerators in rural primary health centres, at railway signals and at warning systems of unmanned rail-road intersections. With current crude oil prices, Parthasarathi feels renewable energy will become even 'more techno-economically competitive and mass market-oriented' (ibid.).

To meet future energy demands from non-fossil sources, the Indian government entered into an agreement with the US government in 2006 to acquire both technology and raw materials. In return, India agreed to open fourteen of its nuclear plants which currently produce power for civilian use to international inspection. This arrangement has raised misgivings in both countries and was awaiting ratification by their respective legislatures (*The Hindu*, 3 March 2006). While the final deal as conceded by the US was a triumph for the internal debate led by India's scientific community, it has undoubtedly pushed India further from its otherwise independent stand in foreign policy.

Unless there is a significant improvement in rail, roads and ports, any attempts to increase India's exports are unlikely to be successful. The dramatic transformation in the operations of the Indian Railways is a hopeful sign. The first breakthrough came when CMC, a public sector company, developed a software system for reservation of tickets on the railway network. It resolved the primary cause of passenger discomfort on Indian railways by making ticket reservations transparent and eliminating opportunities for illegal transactions. Several innovative measures introduced under a new Minister have increased the operational efficiency of the railways and improved its public image and profits significantly, without a noticeable increase in travel and freight charges. Once regarded with some amount of pessimism, the transformation made the minister a sought-after guest at elite business schools in India and the US.

Acknowledging that a good network of roads is vital to industrial development, the 2003–04 Union budget paid special attention to the building of roads. Forty-eight new roads covering a distance of 10,000 kilometres at an estimated cost of Rs 40,000 crores were to be laid. Many of India's air and sea ports were straining under the increased use and plans were afoot to modernise some and build others (*Deccan Herald*, 7 March 2003).

Hailing India as the next knowledge superpower, the *New Scientist* (19 February 2005), predicted that the ideas being generated by employees of a hundred innovative IT and science-based firms will take the world by storm. Further cause for optimism is provided by India's thriving pharmaceutical and biotechnology industries. With India's advantage in skill-intensive industries, the CII-McKinsey study projected an increase in manufacturing exports from $40 billion in 2005 to $300 billion by 2015 with a labour force of 25–30 million. To achieve this, however, the report suggested that Indian exporters should move from a domestic to a global approach (*The Hindu*, 25 October 2004).

Based on their analysis of India's economic performance in the 1980s and 1990s, Rodrik and Subramaniam concluded that India was on a permanently high growth path. 'The pro-business tilt in the 1980s, which was a rectification of previous distortion, may have been the first decade of true import substitution. And, by following up with the reforms of the 1990s, India seemed to have pulled off an interesting experiment in policy sequencing. The limited pro-business reform in the 1980s had great political economy merit of avoiding the creation of losers, and appeared to have built up the kind of dynamic efficiency that stood India in good stead, when the deeper, but more dislocating reforms of the 1990s were implemented' (Rodrik and Subramaniam, *The Hindu*, 15 May 2004). Substantiating their claims with some features of the Indian economy, such as productivity, demographics and institutions, they assert that India had hitherto failed to reap the benefits of its institutional quality. 'In other words, India having done the really hard work of building good economic and political institutions failed until the 1980s, to take advantage of it' (Rodrik and Subramaniam, *The Hindu*, 17 May 2004).

Disputing those critics of Nehru who attribute India's woes to Nehruvian socialism, Inder Malhotra asserted that 'Nothing can be further from the truth. From 1947 until the mid-1960s, there was no escape from the policies Nehru pursued. Without the heavy industry, the infrastructure and the science and technology base that he assiduously built, there could have been no economic development of any kind. While speaking the language of Gandhi, Nehru urged his countrymen to develop a scientific temper and built a network of high-class institutions of science and technology, IITs and the superb atomic energy establishment. But for this pioneering work, India could not have become a "software superpower" and nuclear weapons power (*The Hindu*, 27 May 2004).

That the economic recovery of the early 2000s was largely urban-centred and focused around the new economy, spearheaded by IT, became evident in the 2004 general election. The United Democratic alliance government led by BJP and its allies suffered a setback resulting in the return to power of a Congress-led United Progressive Alliance. Apart from temporary hiccups on the stock market, the change in government was smooth, with the return of the architects of the 1991 economic liberalisation, Dr Manmohan Singh as Prime Minister and C. Chidambaram as Finance Minister.

India was faced with two options: (1) growth by encouraging foreign investment through liberalisation, privatisation and a stable fiscal and monetary policy, or (2) a pre-1990 approach with the state providing economic and social opportunity through education, health care, land reform, and the encouragement of small and medium sized enterprises, and most important of all investment in infrastructure and basic and heavy industry. While the previous government veered towards the former, the government in power was trying to balance the two by avoiding either extreme (Ravi, *The Hindu*, 25 February 2005).

The present government realises the importance of continuing its economic reforms while bearing in mind the implications for the average Indian. While IT which has brought prosperity and prestige to some in recent years will continue to receive encouragement, the government intends to correct a distortion, the unintended neglect of the manufacturing sector, the traditional 'brick and mortar economy' (*The Hindu*, 20 June 2004). No one can ignore, least of all the Prime Minister, the challenges India faces. In warning his countrymen not to be complacent, he listed five challenges to be faced in the near future. They are: revitalisation of the rural economy; improved delivery of essential public services; improved management of urban areas; preparing the financial system for greater inclusion and increased global integration and establishing a regulatory culture to facilitate cost-effective private investment in infrastructure (*The Hindu*, 18 December 2006). *The Economist* (2–9 February 2007) pointed out the areas which are serious obstacles to sustained growth: the infrastructure—roads, ports and power, followed by quality of primary education, primary health, public services and labour laws as serious obstacles to sustained growth. India cannot overlook what I refer to as the underlying anomalies—an educated elite with high rates of illiteracy, widespread ownership of mobile telephones with having to queue up for hours to collect water for personal use; in essence, the co-existence of wealth and poverty. While the opening of the market to the private sector will generate growth, that growth has to be achieved with policies for social equity. Making economic growth inclusive is a massive challenge facing India today.

The United Progressive Alliance led by Manmohan Singh of the Congress Party overcame internal tensions within the coalition over its strategic alliance with the United States aimed at acquiring nuclear technology to meet its energy requirements. Despite the withdrawal of outside support from the left parties, the government not only held on but went on to win the 2009 general election with an increased majority. The result has given the Congress-led alliance a comfortable working majority to carry out some of its policies of economic growth with inclusion, especially the National Rural Employment Guarantee Scheme (NREGA), a policy which has garnered rural support.

Amid the recession that hit the world economy affecting growth in 2008–09 between 6.7 and 7.1 per cent, the government had maintained an 8 per cent average growth during its term (2004–09). This modest achievement was helped by the satisfactory performance of the agriculture and IT sectors. However, the agricultural sector is likely to suffer owing to the delay of the monsoon and the consequent shortfall in rain.

With the recession, the belief that the Indian economy is 'decoupled' from the West has been belied. The sharp decline in the stock markets in response to global cues was the first indication that global developments had retained their hold over Indian markets. While the withdrawal of foreign institutional investors has resulted in a widening of the current account deficit, the most significant indicator is the decline in software exports. Further decline is expected in industry possibly from 8.2 per cent in 2007–08 to 4.14 percent in 2008–09. However, the Indian banking sector remains quite robust with satisfactory credit growth. Other helpful factors are a comparatively lower reliance on exports which amount to only 21.2 per cent of GDP and a gross saving rate of 37.7 per cent of GDP. Its poor infrastructure leaves India open to investments that any stimulus package can offer (*The Economist*, 17 March 2009). In this and in the previous economic crisis (1990), one must note that the state has played a crucial balancing role in relation to the market once again confirming my view that the type of state intervention in the economy is vital.

The strength of India's political and economic institutions enabled it to withstand a major economic crisis while undertaking the largest ever election, in which the governing coalition was returned to power with an increased majority. The stock market showed significant upsurge expecting government to focus on further economic reform. In his June 2009–10 budget, Finance Minister Pranab Mukherjee has paid attention to 'investment in delivery of public services, ensuring greater accountability, efficient targeting of expenditure, weeding out wasteful expenditure and constant monitoring' (*The Hindu*, 1 June 2009). Harsh Mander comments: 'Millions among the men and women who lined up patiently outside polling booths this hot summer have voted for a caring state, for inclusive growth and a secular government. The burden of expectations, therefore, that rests on the shoulders of the government in New Delhi—which has been returned with an emphatic expanded mandate—is daunting and diverse' (*The Hindu*, 31 May 2009).

Prior to the election, the German Foreign Minister, Frank-Walter Steinmeier, while inaugurating the Frankfurt Book Fair, suggested 'that contact with "unfamiliar" India can help us understand our own Europe better. For, contact with India is contact with the world's largest democracy, which unites over a billion people in 28 states and 7 Union Territories in a country in which 400 languages and dialects are spoken, over 20 of which are recognized as national languages, in which the Prime Minister is a Sikh, the President a Muslim, and the largest political party is led by a woman with a Christian background. This India sometimes appears paradoxical, when we see how many different ways of life, cultures, languages, religions and beliefs coexist, and despite all internal antagonisms, both apparent and real, are bound together by the Constitution and the state' (*The Hindu*, 9 October 2006).

3.5 Privatisation

The Indian government policy on privatisation was aimed at retaining partial public control of assets of up to 50 per cent of equity and transferring the rest to the private sector. In 1991, a policy of divesting shareholding in select public undertakings was announced and, between 1991 and 2000, shares in thirty-nine undertakings were sold, reserving a percentage of government equity. A Disinvestment Commission which was set up in 1996 studied the situation and submitted reports before the expiry of its term in 1999, when its role was taken over by the Department of Disinvestment. Early success with 51 per cent of Bharat Aluminium (BALCO) followed by Videsh Sanchar Nigam (VSNL) led to others. However, the initial policy of diluting ownership through partial divestment while yielding limited results faced innumerable controversies. In fact, the sale of Centaur Airport and Centaur Juhu, both located at Mumbai, attracted the attention of the Central Bureau of Investigation (CBI), which launched enquiries into alleged irregularities. Similar questions about the sale of Modern Foods were raised, belying the expectations of policy-makers. Narrating the Modern Foods experience, Vardarajan concluded 'at the end of the day, the story of India's first full-scale privatisation is not a happy one' (*The Hindu*, 5 May 2005).

In deciding that the central government could not go ahead with the disinvestment of Hindustan Petroleum Corporation Ltd. (HPCL) and Bharat Petroleum corporation Ltd. (BPCL) 'without appropriate parliamentary legislation', the court concluded that there were serious flaws in the manner in which they were intended to be privatised (*The Hindu*, 18 September 2003). That decision and the election of the UPA government had far-reaching consequences for privatisation. Some other decisions taken by the previous government have also come in for re-examination. These include the sale of thirteen PSUs listed as strategic sales by the NDA government from which the UPA government has been forced to retreat.

Independent of the legal and political hurdles in the way of privatisation and the process adopted, the government's policy has not been firmly enunciated or implemented. Evidently, the path to privatisation, should the government move further in that direction, is strewn with obstacles. The present UPA government subscribes to a policy of privatising profitable enterprises while retaining government control with majority holding. An argument in favour is that resources released could be invested in social services. Further, there is an underlying feeling that the change of ownership from public to private will automatically result in efficiency (Kaur 2005). However, the calamity faced by the residents of Mumbai during the floods in July/August 2005 has increased scepticism on the part of those who are suspicious of the private sector's capacity to cope with the urgent demands of a major crisis (Jayant, *The Hindu*, 10 August 2005).

3.6 Conclusion

The state in India has played an important role in industrial development by adopting a strategy of self-reliance. That role was dominant during 1950–1990 and declined when the government adopted economic liberalisation. Would India's industrial performance have been better had the government adopted the policy of liberalisation earlier, like east Asian countries? Like other critics of the political economy of state intervention, I am inclined to say that this has more to do with quality rather than extent. Bestowed with a public service that was competent at maintaining political stability through the democratic process but ill equipped to manage the economy, its performance in promoting industrialisation was less than commendable creating instead a restrictive atmosphere, where investment activity had to be approved and scarce resources channelled and rationed through a bureaucratic system of approvals and counter approvals. Any dealings with the bureaucracy were fraught with delays and frustration and actually encouraged unethical practices.

The key issue in understanding state intervention in developing countries is to examine how that power is generated and used to promote change. Illustrative of the context in which economic performance has to be evaluated is the decision of the Supreme Court declaring privatisation of two public enterprises in September 2003 as lacking parliamentary approval and therefore unconstitutional. While Kohli suggests that success or failure of state intervention depends on how good states are in organising power and promoting development (Kohli 2004, 423), Khatkate (1997) sums it up thus:

> The paralysis of economic policy formulation and its fitful course have their genesis in the inner working of the political system which operates in such a manner that, at one extreme, economic policy has punishment as its basis, but without sanction for enforcing it, and at the other, incentive as its rationale, without any built-in mechanism to reward success. It is this nature of economic policy, built simultaneously on punishment and incentive, but without any sanction for enforcing penalty or a system for offering reward, which

largely explains the frequent gyration in economic policy in India (1557).

According to Tickner (1987), 'the development path taken by India since independence is actually closer to the Listian model, with its emphasis on building productive capacity and national power than to the Gandhian version of self-reliance' (167). Other observers of internal political dynamics attribute India's problems to the conflicting views of Nehru and Gandhi whose underlying approaches to development differed significantly (Mascarenhas 1999).

Despite operating in a system which was created for a different era, India has succeeded in laying a solid foundation for industrialisation. The outcomes of the 1991 liberalisation programme must be seen in the context of the policies initiated by Prime Minister Nehru and the many institutes of excellent quality that emerged as a result. Without that foundation of elite engineering education offered at the IITs and the chain of S&T institutes, India would have continued its dependence on technology suppliers and been unable to even hope to become self-reliant. To obtain technology in strategic areas such as defence, atomic energy, space and advanced computing, nations are expected to toe a certain line in international affairs. If not, the consequence is technology denial, which India has experienced at crucial stages of its development (discussed elsewhere in this study). India's strategy of self-reliance spearheaded by the state, has, after four decades, placed it in the top rung of industrialised countries.

Note

[1] According to The Economist (20 September 2003), 'India is now producing companies that can compete with any in the world. These include not just the well-known successes in information technology and pharmaceuticals, but also businesses in "old economy" industries: cars and car parts, motorcycles, cement and steel.' Tata steel, according to a leading information service provider based in the US, is considered the best steel company among 23 steelmakers in the world (The Hindu, 23 June 2005).

4

Development of the Computer Industry

4.1 Introduction

India has emerged as an industrial power in a period of five decades, having laid the foundation with an S&T infrastructure and a broad industrial base. With this in place, the country has moved towards greater diversification, with special attention to the development of ICT, in which gigantic strides have been made since the 1990s. Such changes have enabled India to move, in many sectors, from the industrial age into the IT age, ushering in a knowledge economy and society.

The initial venture into broad-based investment in S&T, which had an indirect impact on the development of electronics, is now looked upon as an unplanned phase in the development of a computer policy. It originated in 1966 within the AEC when its Chairman Homi J. Bhabha headed a committee whose report became the basis of India's beginnings in the computer industry. That decision to examine India's prospects to enter the electronics industry was the result of a US embargo on the export of electronic equipment to India, following its support for Pakistan during the 1965 Indo-Pakistan war. The development of the first digital computer by Srikantan, a member of the computer division of the AEC, was followed by the establishment of a manufacturing unit, the ECIL, in 1969. With BEL already in operation in Bangalore since 1954, the need for a centrally focused agency for electronics policy making was filled with the creation of the Department of Electronics (DOE) in 1970 and the Electronics Commission (EC) in 1971. Although both organisations were technically equipped, their initial impact in the game of Delhi's bureaucratic politics was limited. The next crucial phase was the development of a software policy in the mid-1980s, while the third phase was the dramatic growth in IT in the 1990s accelerated by the transformation in telecommunication technology.

Such growth in ICT has attracted the attention of scholars focusing on different aspects. While one group (Greico 1984, Brunner 1995, Evans 1995) has focused on the role of government policy, tracing developments from the mid-1960s, the other (Sridharan 1996, Joseph 1997, Heeks 1996, Singhal and Rogers 2001, Saxenian 2002) has closely observed the effects of post-1991 economic liberalisation which allowed unrestricted imports, encouraged foreign private investment and offered incentives for exports.

While acknowledging the contribution of some of the studies mentioned above in terms of the insights offered, the present study aims at a broader analysis. In any study of this nature, one has to understand the inter-linkages between several segments of the Indian political and socio-economic system. Within that system, a crucial role is played by the political and administrative system, which although known for its elitist and restrictive regime, does, however, offer a continuity and stability not available in most other TW countries. This elite political-administrative system, has, under successive governments spawned three vital segments to which can be attributed the credit for the current ICT boom. The first of these is the S&T infrastructure described as 'excellence in the midst of poverty' (Maddox and Rich 1984), with the country becoming known as The Next Knowledge Superpower (*New Scientist*, 19 February 2005). The second is the often discredited public enterprise sector within which are included enterprises such as HMT, HAL, ITI, BEL, etc., which have contributed in many ways to the industrial milieu. The third, which is more specific to the IT sector, includes organisations such as ECIL, CMC, C-DAC, C-DOT and ISRO.

While the above achievements are a product of state-directed development, the specific outcome of ICT in the old Mysore region has to be explained both in terms of historical and cultural foundations and in terms of economic liberalisation, market response, regional policies, engineering skills and entrepreneurial ability (see Chapters 7 and 8). These are issues that will occupy our attention in the rest of this study. In this and the following chapter (Chapter 5), I examine policies and strategies that have contributed to the development of ICT in India. Chapter 4 roughly covers the period 1965–1983 while Chapter 5 covers the period from 1983 to the present.

Following the introduction, Section 4.2 of this chapter traces the background of India's efforts to acquire technology in order to develop the computer industry while Section 4.3 examines the factors that influenced the direction of that policy. Section 4.4 traces the evolution of computer policy in the context of current technological change. In Section 4.5, the role of DOE and EC are discussed while Section 4.6 looks at bureaucratic politics as different departments seek to promote their own interests. Section 4.7 traces the gradual shift towards promoting indigenous manufacturing and restricting the role of foreign computer companies, and Section 4.8 analyses the impact that such change might have for the future direction of ICT in India.

4.2 The Beginnings

While India (more specifically Bangalore in terms of this study) has attracted attention for its ICT, it may surprise those unfamiliar with the developments to learn that there was no mention of software in policy pronouncements until the creation of the Software Development Promotion Agency (SPDA) in 1984. Until then, Indian government strategy was to promote an indigenous import-substituting, self-reliant electronics industry under government control. Consistent with its industrial development strategy, this included restrictions on entry of foreign private capital and a system of licensing and import controls which were regulatory and protectionist in character (Greico 1984, Bhagwati 1988, Evans 1995, Heeks 1996).

In 1966, the computer industry, which at the time relied on foreign imports, was examined by a committee chaired by Bhabha, which advocated a strategy of self-reliance to be achieved in the shortest possible time and in the most economical manner (Greico 1984, 21). It visualised that self-sufficiency was achievable within a period of ten years and set out three goals:

- greater Indian participation in the ownership and control of foreign computer subsidiaries;
- all computer needs to be met from domestic sources by 1970, with the exception of large computer systems; and
- access to participation in the manufacture of most advanced systems available internationally by the 1967–72 period (Greico 1984, 9).

To implement such a strategy, the government established priorities and allocated production capacities by licensing prospective investors. While this had been adopted in most industries, the computer industry differed in that it had been developed largely by organisations in the public sector. Although Evans (1995) has questioned this policy on the grounds that the state cannot effectively play the role of producer, he does however acknowledge the valuable contribution of BEL, ECIL and CMC, which are public undertakings. Encouragement of public enterprises was obviously the government's way of restricting the entry of foreign capital while promoting its self-reliant industrialisation strategy. The outcome of such a strategy, however, was the industry's inability to respond to developments in the international computer industry because in the absence of interaction it remained unaware of them.

In analysing technical change, Brunner (1995) adopts the Schumpeterian analysis, positioning himself between Adam Smith's invisible hand and government's guiding hand (17). Viewing the Bhabha Committee recommendations as an effort in leapfrogging, he adopts the concept of generic technologies, and categorises them into, one, the source from which technological know-how springs; and two, by the way in which benefits arising from innovative efforts can be captured. Such differences in generic technologies give rise to distinct technological regimes at the industry level, one entrepreneurial and the other routinised. Brunner suggests that the advent of the microprocessor (1995) was an indication of the emergence of an entrepreneurial technological regime. Such a technological regime enabled a country like India to exploit the special nature of the computer manufacturing industry.

Although opportunities for accessibility of computer technology were available, the Indian computer industry did not use them until 1977 because the industrial policies and the restrictive regulatory framework were more suited to a routine technological regime. In effect, the creation of a fortress type mentality caused India, which had advanced sufficiently in the industrial sector by adopting a self-reliant approach, to reject both foreign investment and technology. Despite much criticism, one wonders if the Indian private sector could have responded, in the way it did after 1991, if barriers had not been erected at all or if they had been removed a decade or two earlier. Doubtless, that regime created both the infrastructure and an industrial public sector, which have together helped the growth of a vigorous private sector. Perhaps the ultimate outcome could have been achieved at a lower economic cost.

4.3 Factors Influencing Indian Policy

In stating the goals for the development of the computer industry, the Indian government assigned clear responsibility to the state (public sector) to shape and direct its electronics industry. To understand why India adopted a policy of state intervention, one must recognise both the size of the economy and the strong sense of economic independence arising from the negative experience of British colonialism (Maddisson 1971, Mascarenhas 1999). It has taken several decades of positive development experience for India to gradually lower its barriers to foreign private investment.

While colonialism created antagonism towards foreign private enterprise, it also left behind an institutional inheritance—the Indian Civil/Administrative Service—that maintained a restrictive regime of controls. The intellectual, scientific and technological human power capable of designing and developing sophisticated technology created through state investment (Mascarenhas 1982) has had to function within the context of a constitutional democracy dominated by a civil service, which retained its pre-Independence 'steel frame' culture imposing a regime of controls in the form of licences and controlled allocation of scarce resources. The other limitation faced is its inability to comprehend the technicalities arising from rapid changes in computer technology. As technical advisors within public service departments enjoy limited power in the policy making process, this often leads to conflict between technocrats and generalists, such conflicts occasionally extending into inter-departmental rivalry (Brunner 1995, Shridharan 1996) (see Section 4.6).

That regime is a reflection of the type of state structure and its capacities for action (Evans 1995). Successful industrial transformation, according to Evans, requires corporate coherence and connectedness or what he terms 'embedded autonomy' (1995,12). Viewing India as an intermediate case, exhibiting partial and imperfect approximation of embedded autonomy, he examines the role of the state in IT from four dimensions. The first two, 'custodian' and 'demiurge', represent variations on the conventional role of regulator and producer while the second pair, 'midwifery' and 'husbandry', focus more on the relation between state agencies and private entrepreneurial groups (Evans 1995,13). Analysing the four options available to governments for the promotion of IT, he suggests that a combination of midwifery and husbandry 'should work better than combinations that rely more heavily on custodian or demiurge' (1995, 14).

For reasons discussed above, India started with the first two i.e. 'custodian' and 'demiurge' and moved gradually to the latter as indigenous skills developed and the industry underwent rapid change. The government of India adopted a multi-pronged strategy in its efforts to promote an indigenous computer industry. Prior to 1970, the industry was primarily dependent on multi-nationals such as IBM and ICL which supplied large computers built overseas. In order to conserve foreign exchange, government decided to adopt a gradual policy of indigenisation. In 1966, an accord was reached between government and IBM on its operations in India, requiring IBM to earn foreign exchange through its export of non-computer products and to use locally manufactured products as far as possible. But IBM's role since 1963 had been limited to reconditioning the antiquated model 1401a and 'its contribution to making India a producer of information technology was questionable'. The relatively weak contribution of transnational capital, according to Evans, rendered self-reliance a more attractive option with the state feeling convinced that it could utilise local technical resources to develop information technology (1995,106).

While negotiating with international companies, government moved on another front by establishing in 1969 a public enterprise, ECIL, with a monopoly to design, develop and manufacture a wide range of components, instruments and computer systems. In expecting IBM and ICL to enhance their manufacturing operations in India, the government expected them to adhere to the requirements of the Monopolies and Restrictive Trade Practices Act, 1969 and the Foreign Exchange Regulation Act (FERA) 1974 to protect the indigenous computer industry.

Evans (1995) considers that the state, in regulating foreign enterprise, was playing a custodial role, but in competing with it, was engaged in a demiurge role. While the establishment of ECIL was necessary in the interests of developing new technology and achieving self-sustaining industrial growth, the later adoption of custodial and demiurge roles, to restrain and stimulate enterprise and risk, was essentially a reflection of a negative view of the private sector. In the creation of a new sector such as computers, Evans feels that the role of midwife is likely to be easier and less risky than the establishment of a state-owned enterprise (79–80). To play such a role and attract private entrepreneurs, the state has to create organisational and institutional resources committed to new sectors. Once persuaded, such firms need encouragement and assistance, as the IT sector, he considers, is suited more to midwifery and husbandry than custodian or demiurge. Equating them to vulnerable seedlings, Evans advocates the use of agrarian skills and techniques associated with husbandry (98).

4.4 Responding To Technological Change

Considering the size and magnitude of the problems inherited, it is not surprising that India deemed state initiative to be essential in the early stages of development. However, in adopting an import-substitution self-reliant strategy, it created a bureaucratic regime unable to sense or appreciate differences between the special characteristics of different technologies and sectors. The framework of rules and regulations suited to a 'routinised technological regime' were not appropriate for the 'entrepreneurial technological regime' which emerged in the computer industry with the advent of microprocessors in the 1970s. As Brunner says (1995), late industrialising countries such as India, 'are more likely to find a window of technological opportunity in an entrepreneurial technological regime than in a routinised regime' (54). Innovations in the latter regime come from large established firms. According to Brunner, 'The special nature of technological change in computer components, specially semi-conductors, has made it possible for firms to spin off intensive components production processes. Computer manufacturers are enabled to purchase the components from outside and concentrate on the assembly of computers designed in-house in relatively inexpensive labour intensive shops. Furthermore, with the speed of technological progress in computers it is unwise to sink vast amounts into production facilities which cannot be adapted rapidly to new products and circumstances' (58).

While the Indian computer industry was initially slow to respond to the technological changes in the international computer industry, when it did, however, it showed remarkable progress both in terms of price and operating capacity. It did this by purchasing components from outside and assembling them according to in-house designs, thus avoiding investment in production facilities. This option worked because of lowered cost barriers of entry for Indian firms with decreasing size in relation to performance of minicomputers and microcomputers.

'With the emergence of the technological entrepreneurial regime internationally, not only was entry feasible, but technologies became, in principle, more accessible under the influence of component standardisation' (Brunner 1995, 62). In order to encourage the domestic electronics industry, especially computers, minicomputers and microprocessors, government introduced special regulations in 1975, intended to overcome the effects of a policy that had 'deterred the entry of firms into specific industries and eliminated competition in certain industries' (97).

The exit of IBM in 1978 and the gradual removal of legal restrictions on domestic operators encouraged the Indian computer industry to respond to technological changes in the international computer industry. With the departure of IBM, government introduced a strategy of import-substitution, requiring domestic manufacturers to phase out import content to 70–80 per cent after two years and 40–50 per cent after the third year. To reduce foreign exchange flow, DOE authorised Electronics Trade and Technology group (ETT), CMC and Semiconductor Complex Limited (SCL) to exclusively purchase standardised components and parts in bulk and sell them to individual producers (Brunner 1995, 78). The Technical Development Council (TDC) established specifically for the electronics industry recommended funding for twenty-six computer related projects—fourteen in education and R&D institutions and twelve in public enterprises. While encouraging the development of the domestic component industry, the policy was intended to protect the infant computer industry and to save valuable foreign exchange.

In referring to the absence of any specific software policy until 1983, one tends to overlook the close links between the development of software and hardware. 'In fact, both technologies form a symbiotic unity, one type spawning ideas for the other type' (Brunner 1995, 126). In the 1960s, the introduction of compatible computer systems enabled programmers 'to define tasks without having to know all the engineering details of the hardware' (128). During the 1970s however, the role of software changed to cater to the needs of users and hardware capability. 'Packaged software was the response to new market pressures for hardware flexibility. In the 1980s, the so called applications software industry became separated from the computer hardware industry' (ibid.). With such rapid changes in technology and market response, computer designers were able to pack in greater speed and operating capacity at lower price and also offer a greater role for systems designers. 'Since one single microprocessor now can contain control unit, arithmetic unit, memory and even an input-output (I/O) unit all in one chip, it has become the designer's task to coordinate the operation of several such tiny computers within an entire computer system.... It is the designer who links such standardised components, operating systems, software packages, to accommodate the user's needs and performance requirements' (Brunner 1995, 129).

The rapid changes made it increasingly clear that the regime of protection adopted as a general strategy for industrialisation in India was unsuitable for the fast changing electronics industry. Noting this, both the Menon (1979) and Sondhi (1979) committees recommended liberalisation. In response to their recommendations, government introduced a market-oriented policy regime which relaxed industrial licensing, liberalised imports and allowed greater access to foreign capital and technology. (Joseph 1997, 25). This marked the beginning of the entry of the private sector into an area, which until the early 1980s, had been dominated by the public sector.

4.5 Role of Department of Electronics and Electronics Commission

The creation of DOE in 1970 and EC in 1971, comprised largely of personnel from the Bhabha Atomic Research Centre (BARC) and the Bhabha Committee on Computers (1966), brought into the IT scene a commitment to an indigenous computer industry. The creation of two technical agencies for the electronics industry coincided with a distinct shift in the Indian political system when Prime Minister Indira Gandhi inducted into her government a new breed of MPs and appointed them ministers of technical departments. Consequently, technocrats were appointed to head six departments, signalling a departure from the old political and administrative culture inherited from pre-Independence India. Both DOE and EC dominated the electronic scene in India in the 1970s and 1980s and were closely identified with ECIL, which enjoyed exclusive power for the manufacture of mini and small computers. In addition, they were entrusted with regulatory and promotional roles. Evans (1995) notes that DOE and EC in their custodial role attempted to protect ECIL from competition by not acting on the recommendations of the minicomputer panel which had suggested licensing a dozen applicants to make minicomputers (113). However, Evans hastens to dispel any notions of self-serving bureaucrats or that of 'rent-seeking'. On the contrary, he sees them as dedicated technocrats: 'protecting ECIL was seen by the company's backers as the only way of implementing the Bhabha Committee's vision. ECIL was making strenuous efforts to follow the committee's exhortations to achieve maximal technological autonomy. The DOE was not convinced that private capital would do the same' (113–14).

In building strong support for the retention of public sector dominance, if not control, DOE/EC were, according to Evans (1995) able to create space for the private sector to work without IBM. That ability to adapt to change was all the more remarkable as it had been 'inserted into one of the world's most sclerotic administrative structures' (114). While both agencies supported rather than resisted changes to policy, technocrats at DOE/EC actively encouraged greater liberalisation because of their 'strong substantive interest in the sector for which they were responsible' (115). They took great pride in the changed department, claiming that they 'broke 26 separate rules to accommodate Texas Instruments Bangalore subsidiary and (were)... willing to break more' (115). However, as technocratic agencies, they were unable to match the traditional departments in playing bureaucratic politics.

4.6 Bureaucratic Politics

The creation of DOE/EC and the departure of IBM in the 1970s raises questions as to why pre-1970s policy-making suffered from internal bureaucratic squabbling. There appeared to be an underlying power struggle between departments such as the AEC which favoured ECIL and the Department of Defence which supported BEL. At this stage, the computer industry was dominated by IBM and ICL as multinational operators; ECIL and BEL had been set up to promote the indigenous computer and electronics industry, respectively. Greico (1984) rejects the view of the Finance Ministry which claims that the failure of computer policy prior to the 1970s was due to lack of expertise within the bureaucracy and conflict between departments. With decision-making dispersed between several agencies, he attributes failure to the bureaucratic struggle for control that developed between the Ministry of Industrial Development and the Ministry of Defence. Being an important consumer of electronic equipment with BEL under its control, the Ministry of Defence became the natural centre for decisions concerning computer policy (110–111).

BEL had a relatively larger share of Indian electronic manufacture than ECIL (16 per cent and 1 per cent, respectively); the balance was either imported or assembled by IBM and International Computers Limited (ICL). The differences between them are reflected in the manner in which they developed linkages with international industry. While BEL based its production on manufacturing foreign licences, ECIL, lacking linkages, was unable to do so as control of licensing and imports resided with the Ministry of Defence (Greico 1984, 114). Such internal politics between the Defence Ministry and AEC had significant repercussions on the electronics industry (115). The situation was such that specialised agencies like DOE/EC were needed to spearhead policy making but the newly set-up agencies with their specialised personnel had much ground to cover.

By contrast, BEL established in 1954, had developed substantial technical expertise. 'In the early 1970s, it was the only company in India able to undertake the full cycle of semiconductor wafer fabrication. Like many high-tech public sector firms, it served as a training ground for engineers. Its massive presence in Bangalore (almost twenty thousand employees by the end of the 1980s) helped lay the groundwork to make India's "Silicon Plateau" the country's most promising technopolis' (Evans 1995, 130). BEL, ITI, HAL and other research, development and academic institutions based in Bangalore served as a training ground for a large number of electronic professionals and have deservedly been credited with making the city a centre of the electronics revolution (see Chapter 8).

Prior to the setting up of DOE/EC, the two public sector units, ECIL and BEL, had been competing for business. Following their creation and a shift in policy towards the indigenous development of minicomputers, BEL was encouraged to develop integrated circuits and peripherals while ECIL undertook the manufacture of minicomputers. Unfortunately, ECIL's performance until the early 1980s was less than encouraging and the entry of local firms into PC manufacture made competition increasingly difficult (Greico 1984, Evans 1995). Over the course of the next ten years, local firms entered the market and completely outstripped ECIL. Noting that setbacks are not unusual for high-tech public enterprises, Evans commends ECIL's resilience and initiative in undertaking special projects like design and implementation of an automated monitoring system for the Oil and Natural Gas Commission's offshore oil and gas wells and developing integrated control systems for public sector steel plants and computerised load dispatch systems for power companies (132). Evans concludes that perhaps public enterprises are inappropriate for the production of commodity goods, although useful in the 'high-tech version of the state's traditional role as a provider of infrastructure' (ibid.).

DOE, which began as a regulator of computer imports with the objective of promoting self-reliance and indigenisation, gradually simplified procedures for the import of computers and later moved into licensing for the manufacture of mini-computers and microprocessors. The impending departure of IBM in 1975 led DOE to establish the CMC with a monopoly to service foreign-installed computers. Most of its employees had previously worked for IBM's customer engineering division. With the entry of Delta Electronic Corporation (DEC) and Hewlett-Packard, CMC was, by the 1980s, servicing forty foreign firms as well as some local companies. That exposure to a range of computer systems not only contributed to the company's technical versatility; it turned out to be an asset as Indian computer specialists learned to work on a variety of platforms.

Some of CMC's seemingly 'mission impossible' contracts cited by Evans include the development of an information system for the Mediterranean Games, the establishment of its international headquarters in London, winning a contract for the London subway and establishing a long-term contract for writing software for ICL. Most complex of all is the IMPRESS railway reservation system developed for the Indian Railways. As to the last, Evans says, 'by combining indigenous software and state-of-the-art hardware, CMC was able to produce a system that was efficient and relatively inexpensive....CMC has specialised in large projects that require a scale few local firms can master and a feel for the idiosyncrasies of local systems and organisation that TNCs [trans-national corporations] cannot easily provide. Such projects are in niches with high rates of social return for which state enterprises may have a 'comparative institutional advantage' (Evans 1995, 133).

In the late 1970s, the government of India established the National Information Centre (NIC) to provide infrastructure for computerised information for central government offices. This was followed with regional centres. To promote computers in the regions,

DOE established the National Centre for Software Development and Computing Technology (NCDCT) at the TIFR. Its purpose was to promote research and training in software technology. In a bid to promote software exports, DOE evolved a scheme through selective organisations (Tata Computer Services, Administrative Staff College of India and ECIL), allowing them to import computers and thus develop software skills. The initiative was taken by TCS which imported sophisticated computers and moved ahead with significant software exports. In 1976–77, DOE streamlined its policy of computer imports as a guarantee for software exports. This scheme extended computerisation within the country and earned foreign exchange through exports (Naidu in Jasswalla and Taylor 2003).

In its excessive zeal to promote the electronics industry, DOE, on one occasion, did overplay that role. By interfering in HMT's arrangements with the Japanese for the production of electronic watches on grounds of jurisdiction, it only served to delay that process (Mascarenhas 1982, 58–59). Bureaucratic power in this case hindered India's entry into electronic watches. The other issue that surfaced here was inter-organisational rivalry which often has detrimental consequences. Similar differences surfaced during DOE's bid to promote speedy introduction of the Internet. The Telecom Department assumed an uncooperative stance fearing a loss of revenue from its two telephone monopolies, BSNL and MTNL (for the role of Telecom Regulatory Authority of India, TRAI, see Chapter 5).

4.7 Political Maturity

The politics of industrial development where newly independent countries seek technology and expertise from multinational companies is analysed from the perspective of two distinctive schools. While the bargaining school subscribes to the thesis that developing countries enhance their power through their politico-economic relations with advanced capitalist economies, the dependency school maintains that developing countries are unable to enhance their power significantly over multinationals. Based on India's experience with computer manufacturers such as IBM and ICL, Greico (1984) supports the position of the bargaining school on the premise that international companies enjoy greater power in the early stages of interaction when the host country has less control. However that bargaining power gradually shifts to the host country as it gains experience in managing relations. Greico's assessment is based on a specific industry and, although supported from other sources, is insufficient to arrive at a firm conclusion. In my analysis of technology transfer in the Indian machine tool industry, I take several factors into consideration. What are the sorts of options available to both buyer and seller of technology? What type of industry is it? What is the level of political and technological capability available within the country? (Mascarenhas 1982). Although that policy of self-reliance is questioned by some critics, in my view it is justified in strategic areas when technology suppliers use it as a bargaining tool. Once India tested a nuclear device it soon became a target of technology denial (see Chapters 2, 3 and 6).

While my analysis of technology transfer was confined to negotiations at enterprise to enterprise level, Greico (1984) based his conclusion on India's dealings with computer multinationals IBM and ICL, where he acknowledged the level of national power achieved by India as an important factor in such dealings (7). A case in point is the major crisis that developed at HMT in its early days when Managing Director M. K. Mathulla asked the Swiss collaborators, Oerlikons, to remain as technical experts and to leave the management of the company to the Indians. This placed responsibility directly on young Indian engineers at HMT to deliver the goods, which they did, the episode becoming a matter of pride in years to come. Over the next twenty-five years, HMT became a leader not only in technology but also in its dealings with government. Leaders of enterprises need autonomy to enable them to be assertive in their dealings with multinationals. In the face of technology denial, India should, according to the Principal Scientific Adviser to the Indian government, become self-reliant and this should not be interpreted as self-sufficiency but as immunity against technology denial (*The Hindu*, 23 January 2004).

Achieving autonomy and technical sophistication in electronics in the shortest possible time was the declared goal of government policy and it became easier to focus on that goal once DOE/EC were given responsibility to review the entire field of electronics (Joseph 1997, Greico 1984). They approached this task on two fronts; one, negotiating with international companies, and two, fostering indigenous supplies of computers. These improvements in computer technology and the achievement of objectives set in the mid-1960s in India's computer industry are attributed by Greico (1984) to central government and to other enterprises outside its control (11).

More policy changes followed, brought on by advances in the international computer industry where companies could choose to focus on design and software alone and import components for in-house assembly. An indigenous minicomputer industry thus became feasible based on systems engineering, with the focus on design, assembly, testing, software and maintenance.

While ECIL was entrusted with indigenous development of design and software to develop an indigenous peripheral industry, the government licensed BEL and Hindustan Teleprinters Limited (HTL) to manufacture dot matrix printers, tape readers and cassette drives for the minicomputer industry (Joseph 1997, 72). ECIL thus gradually emerged as a competitor to IBM, which by manufacturing TDC 12 and TDC 16 series minicomputers, had until 1970 dominated the Indian market. These developments helped the growth of the indigenous computer industry.

Well before this, the government had clearly shown its intention of curbing the operations of IBM and ICL by requiring them to earn foreign exchange through exports and to make greater use of local content in the manufacture of computers. Convinced that it could 'operate without the world's hegemonic computer company' (Evans 1995, 114), the Indian government asked IBM and ICL for greater Indian equity participation. However, IBM was unwilling to share ownership on account of the interdependent nature of its operations and indicated it would withdraw from India rather than share ownership (Greico 1984, 25).

Government pressure on IBM and ICL to adhere to Indian policies of local equity participation, to restrict imports and to encourage the local computer industry left them with little choice: accede or exit. ICL was willing to accede to the conditions, while IBM declined and exited in 1978 (ibid.). IBM did, however, make some overtures by offering to set up a scientific centre and an electronic testing facility in lieu of sharing ownership. While ICL entered into negotiations giving Indians majority shareholding, Burroughs entered into a joint enterprise with the Tatas. The availability of skilled personnel in India was an influential factor in Burroughs' acceptance of equity participation. Another factor that influenced Burroughs to accede to government demands was the choice available to India with increasing suppliers and the potential for growth in the Indian market (11).

Greico views government's attitude on the issue as inflexible (31) and IBM's refusal to concede to government demands as a case of using technology as a bargaining asset to resist the policy on sharing control adopted by some TW countries. (25). As Burroughs was a new entrant and ICL already had local equity participation, Greico wonders whether the objective of participation was actually achieved. Further, he considers that India was by 1972 unable to achieve any of the three objectives it had set itself in 1966 (25)—a judgement which seems less than charitable taking into consideration the advanced projects undertaken by both ECIL and CMC and the range of peripherals being manufactured by BEL.

It is fair to say that both the government and IBM adopted an inflexible approach to the issue of equity participation. Firstly, IBM had been made fully aware of government policy on the role of foreign ownership in relation to India's development policy of achieving self-reliance. Secondly, although the government was unable to achieve its objective of an indigenous computer industry, it, according to Greico, was certainly aware that it had sufficient technological capability enabling it to take a firm stand. Evans portrays it as a case of the Indian government and IBM testing their mutual strength, government using the political card and IBM the technology card (Greico 1984, 5).

While several studies have examined the issue of power in the relations between multinationals and host governments, with reference to the IBM case, analysts have failed to recognise the significant shift in Indian politics that took place in the late-1970s. After three decades of Congress party rule, a coalition calling itself a Janata (Peoples' party) government came to power with symbolic policies on its platform. Of these, a key one was to rid the country of Coca-Cola and IBM. While the latter was already at loggerheads with government on the issue of control over ownership, the issue came to a head under a particular Minister of Industries. According to Brunner (1995), 'Government officials even today point out that it never really was the intention of the government to force IBM to leave, had it not been a personal issue with George Fernandes' (101). While Greico (1984) questions India's actions as inflexible, with hidden costs to the Indian computer industry, the episode turned out to be a blessing in disguise (102). Although not deliberate, the timing worked in the Indian computer industry's favour, opening up commercial opportunities for the hitherto protected domestic industry (Brunner 1995). Forcing out a big player in the international computer industry gave a boost to the indigenous industry, which then launched on a gradual move from mainframes to minicomputers and microprocessors.

Viewing IBM's contribution as questionable, policy makers became more convinced that the state could utilise its own resources to develop IT (Evans 1995, 106). That role grew as IT began to be recognised as 'the master technology of late twentieth century development' (ibid., 95). Evans wonders at the consequences if, in a world of fast-changing international technology, 'states lack the agility necessary to enter as a producer and the perspicacity to act as effective midwives' (ibid.).

4.8 The Impact

Any analysis of the development of Indian computer policy needs to consider the inter-linkages. In the Indian socio-economic and political environment where such linkages can be quite intense, it took a period of four decades for the government to recognise that the electronics industry had to be treated as a special case, quite separately from other industries. That acknowledgment was followed by a sudden shift in policy. Joseph (1997) analyses Indian policy on computers in three phases. Phase one is the pre-1970 period when the computer industry was under foreign control. Phase two covers the post-1970 period when the industry began to develop but was dominated by the public sector. Phase three is the post-1984 period and onwards marked by the entry of the private sector and foreign firms. While that analysis into phases appears elegant, there has been considerable overlap caused by the inter-linkages which one cannot avoid in a vast country like India.

In its early stages, the computer industry was dominated by MNCs. Looking at the evidence, it is obvious that this only delayed India's progress and the situation was further aggravated by the system of bureaucratic control introduced to protect further entry of foreign technology. According to Greico (1984), 'India possesses one of the world's most restrictive, cumbersome and "assertive" regimes regulating foreign direct investment' (16). Two factors contributed to a change in that policy: (1) the establishment of DOE and EC which, while influencing the shape of the computer industry, gave a tremendous boost to public sector units like ECIL, BEL and CMC resulting in the consequent decline of multinationals, and (2) changes in the international computer industry which led to the increasing acceptance of in-house design and assembly of minicomputers with imported components in India.

A fact unnoticed by many observers is that this occurred at a time when software technology was taking on an important role in pushing forward the frontiers of data processing technology (Brunner 1995, 126). This then marked the beginning of a revolution in IT when electronics, computing and telecommunications were converging, bringing about fundamental changes in industrial activities. Dubbed 'informatics', these changes brought about a rapid transformation in the electronics industry. However, the emergence of software and its growth with liberalisation has led to a decline in the hardware industry and this will be discussed in the next chapter of this study.

4.9 Conclusion

The 1960s and onwards constitute an important period in the development of ICT in India, especially intense in computer technology and certainly a defining moment in India's choice of direction. One must realise that the policy-making machinery was being developed while the process was evolving and that those involved had to deal with several power centres pulling in different directions. Credit is due to external observers like Brunner, Greico and Evans whose analysis of the happenings during that period offers an excellent and dispassionate insight into the politics of policy making. Heeks credits India with having developed its own model of state intervention, a model which the World Bank has recognised as worthy of emulation (in Coopey 2004).

In the process of developing IT policy, both the DOE and EC have played a vital role. While encouraging the development of indigenous sources, they entered into negotiations with MNCs like IBM and ICL to protect the domestic industry. Their success heralded the emergence of technocratic agencies capable of shielding public sector undertakings in the electronics sector from bureaucratic interference. In this effort they received support from politicians like Rajiv Gandhi who were keen to encourage the use of new technology in computers and communication.

While some may still question India's early history of state entrepreneurship and, in particular, 'the Nehru model', I hesitate to think what might have happened had India's post-Independence development lacked that guiding hand and instead been left open to all and sundry.

Although not the perfect answer, what was set in place was apparently seen as the best under the circumstances by a country emerging from a long history of colonialism and, despite its cumbersome procedures and inflexibility, that cumbersome and inflexible bureaucratic system did offer the new nation a measure of continuity and stability.

5

Development of Information and Communication Technology

5.1 Introduction

Information and communication technology (ICT), brought about by the convergence of computers and telecommunication, has ushered in a dramatic transformation in the economies of countries. In India, the adoption of digitalisation in the mid-1980s by the telecommunication sector opened up avenues for the computer industry in the form of new products and services and accelerated the liberalisation of the industry itself. While the delay in moving in that direction has been questioned by observers in the light of developments elsewhere, it must be remembered that new technologies, particularly the Internet, challenge the existing institutional and technological structures.

In Chapter 4, I noted that India's computer policy was, until 1984, geared towards hardware with minimal attention paid to software. The creation of the Software Development Promotion Agency in 1984 marks a convenient point in time to distinguish between the policy emphasis on hardware and the shift to promote both hardware and software in the post-1984 period. This fortuitous occurrence coincided with several other factors which favoured the growth of Indian software exports. Triggered by the liberalisation measures introduced by Rajiv Gandhi on becoming Prime Minister in 1984, the industry responded by adapting to technological changes in the international computer industry. The changes enabled manufacturers to assemble computers by importing components designed in-house, a process that allowed computer software to be delinked from computer hardware, i.e. applications software industry was separated from the computer hardware industry (Brunner 1995).

In 1988, as the impact of these changes was beginning to be felt, the turnover in the Indian hardware industry had reached the

$270 million mark. However, by 1989 it had jumped to $400 million, which, according to Brunner, was ten times the sales at the beginning of the 1980s. While such growth had the effect of eliminating the technology gap in mini and microcomputers, Indian computer firms succeeded 'in developing a potential competitive advantage in custom-designed system' (ibid., 164). Directly attributed to government policies, increased incentives, greater domestic competition and the adoption of an entrepreneurial technology regime which incorporated the building of a strong technological infrastructure, such successes indicate, according to Brunner, that technology and policy rather than demand played a key role (164–66).

The new regime of open entry ushered in an atmosphere which encouraged innovation with HCL launching two new products. 'HCL's Horizon 030 was reputed to be the first implementation of UNIX V.3 on the Motorola 68030 chip anywhere in the world. It was followed up with a variation on the theme, one of the first machines in the world to incorporate the Motorola 68030 chip in a multiprocessor design' (Evans 1995, 170).

With its strong technological base in hardware, rapid developments in telecommunication technology and its skilled manpower, India was ready to exploit opportunities in the software industry. This opportunity was first identified by the Committee on Minicomputers which, after observing the practices of international computer manufacturers, suggested the establishment of an indigenous minicomputer industry based on systems engineering with the focus on design, assembly and software and not components and peripherals (Joseph 1997, 71). A requirement of that policy was the liberalisation of imports of components and peripherals with licences granted to public sector units such as ECIL, BEL and HTL to manufacture minicomputers and peripherals. However, the departure of IBM in 1978 and the entry of competitors led indigenous operators to rely on foreign imports ignoring the strong base that was being built in the hardware sector. Such free access to technology acted as a deterrent to indigenous research and development and encouraged a 'kit assembly culture' (Joseph 1997, 82–83, Heeks in Coopey 2004, 294–95).

After briefly reviewing the state of the Indian computer industry until 1984, the rest of this chapter reviews developments in ICT, focusing on the role of institutions responsible for ICT policy as well as related technological changes which influenced development. In

Section 5.2, we explore the basic terms 'hardware' and 'software' used in computers and their linkages to the ICT industry. Section 5.3 analyses influences that shaped the direction of the industry. Section 5.4 reviews the policies introduced in the 1980s to promote the software industry, followed by fundamental influences on the direction of computer policy. Section 5.5 analyses policy initiatives in response to technological changes and Section 5.6 examines deregulation of telecommunication. The conclusion is in Section 5.7.

5.2 Basic Characteristics of Hardware and Software

A computer consists of a central processing unit (CPU), which includes a microprocessor with logic chips, the operating system and applications software, information storage products (disk drives, memory chips), ways of feeding in and extracting information (input-output devices), power supplies and communication devices or networks to link computers to each other (Saxenian 2000, 143). The various components and their special uses pose limitations on manufacturers who are hard pressed to keep pace with technological changes in the industry. Generally, manufacturers tend to specialise in particular components and acquire others from suppliers. According to Saxenian, the very nature of the computer manufacturing industry discourages in-house manufacture, i.e. design and production cannot be accomplished by a single firm; it requires collaboration between firms. 'In an industry that is continuously changing because of pressure to be up with the latest technology, the practice of developing a network of suppliers offers greater flexibility for introduction of new products rapidly. With this objective the relationship between computer firms and their suppliers becomes one of long-term partnership and differs from that of arm's-length relationship that exists in mass production systems' (148).

Software is now an important component of most commercial, engineering, governmental and social activity. In the era of mainframes such as IBM 1401, a data processing unit had to be housed in a large room with air-conditioning facilities. However that has changed with miniaturisation resulting in mini-compressors, mini-processors and minicomputers. By hand-wiring together multiple transistors to the size of a paper clip, Jack Kilby initiated a revolution in miniaturisation in which millions of circuits are housed on tiny pieces of silicon devices from computers to lifts to pacemakers (Reid, *The Melbourne Age,* 23 June 2005). Kilby's 'invention of the integrated circuit or microchip gave rise to the information age and heralded an explosion of consumer electronics products ... from personal computers to mobile phones' (Sullivan, *The Age,* 24 June 2005). Software, whether embedded, customised or packaged, is growing faster than any sector of the economy. As in the hardware sector, governments have a crucial role to play in the development of software. While this should focus on the designing of software needed to enhance competitiveness, Schware (1987) asks if there are specific policy or institutional measures which can assist in this direction (1250).

Software is the set of instructions needed to direct the operations of computer equipment and the information content or data that computers manipulate. While systems software controls the components of the computer system, i.e. the computer operating system, applications software is designed to apply computers to the management of specific areas such as health, transport or a business. The current portability of systems software ensures the ready availability of application programs, thus giving them a market advantage (ibid.). To develop applications software, a country needs trained software design engineers, computer programmers and systems analysts (ibid.).

Corresponding with the growth in specialised users of IT, software developers need to develop programs tailored to specific needs. A productive entry path identified by Schware for TW countries is systems integration whereby a designer combines hardware components with custom software to meet specific user needs (1987, 1251). A system integrator's ability to 'mix and match' can be useful in producing software that can be matched to make assembled components communicate (ibid.). Identifying the various steps as specification, prototyping, coding, and testing, Schware stresses the importance of education and training to develop expertise in (a) developing and supporting applications software, (b) evaluating and modifying software packages, design methodologies and productivity tests, (c) providing special consultancy and software support services, and (d) promoting products and services (ibid.). While these constitute the basic steps of any software development policy, their success rests on a pool of skilled people, combined with efficient telecommunication and transportation infrastructure. Unlike hardware, software is less capital intensive and more labour intensive, has a lower rate of obsolescence and far lower economies of scale.

The growth of the global ICT industry was seen as an opportunity for TW countries to focus on software development through a variety of policy and institutional measures. In promoting the computer industry in general, India initially lacked a specific policy on software development (Joseph 1997). In 1984, a separate Software Development Promotion Agency (SDPA) was set up under the aegis of DOE. Manufacturers were allowed to import components provided that they then exported software. However misuse by importers led to a tightening of regulations, which, according to Heeks (1996), unfortunately coincided with the government's intention to develop the local hardware industry.

With the election of Rajiv Gandhi as Prime Minister, the government adopted a new computer policy with a series of measures intended to liberalise both hardware and software imports. The main objectives of the policy were:

- to enable computers to be manufactured in the country based on the latest technology at prices comparable to international rates and to encourage indigenisation consistent with economic capability;
- to simplify existing procedures so as to enable users to obtain computers from within the country or overseas and to do so mainly through fiscal measures; and
- to promote computer applications that would catalyse the long-term benefits of computerisation in the country as a whole (Naidu in Jasswalla and Taylor 2003).

By reducing customs duties on both hardware (135 per cent to 60 per cent) and software (100 per cent to 60 per cent) and de-licensing software, the policy indirectly allowed companies with 40 per cent foreign equity (under FERA and MRTP) to become software producers (Heeks 1996, 45) and was, according to Heeks, 'almost entirely one of liberalization for software, because it made imports of hardware and software, entry into the industry and access to foreign exchange easier' (ibid.). This was followed by a more liberal policy, exclusively for software, intended to encourage imports with the expected outcome of increasing exports i.e. 'flood in' and 'flood out' (ibid.). India's software policy trends have, according to Heeks, broadly followed the industrial and technology policy, with substantial liberalisation in the mid-1980s, a period of relative stability followed by renewed liberalisation in 1991 and eventually resulted in a policy which allows for inputs and software tools on open general licence (OGL) without needing government permission. 'The government has had no plans for a dominant public sector role in this industry and has not intervened in prices or industrial relations' (1996, 51–3). However, government's role did change to one of 'enabling' when it provided communication and other facilities by setting up STPIs which offered a range of incentives. Credit for this goes to Rajiv Gandhi and senior officials working at DOE/EC who veered away from the controlling role associated with traditional Indian bureaucracy and instead adopted a facilitating role.

5.3 Fundamental Influences on the Direction of Computer Policy

Rapid technological advances in the computer industry render it more efficient to offload the capital-intensive manufacture of components. Apart from relying on manufacturers for such parts, firms interested in R&D need a domestic industry large enough for the spread of investments necessary for a technology-intensive industry. For this to be feasible, the economies of scope must be favourable, i.e. large enough with capital to invest and to market the product. A suitable option, as suggested by Brunner, is an entrepreneurial technology regime (1995, 59). Following its announcement of a liberal computer policy in 1984, government took the initiative to launch such a regime, with ECIL undertaking the manufacture of minicomputers, BEL the manufacture of peripherals and CMC the maintenance of imported computers (by IBM and ICL).

The drawback of such a set-up was that it did not offer enough competition and, while the monopoly remained with ECIL, there was no opportunity for the domestic computer industry to move ahead and keep up with rapid technological advances. Another inhibiting factor was the monopoly granted to CMC, a public enterprise, to 'service computer systems not manufactured in India, and to execute software development and service projects for public sector agencies within the country' (Schware 1992, 150). While this policy deprived the private sector from gaining any experience, one must acknowledge the extraordinary contribution made by CMC to the Indian computer industry following the departure of IBM (Evans 1995).

When government did allow private sector units into the computer industry, instead of encouraging price competitiveness, this actually proved detrimental to the policy of indigenisation. In 1984, institutional barriers were finally removed. While this led to increased growth in the manufacture of computers, the industry continued to be dominated by foreign-based technology (Joseph 1997, 75–77) with imports constituting over 95 per cent of materials used in microcomputers, rendering the domestic computer industry almost completely assembly-oriented (Schware 1992).

Until this time the Indian computer industry had been governed by industrial licensing, low demand, reliance on imported inputs and an indifferent attitude to the use of computers in the private sector. Added to this was the effect on local producers of allowing the import of complete computers. The appearance of the IBM-compatible PC in the 1980s further discouraged indigenous manufacture. Being technically simple, this model was easily reverse-engineered by competitors at a lower cost than the IBM. During the next stage of hardware development when policy changes rendered indigenous manufacture uneconomical, local manufacturing was left with two options: assembly of imported components to in-house design or collaborating with foreign companies operating in India. (Heeks, 1996, 212–220). In the mid-1980s as India moved towards advanced computers, the setting up of C-DAC and C-DOT had a tremendous impact on both the hardware and telecommunication industry (Mani 2003) as reflected in software exports in the late 1980s and early 1990s.

Sustainable growth of the IT industry is dependent on the development of both software and hardware. While the former has been favoured by government policies and some fortuitous occurrences, the very same factors have acted as disincentives in hardware manufacture. The use of import duty on domestic manufacture as an instrument of resource mobilisation was identified by the Task Force on Information Technology as 'one reason for the progressive decimation of the hardware industry'. As rising costs brought on by economies of scale rendered hardware production virtually unviable, the thriving software sector exercised pressure on government to allow it to take the import route. While the hardware manufacturers were forced to become dealers of foreign brands, the software industry urged government to open up the import channels to enable it to engage in direct importing. Further, when the date for the zero import regime was brought forward to 2003 (from 2005), the survival of the remaining units became a matter for concern. As the Task Force concluded, there was a need for the replacement of faulty policies that had contributed to the decline by others that would be conducive to growth and competitiveness (http://it-taskforce.nic.in/actplan/intactO.htm).

The growth of the computer industry is reliant on a strong and vibrant domestic market as a base to create the required expertise. 'While there has not been a conscious strategy to prevent the domestic software industry from developing, it has been slow to develop because the market has been small, unprofitable and, for most companies, difficult to enter' (Schware 1992, 148). Until the mid-to-late 1990s, 'the absence of adequate communications technology ... forced companies to send Indian software developers to work on their clients' premises rather than undertake projects in India' (150). Software developers also suffered from limited opportunities in the absence of large systems platforms, telecommunication earth stations with capacity to support exports and the absence of continuous interaction between client and developer (ibid.) Other factors were the restrictive market environment, poor quality of telecommunication services and an inadequate market. The much-needed reversal came with the change in political leadership in the mid-1980s when Rajiv Gandhi assumed the prime minister's post.

5.4 Related Advances in Technology and Telecommunication

Following the 1980s' changes in computer policy, the industry received encouragement through technological developments in two significant areas: in advanced computers initiated by C-DAC, and in telecommunication equipment spearheaded by C-DOT. ISRO developed satellite technology which provided Internet access to software exporters. Before discussing how various policy initiatives triggered the upsurge in the Indian computer industry, we explore the role of C-DAC, ISRO and C-DOT.

5.4.1 Centre for the Development of Advanced Computers (C-DAC)

Incidents like IBM's refusal to accept the Indian government's requirement of equity sharing resulting in its exit from India in 1978 and the issue of technology denial with regard to equipment for supercomputers were instrumental in India's launch into parallel computing in 1988 and the eventual establishment of C-DAC. Since its establishment, C-DAC has produced 'three generations of PARAM super computers, which have increasingly advanced technologies and computing power, with an equivalent of US $25 million in investment' (Ashok Parthasarathy 2003, 18). Similar high-powered supercomputers are now designed by National Aeronautical Laboratory (FLOSOLVER), the Advanced Numerical Analysis and Research Group (PACE), BARC (ANUPAM) and C-DOT (CHIPPS). Mani (2003) comments that 'though questions remain about both the commercial viability of these systems and the cost effectiveness of government funding for them, it is generally felt that their presence has brought down the cost of equivalent international machines in India and also helped to create a high performance computing culture in India' (13).

Apart from other applications, such computers are used for weather forecasting, seismic data processing and bioinformatics. 'A particularly successful use, which is of crucial economic and social importance, is the modelling of the monsoon by the National Centre for Medium Range Weather Forecasting in New Delhi' (Parthasarathy 2003, 18). C-DAC's initial use of parallel-processing technology has led Parthasarathy to conclude that the price-performance ratio of its computers is better than those of their North American, European or Japanese equivalents (ibid.). The Param 20000 with teraflop capability released in April 2003 is to be used in climate and molecular modelling, genome sequencing, and two-and three-dimensional seismic data processing. 'India's most powerful and the world's fifth super computer PARAM Padma, with a peak computing power of teraflop', developed by C-DAC, was launched on 12 April 2003 at C-DAC Knowledge Park, Bangalore where the Minister for Information Technology congratulated C-DAC on its singular achievement in an area where technology had been denied (*Asian Age*, 12 April 2003). C-DAC later announced its intention to link all supercomputers in the country through an I-Grid-enabled information system. Fifty Indian super computers of the Param 10000 series are now operating in Russia, Canada, Germany and Singapore, and several countries have initiated negotiations for the next generation Param Padma 20000 series.

Having made the breakthrough in supercomputers, it is sad to note that none of the eleven 500 supercomputers now being used in India for silicon chip design, genetic engineering research and geophysical exploration were made in India. Apparently, India has not kept pace and has consequently fallen behind. The former Executive Director of C-DAC, who once promoted the Param series, attributed this to lack of vision on the part of government and the absence of a master plan for super computing.

In 1988, India established the Centre for the Development of Advanced Computers (C-DAC) in Pune, as a response to the United States refusal to allow the export of Cray supercomputers. The development of Param supercomputers by C-DAC has been characterised by Rothermund (2008) as disruptive technology. 'The story of Param supercomputer illustrates the phenomenon of disruptive technology since it outperformed the contemporary Cray supercomputer—at a fraction of the cost of Cray's expensive machine (112). It was based on massive parallel processing (MPP) by acquiring a suitable RISC (reduced instruction set chip) for its new machine the "Transputer" (transistor+computer) which includes its own RAM (random access memory) and is good at communicating in an MPP environment' (ibid., 110). With rapid changes in computer technology and the departure of its Executive Director, Vijay Bhatkar, C-DAC has since been unable to compete with faster designs. Rothermund cautions countries on the limits of adopting 'denial-driven innovation' once denial ends to ensure that disruptive technology does not kill the protagonist of sustained technology.

Meanwhile, BARC began developing the Anupam series of supercomputers. Its Anupam-Amerya, which achieved 1.7 teraflop in 2005 and made a real breakthrough, was installed in several major institutes in India. Following that success, the Department of Atomic Energy (DAE) funded the development of another supercomputer, the Kabru, which was developed by the Indian Institute of Mathematical Sciences. This was done by constructing a cluster of 144 inexpensive computers with Intel-Zion chips working with a Linux operating system. Rothermund sees the collaboration of several young companies as an encouraging sign of India's take-off in the field. Noting that funding for the Kabru was just $500,000, Rothermund comments, 'Kabru provides evidence of Indian ingenuity and it is to be hoped that PARAM, Anupam and Kabru are just stepping stones for even more inspiring achievements' (ibid., 115).

The Computational Research Lab (CRL), a Tata enterprise, has developed a supercomputer which has made it to the fourth spot in the world ranking of high performance computing. In its editorial, *The Hindu* (16 November 2008) advocated that Tatas should maintain their investment in R&D and that government should underwrite part of the cost of purchasing the present Tata system, so as to stem the tendency to buy outright Cray-like supercomputers, which Tata system outperforms.

5.4.2 Indian Space Research Organization (ISRO)

India's space programme, which began modestly in the 1960s with the setting up of ISRO, places great emphasis on communication, meteorology and remote sensing to ensure that its space programme is oriented to the country's needs. Vikram Sarabhai, in establishing the Physical Research Laboratory at Ahmedabad, seen as the intellectual springboard of the space programme, believed that space technologies can help developing countries to solve many basic problems (Maddox and Rich 1984, 600). Today 'India's communication satellites, the Insats, make telephony from the far corners of this large country possible, broadcast TV signals, and relay weather data' (*The Hindu*, 23 September 2003). In terms of the computer industry, the global navigation satellite system (GNSS), consisting of a network of ground control and monitoring stations using satellites placed in orbit 11,000 miles above the earth, plays a major role in telecommunication (*The Hindu*, 27 July 2003). According to Bhargava and Chakrabarti (2003, 39) DOS which is responsible for the overall control and development of the space programme, is, 'without question, the most successful scientific department in the country'.

With the launch of Insat-3E in 2003, which joined the four other Insats already in orbit, India's Insat system, in ISRO's words, became 'one of the largest domestic communication satellite systems in the Asia-Pacific region' with 128 transponders available for communication and broadcasting (*The Hindu*, 30 September 2003). While these achievements are commendable, Nair is well aware of the work ahead. 'In the lucrative and fast-growing communications field, a substantial part of India's space-based TV broadcasts and data communication is being provided by foreign satellites. If ISRO is unable to meet such demand or fails to market itself well, some of the world's leading satellite companies will only be too happy to carve themselves more of the Indian pie' (*The Hindu*, 23 September 2003).

In an era when technology is used for political blackmail, there is the need to develop one's capability. When India's supply from Russia was restricted to a few cryo-engines because of American pressure and suggestions of possible violation of the missile technology control regime, ISRO initiated two projects: the development of GSLV using Russian engines and the designing of indigenous engines. While the development of GSLV experiment is now well on the road to success and the indigenous engine is also at an advanced stage of development, successful completion of both projects would result in savings of valuable foreign exchange (*Deccan Herald,* 12 April 2003). With the conduct of the 720-seconds test on 19 January 2007, India was expected to join United States, Russia, France, Japan and China as the sixth country to develop the cryogenic technology for the launch of satellites. This highly complex technology, whose development has been a multidisciplinary task, is, if successful, expected to eliminate India's dependence on the foreign launchers used to send satellites weighing over 2000 kgs into orbit. Further progress and possibly total self-reliance in the area of rocket technology is expected with the launch of GSLVs with Indian cryogenic engines (*The Hindu,* 14 January 2007).

ISRO achieved another milestone by becoming the sixth country to develop a cryogenic stage in its rocketry at the Liquid Propulsion Systems Centre. This was achieved with the help of an advanced mission computer with the parameters of the test monitored from a sophisticated control room (*The Hindu,* 29 October 2006).

The Vikram Sarabhai Space Centre, a unit of ISRO based at Thiruvananthapuram focusing on advanced technology initiative in air breathing propulsion, has designed and developed the Supersonic Combustion Ramjet. This development, claims ISRO, has enabled it to take a big step forward in its search to reduce launch costs, a key factor in becoming competitive in the global satellite launch market. Although the Scramjet is still in its early stages, India is the second country after the US to have advanced thus far. Its eventual development, ISRO predicts, will go a long way 'in meeting the futuristic space transportation needs of our country' (*The Hindu,* 11 January 2006).

On 10 January 2007, ISRO launched Space Capsule Recovery Experiment (SRE) by which a 555-kg SRE was sent into orbit for eleven days and then de-orbited back to earth in a sequential manner. The PSLV-C7 launch involving four bodies (SRE, Cartosat-2 and one each for Indonesia and Argentina who were charged $8000 to $10,000 per kg) being sent into precise orbit was considered a major design achievement as it posed several technological challenges. The Cartosat-2 images thus generated are used in town and country planning to identify the boundaries of each land area and are helpful for administrative purposes (*The Hindu*, 11 January 2007).

Many space-faring nations have become wary of India's rapid advances in space technology and have refused to share knowledge. Indian scientists and engineers have had to work in a 'hostile environment' with other countries sharing little information and expertise. However, our scientists, according to Madhavan Nair, Chairman of ISRO, are coping with the challenges. 'Today we have data on the moon that no other country can boast of and that too with minimum expenditure' (*The Hindu*, 13 July 2009).

ISRO's latest venture is Bhuvan, a web-based mapping tool using images taken over a year by its seven remote-sensing satellites including Cartosat-1 and Cartosat-2. It provides pictures of Indian terrain barring sensitive military locations. Dr K. Kasturirangan, former chairman of ISRO and currently Member of the Planning Commission, described it as an 'interesting example of marrying space capabilities with information technology' (*The Hindu*, 17 August 2009).

Amid endless questions regarding the justification for a country like India to invest in space technology, the value of such work is now obvious. Launching and operating a massive publicly funded undertaking in the absence of markets defies existing techniques for evaluation. In his review of U. Sankar's *Economic Analysis of India's Space Programme: An Exploratory Analysis* (2007), Chandrashekar comments, '...for many of us who were involved in the early days of the programme it is of course nice to see a clear economic justification of what was originally considered to be an illusion or a dream. The Sarabhai–Dhawan vision for utilising space for socio–economic transformation of the country has indeed become a reality' (*The Hindu*, 10 April 2007). Other technological, economic and social values arising out of India's ventures into space include remote sensing used to monitor land and coastal waters, guidance to rural communities about the location of aquifers and water courses, advice to fishermen regarding the times for the best catch and early warnings regarding storms. Through the communication satellites, which reach remote corners of the country, television coverage and health care are provided to the rural poor (19 February 2005, 33).

Under its technology transfer programme, ISRO has also transferred technologies to the public and private sectors which can be used for commercial purposes. An example announced by Chairman Nair is the Jaipur Foot developed out of polyurethane. The composite material, first researched and developed by ISRO for use in rocket motors, was subsequently developed as integral skin polyurethane foam, a light and durable product, in consultation with its inventor, P. K. Sethi. Expertise in a range of technological and engineering disciplines is offered to individuals and organisations under the ISRO Consultancy Services Scheme (*The Hindu*, 14 October 2006).

A new concept in distance education, EDUSAT, was commissioned by ISRO in September 2004. Its aim is to extend quality education beyond schools and colleges to remote and rural areas in the country. The idea of beaming education programmes by satellite started in 1975–76 with the success of INSAT-based educational services. Intended to meet the demand for an interactive satellite-based education system through an audiovisual medium employing direct-to-home (DTH) quality broadcasting, EDUSAT possesses multiple regional beams which cover different parts of India and is located in a 36,000-km high geostationary orbit co-located with INSAT-3C and KALPANA-1 at 74 degrees east longitude. A pilot project using transponders on INSAT-3B connects a hundred engineering colleges affiliated to Visvesvaraya Technological University in Karnataka, Y. B. Chavan Open University in Maharashtra and Rajiv Gandhi Technical University in Madhya Pradesh. In addition to these three states, a further hundred to two hundred classrooms will be connected once EDUSAT is commissioned in orbit. ISRO will provide the technical and managerial support, while ground systems will be provided by the users. Ultimately, EDUSAT is expected to cover five thousand schools and colleges by supporting two to twenty uplinks with five thousand remote terminals (*Deccan Herald*, 28 July 2004). ISRO has also launched the ISRO–M. S. Swaminathan Rural Foundation (MSSRF) Village Resource Centre Program to help rural women, men and children to meet their basic needs in education, nutrition, health, drinking and irrigation water, agriculture and markets. Plans are afoot to use the Internet and space technology to promote the goals of Mission 2007 by forming a National Alliance to achieve synergy between technology and public policy (*The Hindu*, 18 October 2004). By May 2007, ISRO had set up an interactive VSAT channel with two-way video and two-way audio network facility through EDUSAT bridging the gap between industry, the student community and academia and, according to the Director of Satellite Communication Programmes, alleviating the shortage of teachers, especially in high-end technology-related areas. IBM, Microsoft, Bosch-Rexroth, Infosys, Intel, HP Sun Micro systems among others have agreed to run technology-specific lessons (*The Hindu*, 23 May 2007).

In September 2006, the Rehabilitation Council of India (RCI) signed an understanding with ISRO for the establishment of an EDUSAT up-linking station and studio within its premises, connecting a hundred study centres of RCI which will be attended by physically challenged students (*The Hindu*, 6 September 2006).

5.4.3 Centre for the Development of Telematics (C-DOT)

Established in 1984 as a research and development agency to create state-of-the-art technology to meet the needs of the Indian telecommunication network with Sam Pitroda, an expatriate, at its head, C-DOT revolutionised telecommunication in India and generated its IT boom. Until the establishment of C-DOT, India had relied on electro-mechanical switching and transmission for telecommunication, the equipment being manufactured at ITI, which was under the control of the Post and Telegraphs Department in collaboration with international technology suppliers (see Chapter 6).

Pitroda succeeded in persuading Indian authorities to dispense with electro-mechanical switching and transmission in favour of digital systems. While the former was actually ill-suited to Indian conditions, the latter, he claimed, would boost the development of electronics, software and related industries (1993, 70). C-DOT developed automatic exchanges for both rural and urban requirements with maximum flexibility of design, installation and repairs, all manufactured in India to international standards (ibid., 74). Such success spawned a range of enterprises which were contracted to manufacture C-DOT products, ancillary parts and components.

A new design was evolved to counteract the heat generated through digital switching, to eliminate dust and function under heavy monsoon conditions (ibid., 74. See Chapter 2 on adaptation to local conditions). C-DOT worked closely with the communications industry to develop a family of switches ranging from small 128-line systems designed to work in harsh rural environments to international state-of-the-art 40,000-line capacity exchanges for cities, all mutually compatible

(Parthasarathy 2003, 18). The development of such rural exchanges, twenty-five of which were installed every day, ensured that rural India received access to telephony by early 2000 (Pitroda 1993). Small rural exchanges described as 'masterpieces of appropriate design' are now exported to several TW countries (ibid., 74).

Established initially to develop technology for the growth and digitilisation of the Indian Telecom network, C-DOT has emerged as a multi-dimensional organisation with skills in the related technologies of radio, optoelectronics, satellite and network management. Through this process, the focus has been on developing technology suited to Indian conditions, contemporary and transferable to industry, in public, private or joint sectors. The presence of over twenty-five million lines based on C-DOT technology in the network manufactured by more than twenty corporations amply demonstrates the quality of technology transfer packages and support provided by C-DOT (http:/www.c.dot.com/knowns.htm, 9/3/2003, p. 1–2). According to Evans (1995), C-DOT's combination of 'technological entrepreneurship with a focus on the development of infrastructure and support for local private firms' offered a variation in state entrepreneurship (134). 'By focusing on technological entrepreneurship rather than direct production, C-DOT was able to play technological midwife to potential private-sector producers of telecom equipment rather than confronting them as a competitor. Its electronic private branch automatic exchange (EPBAX) technology was licensed to about forty firms, which, given the modular design of C-DOT's switches, made them potential producers of rural exchanges as well' (135).

As of 31 December 2001, these technological changes enabled the installation of about 45,000 exchanges totalling about twenty-three million telephone lines in India. C-DOT uses the most powerful software available, has developed a wide base of component suppliers, and built a model plant on the outskirts of Bangalore (Ashok Parthasarathy 2003). Even during the period (1995–2001) when deregulation allowed competition from multi-national companies, C-DOT continued to increase its market share (Mani 2003, 33).

Such extraordinary success in a lucrative industry soon attracted the attention of MNCs, who have indirectly brought government pressure to 'pare down research activities or even close down the activities of C-DOT supposedly on time overruns in their R&D projects' (ibid.). Back in 1989, C-DOT's attempts to develop digital main exchanges were undermined by the incoming NDA government which imported them saying that C-DOT was behind schedule considering the long waiting list for telephone connections. However, Sridharan (1996) asserts that the real reason for this was departmental infighting and lobbying by MNCs to frustrate C-DOT's efforts (148–149). Such pressures moved to a political level when the Parliamentary Standing Committee on Information Technology noted the decline in C-DOT's turnover and 'asked it to update its research activity so that it can match the private sector' (*The Hindu*, 26 December 2004). The Committee was obviously unaware that C-DOT had actually initiated the technological breakthroughs that brought about the revolution in Indian telecommunications !

While the proximity of C-DOT's hardware unit, ISRO's space centre and C-DAC's technology park at Bangalore have resulted in an exciting ICT cluster, leading to that city's reputation as a leading technopolis, recognition is due to these three undertakings for their crucial role in countering the pressure of technology denial regimes. The other point to note is the shift in operational aspects of publicly funded agencies from those discussed in Chapter 3. While HAL, ITI and BEL as early ventures were under the direct control of their parent departments and operated as traditional public undertakings, C-DAC, ISRO and C-DOT as later ventures by contrast were more promotional in their operations, reflecting a braver and more enterprising attitude in their leadership.

5.5 Policy Initiatives

Apart from the various policy initiatives such as the encouragement of education and training undertaken by the Indian government to transform the country into a major centre for design-intensive human resources, the specific measures that have had real impact are its efforts to promote software by establishing STPIs, improving satellite communication and allowing the use of venture capital. Enlargement of DOE into the Department of Information Technology in 1999 augmented the structure for coordination and policy making. Such policy initiatives constituted a process of policy learning similar to the changes in state intervention from production to technological entrepreneurship.

In the mid-1980s, the Indian computer industry experienced significant growth, spearheaded by HCL, Wipro, PSI, TCS and their international collaborators. In fact, the policy changes of the 1990s had the effect of drawing IBM, which had exited in 1978 due to its failure to accede to government ownership regulations, back into the country through collaboration with the Tatas. While Dahlman and Utz (2005) attribute the growth of software exports and the growing presence of international firms to liberalisation, it is only fair to acknowledge that such growth is also the result of a long-term vision whose foundations were laid in the 1950s and 1960s (see Chapters 2 and 3). That early foundation was complemented by ongoing state involvement through Software Technology Parks and vital breakthroughs in IT infrastructure. If one must castigate state intervention for India's problems of poor infrastructure, such as in the area of power and transport, one must, in all fairness, attribute its high-quality design intensive capability to state investment in educational infrastructure (Evans 1995, 172). India was able to cash in on a global IT services market because a development programme was planned, focused at the beginning on education and training. The result is that more than two million people graduate from higher education, of which 250,000 are IT graduates. 'That sort of figure leaves most astounded, but the more impressive attribute is the extremely high standards of these individuals. As a group, they are world renowned' (Davies 2004, 42).

To develop an IT services sector that can compete internationally, the focus necessarily has to be on education and training. The IITs set up in the 1960s have earned worldwide reputation for the quality of their graduates. Of approximately 150,000 aspirants who seek entrance to the IITs, only 3,500 (2.3 per cent) gain admission. IIT and other engineering graduates who have worked abroad have contributed in large measure to the growth of the IT services industry. First, their quality of training and skills has created a positive reputation in the US and Europe. Second, many having acquired further education and experience abroad have returned to India and set up business or are employed by local firms or MNCs operating in India. 'In fact, 71 of the 75 MNCs operating in Bangalore's software park were headed by Indians who had lived overseas, and many of the smaller companies are owned by Indian entrepreneurs presently living overseas' (Winters and Yousuf eds. 2007, 46). While Davies (2004) considers that the IITs should be the benchmark by which equivalent institutions elsewhere should be judged, Prestowitz (2005) states categorically that they rank among the 'world's best universities, in a league with MIT, Oxford and

Caltech' (29). Indian institutions range in quality from low to medium level to elite institutions such as the IITs, TIFR and the IISc (Greenspan 2004, 83).

Enrolment in software-related training, principally engineering, rose dramatically as the sector expanded. During 1992–2002, the number of Indian graduates trebled in engineering, IT degrees and diplomas. With the public system unable to provide a sufficient flow of skilled labour, private institutions were allowed to enter to offer training on a fee-paying basis, resulting in the rapid growth of engineering graduates. Such growth naturally showed up in regional variations in quality. To counter that, Karnataka set uniform standards and thus ensured that quality remained above a set minimum. This, according to Ashok Desai (in Commander 2005), was one of the factors behind the rise of Bangalore as the IT capital of India (58).

TABLE 5.1 State-wise Increase in Student Intake in Engineering Colleges in India: 1990–91 to 2003–04

States	*1990–91*	*2003–04*
Andhra Pradesh	8,070	66,205
Delhi	1,290	3,800
Gujarat	2,780	10,325
Haryana	1,085	10,105
Jammu & Kashmir	480	970
Karnataka	19,452	40,920
Kerala	4,512	19,868
Madhya Pradesh	2,265	15,920
Maharashtra	20,425	47,450
Orissa	1,325	10,695
Punjab	1,508	10,701
Rajasthan	1,629	10,785
Tamilnadu	12,855	79,302
Uttar Pradesh	3,029	24,773
West Bengal	2,022	13,269
Total	87,221	3,83,912

Source: Ministry of Human Services, compiled from R. Chandrakanth, *The Hindu*, 27 July 2005, Education supplement.

India's entry into high-tech ICT has generated such demand for engineers that engineering colleges have grown in number from 158 in 1980 to 1346 in 2004. In Karnataka, 116 engineering colleges offer courses ranging from Computer Science and Engineering to Electronics, Communication Engineering, Information Science or Technology and

Biotechnology and Informatics. Entrance to the colleges is through a common entrance test (CET) and students are offered vocational guidance to help with decisions regarding course selection. The state's Board for Information Technology Education Standards (BITES) offers useful information on facilities and the quality thereof on its website based on a study of sixty-six of the 116 colleges. In collaboration with IBM, BITES launched Project INVITE (Initiative to Nurture a Vibrant IT Ecosystem) to encourage academic excellence in Karnataka and 'fuel the growth of IT at the grassroots level ' (*The Hindu*, 30 January 2006). Assistance from the World Bank in 2002 enabled the establishment of a Technical and Engineering Education Quality Improvement Programme which is currently operating at 120 institutions in thirteen states (Dahlman and Utz 2005, 68).

Continued growth in the industry has resulted in increasing demand for specialists such as software analysts, domain specialists, specialists in information security, integration specialists, database administrators, data warehousing and semi-conductor designers. Computer education schools have now proliferated across the country, training 500,000 students a year in more than 2000 centres, franchised by the HCL and set up by the National Institute of Information Technology (NIIT). Such growth, some of it privately funded, has assumed highly undesirable political and ethical dimensions. In order to ensure that standards are met, NASSCOM has suggested the introduction of a system of accreditation on the basis of faculty, facilities and curricula.

Now known as a source of quality manpower, India will soon be faced with shortages in specialised areas. A more serious outcome of such growth is the lack of good quality teaching staff in certain disciplines. Concerned with declining quality of professional education, the All India Council of Technical Education (AICTE) organised a seminar on 'Restructuring Technical Education to meet Global Industrial Needs' in Bangalore recently. The participants suggested raising academic salaries, derecognising colleges with inadequate infrastructure, periodic upgrading of curriculum, increasing interaction with industry and providing incentives for research. 'Despite a five-fold increase in engineering colleges in the past six years, high-quality colleges account for less than one percent, according to AICTE'. With over 500,000 engineers graduating each year, surprisingly there are only 800 who register for a PhD, a conversion rate of one in 625 as against one in nine in the US (*The Hindu*, 4 December 2006). Despite these concerns, one cannot fail to be impressed by the vastly increased sense of maturity and self-confidence, compared with the situation a decade ago (Graeme Philipson, *The Age*, 5 December 2006).

To address the oft-heard complaint that engineering education is too theory-oriented, Hewlett Packard has linked up with ten engineering colleges to offer technology-intensive, hands-on programmes designed to integrate the student into the real world. In promoting industry-academia interaction, HP plans programmes in Software Engineering and Advanced Unix thus giving students first-hand exposure to application of theoretical concepts in an atmosphere of constant innovation (*The Hindu*, 2 December 2006).

Although many IIT graduates had migrated in early years in search of better opportunities, the current burgeoning domestic scene and increasing investment by multinational companies in ICT in India is altering that lamented brain drain into a welcome brain circulation (Saxenian in D'Costa and Sridharan 2003, 2006). According to World Investment Report 2005, many scientists and engineers are staying on. And Bangalore has recently seen the return of 35,000 scientists and engineers with training and experience in the US (see Chapter 8). As Saxenian points out, the zero-sum view of immigration is outmoded (Florida 2005). In India's case, those greener pastures overseas appear to have generated a greater demand for higher education and migrating graduates have certainly benefitted from exposure to cutting-edge technology.

As the computer industry becomes more competitive, the need to provide assistance in other areas has resulted in the following:

- standardisation, testing and quality certification (STQC),
- education and research network (ERNET), and
- STPI.

STQC functions through twenty-two laboratories staffed by 600 engineers and scientists to provide standards, testing and certification facilities for electronic industries. As Indian software companies are largely export oriented, much importance is attached to achieving certification of their quality and standards so that they can compete effectively in the international market. The relatively high proportion of Indian software companies with Software Engineering Institute (SEI)-authorised Computer Maturity Model (CMM) Level 5 certification is explicable in terms of their keenness to obtain quality certification to assure their clients that they can, in the absence of legal protection, fulfil contracts to the clients' expectations.

ERNET was set up with the assistance of UNDP and DOE to provide global Internet connectivity for the academic and research community. It offers electronic mail, file transfer and remote login database access and despite a late start owing to funding delays, it currently supports WAN (satellite-based wide area networks) whose central hub with its VSATs (very small aperture terminals) is located in STPI-B (Bangalore). In 1993, NICNET or National Informatics Center Network, a satellite-based network providing computing and two-way data communication infrastructure for government departments and agencies at central and state levels, was set up.

Real policy support for software was provided only in the 1990s when DOE created STP providing infrastructure and administrative support for software exports. Recognising its suitability for export in a growing world market, the low investment required, and the availability of a skilled, English-speaking workforce, government accorded export-oriented software firms in designated zones with access to high-speed satellite links, reliable electricity and tax exemption for five years. The tax-holiday has helped to attract needed investments and allowed firms 'to avail benefits without constraints on the choice of location encouraging entrepreneurship and integrated growth' (NASSCOM Strategic Review, 2007). At the recently concluded summit, industry representatives requested that the schemes, which are due to expire in 2009, be continued (*The Hindu*, 8 February 2007).

Established in 1991 to promote India's ICT globally, STPI has fulfilled the aim of its creator, N. Seshagiri of DOE, by playing a crucial role in the development of the software industry. STPI operates as a purely export oriented scheme using communication links or physical media, including export of professional services. It provides single-point contact services to member units and acts as a research centre by offering infrastructural facilities like ready-to-use built-up space, a centralised computing facility and high-speed data communication facilities. There are twenty-seven such parks operating in India, four of which are in Karnataka, serving 7200 software exporting companies. Incentives and facilities offered include:

- a single window clearance mechanism for approval of schemes;
- 100 per cent foreign equity;
- duty-free imports to STP;

- the import of second-hand capital goods;
- exemption of domestic purchases from local taxes;
- sale of up to 50 per cent of the exports in the domestic market; and
- exemption of STP units from corporate income tax up to March 2010 (Naidu in Jasswalla and Taylor 2003, 139).

In addition, STPI provides high-speed data communication (HSDC) services through SOFTNET which has set up its own international gateways at twenty-six locations to provide HSDC links to the software industry. It also provides worldwide connectivity to software export units and radiates more than 160 Mbps using around twenty-eight carriers from its earth stations to various destinations. In 1993, the government permitted the use of private dedicated links so that work done in India could be transmitted abroad, thus reducing the need for programmers to travel. Such communication facilities according to Naidu are the backbone of the successful development of offshore software activities. As an autonomous government agency and an instrument of state intervention, STPI has always risen to the industry's expectation and 'is considered to be much more corporate than average corporate enterprises' (Naidu 2003). In recent years, STPI has set up the India Infotech Center at San Jose (Silicon Valley) to assist Indian companies to export to the US and to act as a nodal agency for US companies interested in doing business in India. Its management model, seen as eminently suitable to other TW countries, is currently being replicated in several developing countries.

It is often assumed that the Indian IT sector is a homogeneous category. That glib assumption is being rudely shaken by the ongoing economic crisis in which the sector is deeply enmeshed. Nothing highlights this better than the nature of the reaction from employers and employees of the 'sunshine sector' to proposals in the 2009–10 Union Budget to end the funding for the STPI. While big players like Infosys, Wipro and TCS had prepared for the end of the scheme, smaller players have learnt that they have nowhere to hide in the current crisis. That reaction confirms the view that programmes with government funding or subsidies tend to create a sense of dependence and any attempts at withdrawal are resisted. It also answers critics who assume that the success of the IT sector has been a product of economic liberalisation, which it is not.

Unlike other departments which tend to adopt a controlling approach, the officials of DOE adopted an enabling role by establishing close links with manufacturers and consulting them in policy development. According to Evans (1995), 'DOE has tried to market the electronics industry, behaving like a 'product manager' for electronics, especially vis-à-vis other parts of the government' (115–16). 'The DOE thus represents a very different model for India from the older generation of 'strategic' ministries that sought to specify, develop, and directly regulate technology and industry structure' (Saxenian 2003, 175). This difference in approach is attributed to certain key players, namely, Dr Seshagiri, S. Vijaykar and N. Vittal (discussed in Chapter 6), who guided the direction of policy in the 1980s with the support of Prime Minister Rajiv Gandhi. According to Heeks (1996), Seshagiri is 'credited with being the 'architect' and the 'moving spirit' behind the 1984 ...liberalisation' (320). Liberalisation came about only after an intense struggle over policy and with support from Rajiv Gandhi and not because of private sector pressure or general reorientation of industrial policy (Sridharan 1996, 181). An example of the positive attitude of DOE officials is the assistance provided to facilitate the entry of Texas Instruments' Bangalore subsidiary. N. Seshagiri took particular pride in the department's new orientation saying, 'We broke 26 separate rules to accommodate Texas Instruments Bangalore subsidiary and are willing to break more' (Evans, 1995, 115). In allowing the entry of Texas Instruments (TI) into Bangalore in 1986, the Department of Electronics took an unprecedented course which had tremendous consequences for the industry. However, as Seshagiri became increasingly identified with total liberalisation which he publicly supported, those who opposed it were instrumental in sidelining him to the National Informatics Centre in early 1988 (Heeks 1996, 331). N. Vittal, who succeeded him, was less passionate in his pursuit of liberalisation.

In 1999, when DOE formally became DIT, some entrepreneurs expressed relief at the new organisation's declaration of its 'hands off' approach (Greenspan 2004, 79–81). As a successor to DOE and not a new creation, DIT was only reiterating existing practice. Far from being meddlesome, both EC and the DOE have played a supportive role shielding the burgeoning IT industry from other bureaucratic agencies which would otherwise have thwarted progress. DIT's role in creating awareness of government policies by organising seminars and exhibitions has brought government and industry closer, resulting in the establishment of NASSCOM and Manufacturers' Association of Information Technology (MAIT) which have been active in ICT policy-making and in setting up the STPs as autonomous units.

Two events, both attributed to DOE, which accelerated ICT development in India are the exit of IBM in 1978 and the entry of Texas Instruments in 1986. IBM's exit (see Chapter 4) provided an unexpected fillip to the industry, giving 1200 trained staff the opportunity to service various models imported from different manufacturers and thus acquire a range of skills. 'Indian programmers thus learned to work on a variety of platforms, which proved helpful in acquiring contracts for maintenance of various legacy systems. More important, computer manufacturers in the 1980s had no alternative but to rely on Unix (the first portable, machine-independent, multi-user operating system) even though foreign companies were developing proprietary systems at the time. By the 1990s, however, when Unix became the system of choice for PCs and work stations, India's Unix programmers had acquired a skill that was extremely scarce elsewhere in the world' (Saxenian 2002, 175–76) (see Chapters 6 and 8). At the turn of the century, when the Y2K scare engulfed the computer world, the major breakdown that was feared did not happen. However, Indian software companies reaped the benefits as its employees were engaged to carry out the laborious task of reprogramming.

With software export promotion in mind, the merged Ministry of Communication and Information Technology (which includes DIT) established the Electronics and Software Export Promotion Council (ESC). Its objectives in collaboration with NASSCOM are:

- to interact closely with government in formulating Information Technology policies specifically software;
- to maintain a state-of-the-art information database of software related activities for software developers as well as companies overseas;
- to encourage members to provide world-class products, services and solutions in India and overseas;
- to take effective steps against software piracy;
- to provide value added services to its members;
- to actively help in the development of human resources required for the software industry; and
- to promote profitable growth of the Indian software industry (Naidu in Jasswalla and Taylor, 2003).

In response to criticism about the undue emphasis given to exports, which has caused the neglect of the domestic market and dampened the development of the indigenous hardware industry (Heeks 1996, 54), the government in 1998 appointed a National Task Force for Information Technology. The Task Force suggested the following measures to promote the software sector:

- that the compound annual growth rate of 55 per cent (1992–97) be increased to 80 per cent by 2008;
- that schools, polytechnics, colleges and public hospitals be provided with access to computers and the Internet by 2003;
- that a policy framework and investment climate be created similar to that of Singapore to enable software and hardware manufacturing units to meet local demands and exports; and
- that the IT culture be dispersed through all walks of life by strengthening the industry to meet the demands of a duty-free regime according to WTO requirements (Naidu in Jasswalla and Taylor 2003, 131–32).

Discussions arising from the recommendations of the Task Force focused on concern about the lack of a domestic base. The absence of a dynamic domestic market, along with the use of low installed base of hardware and the absence of intensive interfacing between users and producers, has been cited by D'Costa as the reason for India's IT preoccupation in providing a low level of services to foreign clients, impeding its logical progress into the more creative and profitable market for software packages. A viable way out of this situation, he suggests, is diversification into high value software such as systems integration and packaged software and indigenous developments like the Simputer and super computer which could be used to raise the technical and commercial profile of the Indian software industry (D'Costa and Sridharan 2003, 20).

5.6 Deregulation of Telecommunication: The Era of Internet

While the departure of IBM and the entry of Texas Instruments were important events in the growth of ICT in India, a far more significant change was the development of the Internet, whose impact on business in a global world has brought about a 'new economy' and challenged different economies in different ways. The application of microprocessors to telecommunications brought about by digitalisation enabled computers and telephones to become compatible (Duysters 1996, 54–55), launching the informatics revolution and the concept of cyberspace. The term signifies the space where electronic data is stored or exchanged. While the convergence virtually obliterated much of the distinction between the two technologies, there were however some anomalies caused by the fact that one (telecom) was regulated while the other (computers) remained regulation free. However, the potential for new products and processes caused pressure to be brought by major players in the field for the deregulation of telecom. Such developments have revolutionised communication between individuals and between communities and organisations, offering numerous avenues for the use of electronics in daily life.

McKnight, et al. (2003, 368) consider that retention by the state of substantial ownership of telecom is preferable to the mainstream approach of rapid and complete state divestment. Although India approached the task of telecom reform belatedly, its leaders nonetheless responded rapidly to technological changes by gradually involving the private sector. And recent changes in policy suggest, according to McKnight et al., 'that the next wave of creative destruction and institutional innovation in telecommunication will sweep away the notion that the state has no role to play in enabling market success.' (390).

The restructuring of telecommunications in India which followed the introduction of digital switching and the success of ISRO in satellite communication was essential to the development of IT. Long castigated for its unreliable communication system, Indian telecom, has, in a period of fifteen years, not only reversed that image, but also injected a new concept in telephony, the focus being on access, not ownership. By developing a simple device which attaches a meter to the telephone and selling the product to small entrepreneurs, Sam Pitroda revolutionised both quality and accessibility. Almost every town and village across the country has small public call centres (PCO) which offer inexpensive telephone access and provide employment for millions (also see Chapter 2, Section 2.4) (Singhal and Rogers 2001, Mascarenhas 2004). In 1985, the erstwhile Posts and Telegraph Department was restructured into the Department of Telecom (DOT) under the Ministry of Communication. In 1986, DOT set up two commercially oriented public undertakings, Mahanagar Telephone Nigam Limited (MTNL) for Delhi and Bombay markets and Videshi Sanchar Nigam

Limited (VSNL) for overseas telecommunication, to be run on best commercial principles.

The establishment of Telecom Regulatory Authority of India (TRAI) in 1997 by the government is a clear indication of its commitment to a strong and independent regulator with comprehensive powers and clear authority to effectively perform its functions. When Sam Pitroda was appointed Chairman of DOT, he set up the Telecommunication Commission under the umbrella of DOT 'to speed up telecommunication decision-making and licensed vendors to manufacture C-DOT's automatic exchanges, EPABXs and telephone equipment, breaking, for the first time, government's monopoly in telecom equipment production. Long-distance direct dialling services were introduced....And public call offices were introduced throughout India increasing telephone access ...India's telecommunication revolution was thus instigated by a technology minded politician working closely with a visionary technologist' (Singhal and Rogers 2001,194, Mani 2003, 25–26).

With the deregulation of the sector, 'a sea change occurred in the telecommunications scenario: by 1999, India had installed a network of over twenty-five million telephone lines spread across 300 cities, 4,869 towns, and 310,897 villages, making India's telephone network the ninth largest in the world ' (Singhal and Rogers 2000, 186). In poor countries where telephone connections are expensive, PCOs provide easy access and generate employment. 'A staggering 117 billion metered calls were made in India from these PCOs in 1998,' leading to a five-fold increase in DOT's revenue in ten years from $790 million in 1988 to $4.3 billion in 1998 (Singhal and Rogers 2000, 189). Notwithstanding the dramatic growth in telephone subscribers, a strategy of access through PCOs remains a viable option to ownership. Between 1988 and 1998, the number of villages with telephone access increased from 27,316 to three lakhs. 'By 2000, some 650,000 public call offices providing reliable telephone service, where people can simply walk in, make a call and pay the metered charges, had mushroomed all over India, including the remote, rural, hilly and tribal areas' (Singhal and Rogers 2001, 186). Under the Bharat Nirman Programme, 92 per cent of villages have already been provided with Village Public Telephones (VPT) and there were plans to provide VPTs in 66,822 uncovered villages by 2007 (Department of Telecommunications, Annual Report 2006–07).

Credit for such growth must, in all fairness, also be attributed to the country's advances in space technology. ISRO has acquired the capability to build world class communication satellites and tries, through its Insat system, to serve most of the country's communications and broadcasting needs. ('Insats flying high', *The Hindu*, 30 September 2003).

The changed scene is attributed to two factors: firstly, government's decision to share its revenue instead of charging telecom operators a licence fee and secondly, the shift to uniform licensing in 2003. This change gave a significant boost to government revenues to Rs 5,000 crores in fiscal 2004–05 (*The Hindu*, 24 February 2006). Basically it is 'a recognition that technology has made separate licenses for different telecom services irrelevant and inefficient'. Evidence of the growth in the Indian telecommunication industry is clear from the figures: five million telephones in 1990; thirty million in 2000 and a hundred million in 2005. By September 2005, subscriptions of fixed and mobile telephones had touched 113 million, and teledensity (a measure of telephone ownership, in percentage) had reached double figures at 10.36. By December 2006, telephone connections were estimated at 198 million, doubling the figure of ninety-eight million connections as at March 2005. Overall teledensity increased from 8.95 per cent in March 2005 to 16.8 per cent in December 2006. On an average, over five million phones per month were added over the last nine months of 2006–07. The number of broadband and Internet subscribers increased from 6.9 million and 1.3 million, respectively, as of 31 March 2006 to 8.6 million and 2 million, respectively, as of 31 December 2006. A further 710 cities have been provided with broadband connectivity by public sector undertakings. (Annual Report, 2006–07). Broadband relates to the use of signals over a broad range of frequencies and once provided is available to all users in designated areas, while Internet is the international computer network linking computer users.

Since deregulation and partial privatisation, the telecommunication sector continues to register significant growth and has emerged as a key sector responsible for India's resurgent economic growth. A sector that was growing annually at 20 per cent to 25 per cent during 2002–03 has moved to a higher growth path at an average rate of 40 per cent. 'This rapid growth has been possible due to various proactive and positive decisions of the Government and contribution of both the public and private sectors. The Department of Telecom (DOT) has set a target of providing 250 million connections in 2007, a teledensity of 22 per cent' (Annual Report, 2006–07).

Telecommunications, which until the mid-1990s had been wholly government-owned, shows a different picture in less than a decade of deregulation. The share of the private sector in total telephones increased from 57 per cent as of 31 March 2006 to 65 per cent as of 31 December 2006. Of the 478.29 lakh additional phones provided during 2006–07, the major share, 424.38 lakh (about 89 per cent), was provided by the private sector.

Amidst this phenomenal growth, the preference for mobile phones, which increased from 71.69 per cent as of 31 March 2006 to more than 79 per cent as of 31 December 2006, surpassed landlines, a trend which was likely to continue (Department of Telecommunications, Annual Report 2006–07). In October 2005, 2.9 million new subscribers had joined the mobile network, taking the total number of cell phone users in India to 68 million (*India Today*, 26 December 2005). A study carried out by ASSOCHAM Eco Pulse in 2005 predicted a monthly increase of three million telephone subscribers, with the subscriber base expected to touch 278 million by 2007–2008 (*The Hindu*, 29 August 2005). However, that figure has jumped to six million mobiles a month, making India the 'world's fastest-growing cell phone market—176 million strong as of last month' (*The Hindu*, 10 December 2006).

TABLE 5-2 Growth of Internet and Telephone Ownership in India

Year	*Internet users (in thousands)*	*Landline (in millions)*	*Mobiles (in millions)*
1995	10		
1996	250	14.5	0.3
1997	450		
1998	700	21.5	1.3
1999	1,400		
2000	2,800	28	3.2
2001	6,668		
2002	10,684	41.4	12.6
2003	29,000		
2004	31,753	44	47.3
2005	69,000	98	101.8
2006	86,000	189	149.5

Source: Information on Internet usage from NASSCOM, World Bank 2005, *India and the Knowledge Economy*, Washington DC, Department of Telecom, Annual Report, 2006–07.

TABLE 5-3 State-wise Subscribers of Broadband Connectivity in India—as of 31 December 2007

States	*2007*
Andhra Pradesh	2,34,099
Assam	12,475
Bihar and Jharkhand	37,278
Delhi	4,09,057
Gujarat	1,88,628
Haryana	40,208
Himachal Pradesh	6,693
Jammu &Kashmir	9,597
Karnataka	3,31,937
Kerala	1,40,306
Madhya Pradesh	80,738
Maharashtra and Goa	6,54,308
Orissa	20,973
Punjab	1,06,892
Rajasthan	57,934
Tamilnadu	4,06,654
Uttar Pradesh and Uttarakhand	1,10,641
West Bengal	1,65,273

Source: Compiled from Rajya Sabha Unstarred Question No 2187, *The Hindu*, 3 October 2008.

To meet the huge demand for mobile phones, Nokia's factory at Sriperambudur had, within six months of starting production, manufactured one million sets. At the inauguration, Nokia executives explained that they were there to capitalise on the telecom boom in India as they expected it to become the world's second largest mobile device market in terms of volumes by 2010. With this in mind, it has also set up a design centre at Bangalore.

The growth of mobile telephones in India at 300,000 subscribers a day led the Minister for Communications and Information Technology to declare, ' We have a goose that lays golden eggs' (*The Hindu*, 1 November 2008). This phenomenal growth, referred to as the telecommunication revolution, began with the setting up of C-DOT which replaced mechanical with digital switches and was followed by the steep reduction in transmission costs because of the availability of communication satellites operated by ISRO. Here, one must acknowledge the contribution made to improved connectivity by the public sector operator BSNL which extended the fibre-optic cable network throughout India. With this new technology and the worldwide boom in telecommunication equipment, India encouraged the entry of private operators such as Reliance, Tatas and Airtel by deregulating the sector.

While such growth in mobile telephones in a country with low literacy levels is surprising, Schmidt of Google recognises it as 'the technology most adapted to the essence of the human species: sociability.' Arthur Modella, Director of the Smithsonian Centre for the Study of Invention and Innovation, calls it 'the ultimate tool to find each other. It is a wonderful technology for being human' (Joel Garreau, *The Age*, 24 March 2008). Despite such growth, one cannot overlook the discrepancy between urban and rural access to telecommunication, a challenge that India needs to overcome. An attempt has been made to address this discrepancy through the allocation of 2G spectrum licences, as advised by the Minister for Communication and Information Technology (*The Hindu*, 1 November 2008).

The downside to the new technology was demonstrated in the 26 November 2008 attack in Mumbai when terrorists exchanged messages using satellite telephones which were virtually undetectable. It is essential, therefore, according to Anand Parthasarathy, to 'stay one jump ahead of the bad guys' by 'fighting technology with technology'. One such technology that is in focus, according to him, is the face recognition technique formed on a database of known suspects, which 'might yet be the *agni asthra* that will stop terrorists in their tracks well before they can do damage' (*The Hindu*, 4 December 2008). His hope of an Indian response rests on work being done at IIT Chennai and C-DAC in natural language processing technology. While alerting readers to the perils of the Mumbai happenings, the writer warns of the greater danger posed by the Web, citing Symantec's report on the underground economy. Other work in the area of surveillance is being carried out by Ittiam, eInfochips and eCon Infotech (*The Hindu*, 4 December 2008).

In the context of India's extraordinary growth in mobile technology, Motorola, at the first ever MotoDev conference held in India, posed a challenge to software developers to develop applications for an open framework. A single standard is preferable to the present multiple platforms with the temptation of a $1.3 trillion market out there. With the purchase of almost ten million phones each month (to total 261 million), India has overtaken the US to become the second largest wireless nation after China. The continuous growth of the market in India led Malcolm Dawe, Vice President, Motorola, for India and South

West Asia, to conclude that it makes sense to develop products tailored to local needs. 'However, the world banked on Indian developers' ingenuity, not just Indian customers', he said (*The Hindu,* 18 May 2008).

The emergence of the Internet, basically a result of the convergence of computers and telecommunications, is reliant 'on two technological components: a network among distributed computers and the digitilisation of content' (Kogut 2003, 2). It also 'relies upon several essential subsystems: the physical infrastructure, terminals and servers, software and technical agreements' (ibid., 8–9). In addition, protocol agreements are necessary because it operates within a regulatory and legal environment where the state or the telephone monopoly controls and issues licences.

Initially, DOT was reluctant to allow the use of Internet on a general basis for fear that the public sector telecommunication companies would lose revenue. However, it had been in use as a link between the IITs through the National Centre for Software Technology set up in 1986 and was followed by ERNET set up by NIC and Softnet set up by STPI to provide high-speed data communication links to Indian firms engaged in software exports. NICNET set up in 1993 by NIC linked various central and state government departments. After priority sectors like research, software and government were linked, VSNL offered Internet services to the public from 1995 (Kudaisya 2001,163).

Two other developments that occurred in January 2005 have brought with them further potential for change. The first is 'In', the official Internet domain of India developed by the National Internet Exchange of India (NIXI) and the other is broadband (*The Hindu,* 7 January 2005) described as 'the seed for a new information explosion' (*The Hindu,* 31 January 2005). In February 2005, Bharat Sanchar Nigam Limited (BSNL) launched its broadband service in Mysore, offering Internet connections 17.5 times faster than dial-up connections with home users being allowed a minimum download speed of 256 kbps, the use of telephone and all for Rs 500 a month (*The Hindu,* 10 February 2005).

While these services and facilities are rapidly utilised by the increasingly affluent middle class, there are millions who have no access to a computer, leading to the comment, 'No developing country has benefitted more from the digital revolution than India, and in no country is the digital divide wider or deeper' (Abbot 2004, 57).

(Challenges India faces to overcome the digital divide, see Chapter 6 Section 6.5). Through the first half of 2003–2004, sales grossed 12.58 lakhs, registering a growth of 32 per cent over the same period in the previous year. That trend continued, according to technology monitor IDC (India), which claimed that Indians bought 4.3 million PCs in 2005, the growth in consumer models being 29 per cent, twice that of business (use of computers for commercial purposes as distinct from personal or research use) which registered only 14 per cent growth. While demand for the notebook (a small portable computer that runs on one battery and works like a desktop computer) was high with sales of 4,74,000 units, indigenous models like 'Lakshman Rekha' priced around Rs 10,000 had few buyers. Further, the government-sponsored 'Mobilis' hybrid machine, combining laptop and desktop, announced in 2006 has not progressed beyond sample quantities. MAIT estimated the total number of PCs in India at fourteen million—a penetration of fourteen per thousand, which was low in comparison with other countries (*The Hindu*, 20 February 2006). Just as PCOs substitute for the lack of telephone ownership, Internet cafes are helping to overcome the affordability of computers. Despite low computer ownership, Internet usage has grown steadily—from 9 per cent to 31 per cent in 2003 (Abbott 2004, 66) (see Tables 5.2 and 5.3).

Cyberspace, the imaginary place where the storage and exchange of electronic data occurs, provides a wealth of information and services to users via a multitude of websites and search engines. The prospects of direct communication between total strangers and the opportunities for the direct marketing of products have their advantages and disadvantages along with an element of danger. With the spread of online banking, consumers have to deal with the threat of cyber piracy. When the creation of a blog (web log) is within the reach of any interested Internet user, anyone can become a publisher of sorts. Misuse of such technological power can leave one feeling powerless. In an interview with Debelle (*The Age*, 4 August 2007), Boyd laments that 'her combined interest in the study of people and the science of the internet has given her a rare insight into what is going on online and how the internet has in some ways failed to live up to its promise'. That science is a 'two-edged' sword to be handled with care is reiterated by Sardan and Ravetz who comment that 'no product is on the market unless someone derives a benefit from it; and so here the situation is analogous to that in biomedical engineering, where any technique, however bizarre its human or ethical aspects, can be defended as bringing happiness to someone' (1996, 51–2)

In a bid to remove the hype attached to the term 'cyberspace', Ryan (1999) suggests that it would be easier to understand if the listed components were presented as 'the diverse applications of computing power and not as the facets of global experience. Let's replace 'cyberspace is' with 'computers can do these things' and we will realise that the territory of cyberspace covers nothing less than all recent, future, or merely conceivable applications of electronic technology' (Ryan 1999).

Undoubtedly, the Internet has in the short time of its existence introduced a totally new element into our lives in terms of virtually instant communication and access to a wide variety of search engines and websites. MySpace, YouTube and Facebook have entered the political arena through their use by politicians standing for election in the USA and Australia.

In her analysis of Internet usage in search of patterns, Boyd (*The Age*, 4 August 2007) discovered 'that users of MySpace and Facebook reflected broad social and class divides' and that 'social stratification was deeply embedded in the supposedly egalitarian internet'. She observed that users of Facebook which originated at Harvard 'were primarily white and looking forward to go to the prom and then college' while users of MySpace were of Hispanic or Latino backgrounds intending to leave school and take up a job. Further, citing the use of CyWorld by 50 per cent of Koreans and that of LunarStorm by most Swedes, Boyd concludes that 'national and cultural divisions between people are just as much an impediment to communication as they are in real life'.

While early versions of the computer technology were used to solve complex problems in physics and mathematics, later versions offer options to a range of users depending on their needs and abilities. The computer is in that way a perfect example of built-in redundancy where the scope for failure is non-existent, unless there is a mechanical breakdown due to wear and tear or power failure, like the outage in north-east US in 2005. The versatility of computers is unique, ranging from a very basic level as a glorified typewriter to the most complex problem solver.

A new and exciting development is biometric technology, the use of thumb impressions for personal identification in digital form (*The Hindu*, 8 April 2007). Bangalore-based Integra Micro

Systems has developed Financial Applications Secure Terminal or iMFAST, a portable platform which can be used in a variety of rural applications including banking, loan management, ration and subsidy disbursement. 'It's a table-top gadget fuelled by 'Geode' processor chip from AMD and harnesses a contactless smart card using Radio Frequency Identification (RFID) to identify the owner. It grabs the thumb impression with a biometric scanner and connects the banking or other system, using friendly voice prompts in the local language. The communication link can be anything: a mobile phone, a telephone landline or an Internet connection'. The iMFAST terminals are being used in a pilot run by a nationalised bank in Doddaballapur taluk on the outskirts of Bangalore to offer banking services in villages which do not have a branch. When showcased earlier this year at the CeBIT computer fair in Hanover, Germany, it drew much interest from agencies in Africa (ibid.).

Mani (2003) notes the lack of attention paid to the Indian telecom equipment industry by researchers. Examining a number of R&D projects currently in operation, he notes the three areas in which India possesses considerable innovative capability: digital switching (see Section 5.4.3 above), wireless local loop (WLL)-based access technology and telecom software. A team of engineers from IIT in Chennai led by Jhunjunwala in conjunction with Analog Devices, Massachusetts, developed a wireless alternative, known as corDECT. Systems developed on WLL technology are useful in areas where there is no electricity as it involves the use of radio waves to beam telephone signals from telephone exchanges into locations within ten kilometres radius, and even up to a radius of twenty-five kilometres when solar-powered relay stations are used. 'Once they reach a local exchange, however, the signals are digitilized and beamed to houses and businesses, where a small, wall-mounted device is used to receive them. By splitting voice and Internet traffic at the local exchange, the system provides a separate phone line with each Internet connection' (Jayaraman 2002, 358). By enlisting Local Service Providers (LSPs) and local companies they hope to extend Internet services to rural areas. 'The first trial system was installed in February 2000. Today, some 50,000 villages across India are hooked up, and more than a million people brought into the system last year alone. Telecom companies in South Africa, Tunisia, Kenya, Kazhakistan, Fiji and Yemen have also adopted the system' (David Cohen, *New Scientist*, 19 February 2005,

53). Mani predicts that 'corDECT technology will reduce significantly the access cost of telecom service especially in rural areas...(and) hasten the diffusion of internet services in the country and especially in the rural areas' (Mani 2003, 39) while the telecom software segment is likely to be 'the fastest growing and the most profitable segment of the software industry in India' (Indiatel 2002 cited in Mani 2003, 32–33) with exports helping to move it up the value chain.

In 1999, major changes to the telecommunication infrastructure were introduced on the recommendations of a government-appointed National Task Force on Information Technology and Software Development. Under a Ministry of Information Technology that was set up for overall coordination, the new policy opened up the Internet market allowing private ISPs to operate fee-free in competition with VSNL. Such changes have resulted in significant growth in software exports, increased the number of countries in which Indian software companies now operate and accelerated growth in the diffusion of the Internet. In 2002, VSNL's monopoly services were officially terminated and subsequently sold to the Tatas.

BSNL and MTNL have introduced broadband at competitive prices hoping private operators will try to match them. While affordability of Internet is one aspect and low computer ownership is another, more important is the paucity of content in Indian languages, which the Task Force on Information Technology has pinpointed as the way to reach the other India and achieve large-scale use of IT in Indian languages. Encouraging signs in this direction are Microsoft's recent launch of its Hindi MS Office and its 'Project Bhasha' which involves working with the education and governance programmes of the state governments of Karnataka, Orissa and Haryana. In addition, C-DAC has released a set of Hindi Software—tools and fonts on compact discs (CD)—and has plans to produce similar CDs in other Indian languages for free distribution.

When one reviews telecommunication policy and the significant changes that occurred in the late 1990s, it is clear that those changes were inevitable, irrespective of the government in power, as they were technology driven. India's strides in software exports necessitated the opening up of the telecommunication sector to market competition, particularly in the context of limited investment capacity within the country. It thus became possible to offer cellular mobile telephony, e-mail and V-Sat data network through private sector companies. In the context of convergence, it became necessary to separate functions like licence, regulation, infrastructure and services which Chowdhury (in Keniston and Kumar 2003) claims was a 'terrible combination unheard of anywhere in the world' (51). Further improvements to information technology services will occur with the government's new broadband policy intended to promote the use of 'always-on high speed' Internet which will remain technology-neutral. 'In other words, operators will be free to employ any technology of their choice but the spread of fibre networks will be emphasised because in the long term it can provide huge amounts of bandwidth in the last mile as well as a true converged network' (*The Hindu,* 15 October 2004).

In October 2005, TRAI suggested a change in direction to increase teledensity in rural areas by moving from Universal Service Obligation to Universal Service Opportunity (*The Hindu,* 4 October 2005). In January 2006, Beecam Communications, creator of the world's first chipsets for mobile WiMax platforms, sponsored a wireless Broadband Summit at which attendees were informed of WiMax-——the faster, longer range version of WiFi (the technology to wirelessly access the net) which can be harnessed by India to achieve its objectives with its huge base of copper-wire and fibre optic connectivity available with BSLN and extend its reach to inaccessible areas by using wireless for the last mile (The *Hindu,* 11 January 2006).

'The rapid growth of telecom networks and adoption of IT is fostering a market place that is ready for converged solutions'—the capability of the same technology to offer various services (Neelam Dhawan of Microsoft, *The Hindu,* 23 November 2005). As regulator, TRAI has sought to encourage greater consultation with stakeholders in its plans to move to next generation networks (NGN) which have the potential to help distance education and telemedicine applications (*The Hindu,* 22 February 2006). The proposed merger of BSNL and MTNL will bring together 35,000 telephone exchanges, forty million POTS (plain old telephone services!) customers and PCOs in 50,000 villages with an optical fibre network covering over 350,000 route kilometres. In that context, one has to understand that the push towards telecommunication liberalisation is essentially technology driven and that governments are unable to steady the pace, even if they so wished. As witnessed, the changes in telecommunication taking place in India in the last decade have had and will continue to have a domino effect.

5.7 Conclusion

In this study, I have looked at the development of the Indian computer industry in two phases, 1965–1983 and 1983 to the present. During the first period, government policy was largely confined to the development of computer hardware, while software was overlooked. The period 1983 onwards recognises the gradual separation of software from hardware with growing recognition of the role of software designers and systems integrators. As the Indian government awoke to the tremendous opportunities for software exports around 1984, it developed promotional policies in that area. With the election of Rajiv Gandhi as Prime Minister in 1984, policies to liberalise the import of computers and export of software were introduced. While these were described by observers as a mere removal of the barriers, real liberalisation occurred only in 1991. Telecommunication in India really surged ahead in the mid-1980s with the election of Rajiv Gandhi and the key contribution of Sam Pitroda (Chowdhury in Keniston and Kumar 2004). With Rajiv Gandhi's support, Pitroda, as head of C-DOT, engineered the move from electromechanical to digital switching and revolutionised rural telephone exchanges in India, continuing this in his role as Chairman of the Telecom Commission. While DOE played a crucial role, two unforeseen events, which proved fortuitous, were the exit of IBM and the opportunities that came with the 2YK scare.

As with hardware, government played a significant role in the development of the software industry until the private sector could assume its place. The early stage of software exports characterised by low skill on-site work, pejoratively referred to as 'body shopping', did have a positive effect on the industry in general, particularly in the context of surplus engineers who would otherwise have been unemployed or moved overseas. The mid-1980s brought major changes when C-DOT transformed telecommunication with digital switching and ISRO offered satellite communication. Further encouragement came through deregulation and partial privatisation of telecom in the mid-1990s. In this environment of rapid technological change, India's liberalising policies of opening up the IT sector and setting up agencies to assist domestic operations triggered a transformation with young entrepreneurs moving from traditional businesses into the burgeoning IT world. Once eager to emigrate, young entrepreneurs are leading the way in the new economy. India's uniquely evolving multi-dimensional model, marking a change in the role of the state from public ownership and regulation towards promotion, is drawing much worldwide attention, not the least from World Bank ideologues (Heeks in Coopey 2004).

6

Evaluation of Policies

Growth and Impact of ICT

6.1 Introduction

Since gaining independence from British rule in 1947, India, has, in a period of six decades, achieved a remarkable level of technological advancement being one of the few TW countries capable of indigenously designing and developing advanced computers and launching communication satellites. Such an achievement, accompanied by the enormous growth in software exports, is the product of state investment in industrial transformation. Government emphasis on self-reliance has resulted in the achievement of an admirable level of maturity on the part of Indian manufacturing with ability to produce high-tech products. In earlier chapters, I have traced the various stages of that involvement, beginning with the creation of an S&T infrastructure and investment in higher education. Current excellence in the quality of human capital, while showcasing India's ICT sector, continues to attract multinational investment.

With knowledge becoming important for social and economic transformation, the crucial test for ICT lies in its capacity as a vehicle of broad-based socio-economic development. Modern communication networks, access to computers and the Internet have become essential to industry, education, healthcare and the rural economy. With digitalisation and deregulation of telecommunications, India has made considerable progress; yet access to ICT is still outside the reach of millions. Viewed now as a world leader in software, India's efforts in attempting to bridge this digital divide will be watched by other TW countries which face similar problems but lack India's abundant and highly qualified manpower.

Having analysed the policies for the development of ICT in the previous chapter, I intend to evaluate them in terms of growth and impact. If growth is measured in terms of data on the number of computers, access to telecommunications and the number of software professionals involved in IT and their output (particularly exports), impact is illustrated by the effect of such technology on business, the economy and politics. This has to do with broad-based industrial and social development and requires the adoption of a comparative political economy approach. Indicative of the application of ICT in present-day engineering and industry is its overall impact within India, where some states like Karnataka with advanced manufacturing capability have been able to utilise the new or knowledge economy to a greater extent than others.

In its early stages, the Indian software industry was largely export-oriented, sending skilled personnel overseas to undertake assignments in the developed world. While this did bring in badly needed foreign exchange to pay for imports, domestic development remained negligible. Such a scenario was the outcome of past policies which had restricted investment through a system of bureaucratic controls. Until the 1991 liberalisation and the deregulation of telecommunication in the mid-to-late 1990s, the bureaucratic strategy of controls for the protection of industry proved detrimental as it drove overseas the engineers and scientists crucial for a knowledge economy. Since then, economic liberalisation and deregulation of telecommunication with active policies to promote IT have dramatically transformed the scene. However, that transformation is restricted to the urban educated leaving large rural areas untouched.

Following this introduction, in Section 6.2 of this chapter I examine the data on the growth of IT. Section 6.3 looks into the use of ICT in government and business. Section 6.4 examines the reasons for the boom in software exports. Section 6.5 discusses the various strategies adopted to overcome the digital divide and their current prospects. In Section 6.6, I attempt a critique of the current trends in IT in India while Section 6.7 discusses the backlash to the outsourcing of software jobs from US to India. Section 6.8 evaluates the social consequences of ICT and the next section concludes the chapter.

6.2 Growth of Information Technology in India

The convergence of electronics, computing and telecommunications in the late 1980s and early 1990s heralded the onset of the IT boom worldwide (Duysters 1996). In India, that genesis can be traced to the concerted policies for the development of electronics which began in 1965, followed by subsequent policy changes in both IT and telecommunication (see Chapters 4 and 5). Despite the limited domestic market for software at the time, the resulting improvement in telecom and internet access led to a sudden spurt in the growth of India's software exports.

In the current debate on the relevant strengths of emerging economies like India and China, a key factor that is often highlighted is the quality of institutions. While India involved itself in the hard work of building sound economic and political institutions in its post-independence period, it failed to fully utilise them until the mid-1980s. By contrast, China, which has grown rapidly, faces the challenge of large-scale institutional transformation (Rodrik and Subramaniam, *The Hindu*, 17 May 2004). Commenting on the World Competitiveness Report presented at the World Economic Forum, Tim Colebatch, economics editor for *The Age*, writes, 'China has a great economic scorecard but low-grade institutions, universities and "technological readiness". India has worse economic grades but leaves China for dead for institutional quality, efficiency and innovation' (*The Age*, 28 September 2006).

With the domain knowledge developed over the years in manufacturing combined with process knowledge acquired in IT outsourcing, Indian companies have been able to make inroads into engineering services. As designing becomes increasingly electronic, Indian designers in diverse locations are able to cooperate on project design, encouraging international companies to outsource engineering services to India. With 28 per cent of global engineering talent, India is seen to be at an advantage because of access to domain expertise from public sector companies, defence research establishments and private sector organisations, and the ability to communicate in English.

In 2006–07, Indian electronics production witnessed a healthy growth, its total exports reaching Rs 141,800 crores (US $31.8 billion), an increase of 36 per cent over the previous financial year, the domestic market (after a growth of 22 per cent) being expected to touch Rs 37,800 crores (see Table 6.1: Annual Turnover in Software 1996–2006). According to NASSCOM, the IT and IT-enabled service sectors turnover accounted for 4.8 per cent of GDP with an estimated workforce of 12.87 lakhs (exports accounting for nearly two thirds of the total production). While service and software exports remain the mainstay of the sector, exports of BPO were expected to exceed

$8.3 billion in FY 2006–07, growing at 32 per cent over the previous year. In the area of offshore product development and engineering services, the expected growth was 22 per cent, earning US $4.9 billion in exports in FY 2006–07. Based on current performance, NASSCOM is confident that India can achieve its export target of $60 billion by 2009–10 (NASSCOM, Strategic Review 2007).

TABLE 6-1 Annual Turnover in Software 1996–2006 (in Rs crores)

Year	*Exports*	*Domestic*	*Total*
1996–1997	3,900	2,410	6,310
1997–1998	6,500	3,510	10,040
1998–1999	10,340	4,350	15,290
1999–2000	17,150	7,200	24,350
2000–2001	28,350	9,410	37,360
2001–2002	36,500	10,874	47,374
2002–2003	46,100	13,400	59,500
2003–2004	58,240	16,250	74,490
2004–2005	80,180	21,740	1,01,920
2005–2006	1,03,200	26,400	1,29,600
2006–2007	1,41,800	37,800	1,79,600

Source: NASSCOM and Department of Information Technology.

India's performance during the decade 1997–2007 has shown that the country possesses a sound technological base with professional competence to compete in high-technology exports. Its share in global sourcing has grown from 62 per cent to 65 per cent in IT and from 39 per cent to 45 per cent in BPO. A crucial element of that is the abundant talent popularly identified as India's demographic dividend with 50 per cent of the population under the age of twenty-five.

In a competitive world economy, it is important for Indian companies to aspire towards internationally acceptable quality and delivery efficiency. Software exporting companies seek certification by a method known as CMM (Capability Maturity Model) developed by Carnegie Mellon University in conjunction with the US Department of Defense. Developed in 1991, CMM has five levels of standards for organisations and is sought by companies once they have achieved ISO 9001 certification. India has ninety companies certified at SEI CMM level 5—higher than any other country in the world (NASSCOM Strategic Review, 2007) and includes the multinationals Wipro, Tata Consultancy Services and Infosys.

While CMM certification is an across-the-board quality certification, the granting of the 'Wi–Fi Certified' stamp to Ittiam Systems, Bangalore-based semi-conductor designer, for design and intellectual property by the Wi-Fi Alliance, the global industry body behind wireless networks and products, is regarded as a major recognition (*The Hindu*, 7 April 2007). While some like Kogut (2004, 261–81) might view such aspirations with cynicism, these efforts have to be commended as they indicate a desire to perform at the highest level and provide an assurance to clients in the absence of legal protection. As leaders in the software sector, such companies stand out as role models of good governance in their adoption of innovative methods such as modern accounting practices, the use of venture capital and offering incentives like shareholder value to staff. Following Infosys's listing on the US NASDAQ, the latter has started trading from Infosys's Mysore campus, a first for any company.

Another company which has drawn attention to its management practices is HCL Technologies. HCL has developed a system described by Leon Gettler as unusual. He writes, 'Out of India we have a performance appraisal model that stands in contrast to the fixture of organisational life that everyone dreads' (*The Age*, 7 June 2006). Its 30,000 employees in fifteen countries are asked to rank their boss and other company managers and the results are posted online leaving nobody a place to hide. Further, 'HCL has a system that allows employees to raise their concerns about anything, from compensation issues to personality clashes, by way of creating an electronic ticket. The ticket is then placed with a manager to be resolved. And it can only be closed by the employee when that issue is resolved' (ibid.). All employees including the Managing Director are trained in negotiation and conflict management and expected to undergo online tests, the results of which are published online. These innovations have, according to HCL's Managing Director, created an environment of openness and transparency and helped to reduce attrition rates from 10 per cent to 3 per cent.

A significant influence on the Indian software industry is the technological spillover through MNCs which have brought with them differentiated input technologies and organisational strategies. The R&D outsourcing market for IT in India is expected to grow from $1.3 billion in 2003 to over $8 billion by 2010. Their success, according to an Irish study, is due to good management, an emphasis on quality and strong ties to universities (Cooke and Piccaluga 2006). That the working of Indian software companies has gained much attention in academic circles is borne out by the visit of two US business schools, Cornell and Stanford, to Infosys to study its experience (*The Hindu*, 15 January 2007).

The prospect of a huge market for engineering services is likely to present challenges such as availability of engineers, adequate infrastructure and cooperation among public sector manufacturing firms, engineering service providers and education institutions. The issue of the availability of qualified human resources has become serious with increasing demand for diversified skills and greater specialisation. The number of IT and ITES–BPO professionals employed in India is estimated to have grown from 284,000 in 1999–2000 to 1,287,000 in 2005–06, growing by over 230,000 in 2005–06 alone. In addition, Indian IT—ITES are estimated to have helped create an additional three million job opportunities through indirect and induced employment (Department of Information Technology, Annual Report 2006–07).

In trying to attract qualified people, ICT firms offer higher salaries, various incentives and an improved work environment. Such demand has encouraged young students to move from courses in science and engineering towards computers and business management and has spawned several educational institutions offering a wide range of courses of varying quality.

Continued growth and the demand for manpower is likely to affect quality. Acting on the report of a NASSCOM study which projected a shortage in software professionals, the Government of India set up a high level task force chaired by F. C. Kohli of Tata Consultancy Services. While its recommendations covered changes to policy, reform of delivery institutions and the adoption of regulatory mechanisms and fiscal incentives, overall its concern related more to the nature of skills, the training imparted and the need to update the curriculum rather than to the availability of seats in colleges (*The Hindu*, 15 February 2004).

The committee's recommendations, to be viewed in the context of future developments spelt out in the information technology vision, have the following objectives:

- to accelerate the establishment of IT infrastructure by spreading fibre optic, satcom and wireless networks and establishing links between local, national and global networks to ensure use of Internet, extranet and intranet,

- to create an appropriate policy framework so as to achieve a $50 billion annual export of IT software and IT services by the year 2008, and
- to accelerate the penetration of PC access from one per 500 to one per fifty along with universal access to Internet/extranet/intranet by the year 2008. Existing public telephone/public call offices (PCOs)—over 600,000 in number—are to be transformed into public tele-info centres offering a variety of multimedia information services (Information Technology Action Plan, http://it-taskforce.nic.in/itintro.htm, 9/1/03).

Such a bold vision is a reflection of the confidence generated by the industry, the important role played by technocrats in both the DOE/EC since the 1980s, (see Chapter 5) and the response of state governments and the private sector.

6.3 Spread of ICT in Business and Government

Since the late 1990s and early years of the new century, India's software industry has been acknowledged as a success story judged by its international presence, its generation of employment and its contribution to foreign exchange earnings. As facilitators of innovation, software firms tend to be centrally located and have, owing to the concentration of professional expertise, important implications for local industrial development (Cooke and Piccagula 2006). It is not surprising, therefore, that Indian software companies are concentrated in major urban centres like Delhi, Mumbai, Pune, Kolkata, Hyderabad, Chennai and Bangalore. These are areas with a sound S&T infrastructure, research universities and STPs set up in 1991 in some areas to provide satellite communication. Initially intended to circumvent the obstacles placed by the Telecommunication Department, the Parks also provide access to duty free imports of capital goods and inputs to export firms located within the parks. While Commander (2005) suggests that this encouraged spatial agglomeration, such agglomeration in India has also been driven, he adds, by high transactional costs resulting from infrastructure constraints. Convincing as such reasoning is, one must also acknowledge that tacit knowledge being a feature of such high-tech industries tends to be sticky and attracts resources.

While foreign exchange earnings are expected to have touched $50 billion by 2008, there appears little prospect of similar growth in domestic software. In 2003, the World Bank praised such phenomenal growth but expressed concern that the benefits were flowing to an exclusive few with the great majority untouched (NASSCOM, 30 July 2003). Concerned with low domestic utilisation, NASSCOM undertook a survey with the intention of revealing the benefits that can accrue from IT usage such as enhanced efficiency, reduction of costs, improved decision-making and better customer service. The survey revealed that a major reason for low adoption was protection and over-regulation resulting in lack of competition. Competition, it was felt, should be welcomed as it contributes to efficiency and encourages further use of IT. Another reason for the low level of diffusion to other sectors of the economy is the poor infrastructure, inefficient communication and energy shortages. Further, domestic demand for software services remains low 'on account of a combination of income levels and other constraints, such as labour legislation, and the relatively slow and regionally patchy adoption of ICT by government and the public sector' (Commander 2005, 23).

The high cost of hardware due to taxes is certainly a valid reason for low usage by Indian businesses. There have, however, been some changes in designated zones including local taxes in Karnataka (see Chapter 8). An industry accustomed to tax concessions has had to wake up to changes in customs duties, value added tax and additional countervailing duty introduced by the newly elected United Progressive Alliance (UPA) government in the March 2005 budget. While the changes adversely affected India-based local assemblers, India-branded companies and MNCs operating here, they favoured importers of fully assembled PCs and laptops, rendering access to IT equipment difficult for ordinary users (*The Hindu*, 31 March 2005). It appears that the government elected in 2004 responded to the perception that the IT industry had benefitted from favourable treatment from the previous NDA government and therefore acted to set the sectoral balance right! Questioning the timing of the withdrawal of tax concessions to BPOs in the 2006 budget, *The Hindu* (14 March 2006) acknowledged that ITES had largely benefited developed countries. Adding that the time had come for Indian business to take advantage of the experience gained by Indian ITES firms, it advised BPO firms to understand the needs of domestic manufacturers instead of mainly 'servicing under a false identity and with contrived accent faceless foreign consumers'. Instead of continuing to provide 'crutches' to export firms, it expressed the hope that government would instead encourage nascent domestic firms. This view was reiterated in 2007 by NASSCOM which called for greater investment in the domestic IT market as 'an important lever for sustaining the competitiveness of the Indian IT firms and transforming India from a global services hub to a global innovation hub' (*The Hindu*, 29 January 2007).

A recent NASSCOM–Boston Consulting Group survey revealed that industry leaders are keen for a government-led initiative to build on the success of the IT-ITES sector and develop a coordinated approach to upscale IT applications in the domestic sector and bolster India's weak ecosystem. This initiative, it was suggested, could be in the form of a team to coordinate IT companies and users starting with the public sector, with NASSCOM acting as a catalyst. Further, the survey identified challenges facing the industry such as insufficient mentoring and networking support for start-ups and entrepreneurs, lack of focus on intellectual property development in emerging technologies, lack of knowledge-sharing between IT-ITES firms and key user industries, insufficient funding at seed stage, a tenuous partnership between industry and academia, and lack of collaboration between industry and research institutions (*The Hindu*, 15 August 2007).

It is well established that successful industries, in order to compete globally, need demanding local customers, aggressive home-based suppliers and strong domestic competition, which together contribute to the competitive advantage of nations (Porter 1990). As India's software firms have grown up in an environment totally different from traditional business houses, they have pursued better returns in export rather than domestic markets. Notwithstanding the widening gap between export growth and domestic demand for software in the 1990s and the first decade of the twenty-first century, dramatic growth in the economy has brought about significant improvement in domestic demand. Driven by huge investments across various sectors of the economy, the domestic IT sector in India is expected to cross US $15.9 billion (in production), a growth of 21 per cent in 2006–07 (*NASSCOM Strategic Review, 2007*). As the evidence for such a change is too recent, the following analysis may offer some explanation of why the process has taken so long.

6.3.1 Application to Business Operations

Although one cannot categorically state that domestic demand was actively discouraged, it must be acknowleged that the development of

TABLE 6-2 Annual Electronics Production 2000–07 (in Rs crores)

Item	*2000–01*	*2001–02*	*2002–03*	*2003–04*	*2004–05*	*2005–06*	*2006–07*
Consumer electronics	11,950	12,700	13,800	15,200	16,800	18,000	20,000
Industrial electronics	4,000	4,500	5,550	6,100	8,300	8,800	10,400
Computers	3,400	3,550	4,250	6,800	8,800	10,880	12,800
Communication and Broadcast Equipment	4,500	4,500	4,800	5,350	4,800	7,000	7,000
Strategic electronics	1,750	1,800	2,500	2,750	3,000	3,200	4,500
Components	5,500	5,700	6,600	7,600	8,800	8,800	8,800
Sub-total	31,100	32,750	37,500	43,800	50,500	56,600	66,000
Software for exports	28,350	36,500	46,100	58,240	80,180	103,200	1,41,800
Domestic software	9,400	10,874	13,400	16,250	21,740	26,460	37,800
Total	68,850	80,124	97,000	1,18,290	1,52,420	1,86,260	2,45,600
Growth %	31.3	16.4	21.1	18.2	28.8	22.2	29

Source: Department of Information Technology.

the industry was by way of special assistance geared towards exports. Despite that, we see some strikingly successful cases of IT applications to domestic business. Software developed by Indian firms has enabled computerisation to be extended into banking, insurance, stock exchanges and other financial services. This includes I-Flex used in 240 financial institutions in sixty-nine countries. Polaris has developed Polaris Point, software for retail banking, while Infosys has produced banking solutions adopted by twenty-two domestic and sixteen overseas banks across twelve countries (Joseph, in Pariyil ed. 2006 91). With the 1991 economic liberalisation and global growth of the IT sector, varied successful software development projects have emerged in other sectors including railroad management, hydrology, energy, power generation, and electronics. The Institutes of Management have developed computer applications for government and public enterprises and the National Informatics Centre (NIC) has developed over a hundred software packages for district planning and computer aided design and computer aided manufacture (CAD/CAM). 'In developing their own software, these organisations and enterprises have acquired expertise and software, which could constitute an area of opportunity for India's exports of manufactured goods' (Schware 1992, 150). Much more needs to be done to bridge the 'large gap between development in India for local needs and marketing of software packages at the international level' (ibid.) and address weaknesses such as delays in importing of computers and spare parts, poor communications and inadequate financing.

With the hope of encouraging extensive use of ICT among various sections of the knitwear export business, and enhancing manufacturing competiveness in small and medium enterprises, Microsoft has set up a Tirupur Exporters Association (TEA) Readiness Centre at a cost of Rs 50 lakhs. The centre will assist knitwear units to improve productivity and reduce production costs by introducing inventory management systems. Offering a platform for buyers, sellers, various workers and exporters, it is intended to become a hub for IT-related requirements for the textile community. Entrepreneurs will be able to visit the centre and look at various solutions and after '... interacting with various IT majors and their customized offerings, they can choose the best solution'. Other benefits expected are the upgrading of technology, reduction of sourcing costs, increased marketing opportunities and assistance in production planning.

Tirupur is an interesting example of how domestic industry can respond successfully to pressures from export markets. India's garment capital has three thousand apparel units, some using computer-controlled cutting and stitching machines to produce garments for export to Carrefour in France, Wal-Mart in Canada, Mothercare in Britain and Health Tex in the US. Responding to the announcement that export quotas were to be lifted on 31 December 2004, 'the more savvy among Tirupur's knitted kings geared themselves for the future—laying new automated production lines, vying for quality certification ... harnessing Information Technology every way they can....' With the objective of securing at least $2 billion out of a world market of $200 billion (*The Hindu,* 1 April 2004), the Network Clothing Company and Jupiter Knitting Co. agreed to cooperate on a modern Enterprise Resource Planning (ERP) system to ensure that complex supply logistics will be automated so as to meet deadlines for export orders.

Anticipating decline in profit margins with the removal of quotas, the Indian Textiles Committee worked out a programme to help knitwear exporters obtain better prices by bringing in expertise from the Netherlands. Their role was to assist exporters to anticipate designs for the European Summer 2008 collections entailing a shift from their traditional role of cutting, making and trimming (CMT) to design-oriented manufacturing (*The Hindu,* 23 October 2006). Like Tirupur, the sari weavers of Ilampillai have shifted to value-added finished fabrics like churidars and half-saris using computer-aided designing. While many fabric designing centres have sprung up in the area to service their needs, the software for such enterprises is being sourced from Bangalore (*The Hindu,* 1 August 2006).

Historically, India has been a major player in the global textile industry. To further promote itself in an era of great global competition, TEA set up, with central government assistance, the Netaji Apparel Park, providing employment for seven thousand people. The Park has a 2.2 MW captive power plant, a telephone exchange, a bank, its own sewage treatment system and uninterrupted water supply. Following the provision of recreation and child care facilities, there are plans for the establishment of twenty-five integrated textile parks with a maximum grant of Rs 40 crores each. While such facilities are welcome, a major problem facing Tirupur, the export town, is lack of skilled labour.

In anticipation of the need for radio tags for all their export pallets in response to demands from US and European supermarket chains, the Information Technology Ministry asked industry to explore the potential of RFID. A Delhi-based firm named Avanna, which has established itself in the RFID applications market, is working with Hewlett Packard to set up an RFID Centre of Expertise at Delhi. Other software companies in the field are Wipro, Infosys and the US-based Indian IT provider Netkraft. The present market for RFID application is $2 billion and could, according to a Frost and Sullivan report, grow to $11.7 billion by 2010 (*The Hindu*, 8 November 2004). A novel approach to RFID use is the provision of a special card with an RFID chip to patients at the Outpatient Department of the Bhagwan Mahaveer Jain Heart Centre. Developed by an Indian-founded, US-based company, Aventyn, the chips have tiny embedded radio transmitters which form the communication backbone of the Clinical Information Processing Platform (CLIP) used at the hospital. It is probably the first such application in the healthcare industry (*The Hindu*, 3 June 2007).

A study undertaken by the Indian Semiconductor Industry Association and Frost & Sullivan estimates that the total consumption of electronic equipment will rise from $28.2 billion in 2005 to $36.3 billion by 2015, a growth rate of 29.8 per cent, creating thirty-five lakh jobs in the process. With such projections, a growing economy and the promise of substantial financial incentives from the central government, it is not surprising that Andhra Pradesh, Tamil Nadu and Karnataka recently engaged in overt competition, coming up with attractive proposals, to entice a prospective investor, SemIndia, which was in search of a base to set up a $3 billion silicon wafer manufacturing unit to meet the demand for that product needed in mobile phones, PCs, set top boxes and DVDs. The decision by the Minister for Information and Communication Technology went in favour of Hyderabad, with a grant of $100 million towards the venture.

With India destined to become a major electronics consumer in the not too distant future and with quality chip designers, it is time for the nation to set up a semi-conductors manufacturing unit. A wafer manufacturing plant based in India with locally-designed chips and Broadband connections provided by BSNL and MTNL would bring down prices of computers as well as generate local employment. The need to move from R&D to manufacturing has been reiterated by Vinod Agarwal of SemIndia who summed it up thus: 'If we do not start manufacturing today, we will be left behind forever' (*The Hindu*, 4 January 2006).

While industry has moved to adopt ICT in a big way, India's other major undertaking, Indian Railways, has not been far behind. A service, remarkable for its transparency and ease for users, is Imprest, the reservation system developed by CMC, a public sector organisation, for Indian Railways, probably the largest and most complex enterprise anywhere in the world. Its recent success, a surplus of Rs 20,000 crores during 2006–07, has attracted worldwide attention including a delegation of defence personnel from the United States which was informed by the Minister of Railways that Indian Railways is the lifeline of the country, employing over fourteen lakh people, operating four different railway gauges and heritage trains and carrying sixteen million passengers and two million tonnes of goods every day along a network of 63,000 km, out of which 18,000 km are electrified. Claiming that the turnaround of the railways is due to 'strong determination and vision', the minister announced the construction of 'dedicated freight corridors, modernisation of track and signals, manufacture of low weight wagons, extension of e-ticketing and online enquiry throughout the country' (*The Hindu*, 2 May 2007). Its operational success has resulted in improved services and passenger amenities such as accommodation, ATMs for banking and restaurants at select railway stations through the newly created Indian Railways Catering and Tourism Corporation (IRCTC), which is linked up with Delhi-based call centre Bharat BPO. Through its Integrated Train Enquiry System (ITES) operating from four centres situated at Noida (Northern Railway), Bhubaneshwar (Eastern), Ahmedabad (Western) and Mysore (Southern Railway), which are equipped to handle twenty million enquiries a day, information is available on train arrivals and departures and online reservations. Services will be extended to include hotel reservations, tourist information and taxi services. (*The Hindu*, 23 June 2007). Both Indian Railways and its counterpart, the Telecommunications Department, once regarded as laggards of the public sector, have been transformed into showcases of 'turnaround management'.

Unlike traditional management approaches when organisations operated on an exclusive basis, one notices the need for greater synergy in the application of IT to solve operational problems. When the Karnataka State Road Transport Corporation launched the country's first online ticket booking system for bus services, Any Where Any Time Advance Reservation (AVATAR), developed by a consortium consisting of BEL, IBM, Radiant Infosystem and the Central Railway Information system, the response was such that the website suffered server overload! Immediately faced with the need to increase its capacity to at least two thousand hits, the corporation called on the consortium for help—a trend in cooperative functioning that is becoming increasingly evident in software development (*The Hindu*, 14 May 2007).

Another case of application in the area of transport is the indigenous adaptation of the Global Positioning System (GPS) vehicle tracking service launched by a Bangalore-based company, BOW (Bharat on Wheels) Network, in March 2003 to assist three million goods carriers. A specially designed BOW card can be used by a truck driver to establish links with his owners and keep them informed as to his location in case of delay or breakdown. Drivers with such cards can use tracking points through STD booths located on trunk routes. 'Details of the truck are coded on the card together with a simple numbered message to a local telephone number using a Voice Response system. At the receiving end, a franchisee of BOW uploads all incoming messages by email to a central hub, where it is processed and placed on a website'. The initial cost of a card is Rs 1,100 with a monthly fee of Rs 100 for a local permit and Rs 300 for a national permit and this works out cheaper than the average monthly cost of STD calls made by drivers which comes to Rs 2500 on an average (*The Hindu*, 18 September 2003).

With India's advances in space technology, there is now the potential for GPS to locate a postal item while in transit, for use in airports for airline landing and takeoff and to locate an address using a personal navigator, all of which have been developed with the aid of locally developed technology. As more geographic and cartographic software is developed, a variety of GPS-based transport logistics is being offered. 'Some of them like Bangalore-based EI Labs easily mix-o-match location techniques based on GPS as well as OSM-GPRS mobile phone network to create solutions like Transdata that aim to be cost effective in India. The Aerial Delivery Research and Development Establishment of the Defence Ministry has embedded GPS technology in parachutes, so that they can land with pinpoint accuracy' (*The Hindu*, 10 March 2007).

The potential of GPS technology was publicised at the national conference of 'Spatial Information Technology for Power Systems' held at Bangalore in 2003. Dr Chennakeshava, Advisor, Central Power Research Institute suggested the use of GPS to fix coordinates on earth to help the Indian power sector to become both profitable and self-sufficient. A decision support system called Geographic Information System (GIS) developed by Bangalore-based Magnasoft Consulting that can be integrated with Network Analysis System is now being used by state electricity boards. (*The Hindu,* 13 November 2003). While Indian power agencies are grappling with inefficiencies, Indian IT companies are providing services to power utilities abroad. A case in point is WTI Advanced Technology Limited which, in alliance with Tata Consultancy Services, is using GIS technology to map services for electricity and gas companies in the US and UK.

Computers are extensively used in both manufacturing and distribution to assist quick business processing. This is done by adopting Supply Chain Management (SCM), which was created by I2i, a Texas-based company founded in 1988 by Sanjiv Sidhu and Ken Sharman. Now serving about 150 companies worldwide, its solutions are used to sell phones (Nokia), computers (IBM, HP, Compaq), potato chips (Frito Lay) and paints (Asian Paints). To assist in-house purchase and procurement, a new business process called Procurement Solutions Provider (PSP) has been designed. Wipro was the first to set up PSP for companies like Gillette, ICI Paints, HSBC and Hindustan Lever.

Texas Instruments uses SAP as its core Enterprise Resource Planning Tool and i2 as its supply chain solution to reduce response time to technical and commercial enquiries. To get whole enterprises to work in real time, it uses Optimal Solutions Integration Inc (OSI) founded by Gurvender Suri. OSI real time architecture is used by the US Department of Defense to enable rapid deployment of logistics and material in military theatres.

While quality and service are primary objectives of any business, it is equally important for IT organisations to ensure that goals are met. This comes down to a firm knowing what to do and when and how to do it. Identified as the Rational Unified Process (RUP) model which is becoming a standard in the software industry to develop quality software on time, it helps a business to compete and to meet customer requirements. Its success rests on successful implementation, i.e., on tailoring the model to suit the organisation's requirement and mentoring. By adopting RUP, companies can reduce software development time and cost and improve delivery schedules. Wipro Technologies, a global IT service provider, has included RUP in its set of process offerings in addition to setting up a Rational Centre of Excellence dedicated to developing practitioners in the area. It currently has around twenty-eight projects running on the same model.

While the above developments assist manufacturing operations, Neil Gregory and Stanley Nolan (2009), authors of *The Emergence of the Software and Hardware Industries in China and India: New Industries from New Places* (International Finance Corporation, World Bank), suggest that India like China must focus more on the domestic market and on closer integration with the manufacturing sector. Such collaboration with industry is necessary for long-term growth (*The Hindu*, 26 May 2009). In developing a road map to cope with the current recession, Mr Mittal, President, NASSCOM, suggested a collaborative effort between industry, government, academia and support structures such as NASSCOM (*The Hindu*, 30 April 2009).

Yet another remarkable development is India's move into animation with e-cinema being digitally delivered and exhibited in 130 or more theatres. India was one of the first to adopt digital delivery and exhibition (*The Hindu*, 18 June 2004) with the animated *Bhagmati: Queen of Fortunes*, an indication of the burgeoning animation business which builds on India's English-speaking workforce, high-quality software engineers, good studios and low cost. Further, the involvement of Indian companies in full-length animated feature films such as the *Legend of the Buddha*, *Gulliver's Travels* and *Tommy and Oscar* has given the country 'a worldwide profile in the industry' (*The Hindu*, 13 September 2005). The extent of Indian contribution to computer graphics imaging (CGI) was displayed at the 'Frames 2006' event in Mumbai organised by the Indian Chambers of Commerce and Industry (FICCI) (Anand Parthasarathy, 'India's Edge in Animation', *The Hindu*, 30 March 2006).

6.3.2 E-Governance

In this selective survey of ICT applications in a large economy like India, one has to include Khajan, a software system developed by STPI-Bangalore for the Karnataka Finance Department which was awarded the first prize by the Administrative Reforms Department in 2005. *Bhoomi* ('land'), a system being used to maintain land records in Karnataka, has been studied by the World Bank and deemed to be worthy of replication in other TW countries (*The Hindu*, 3 February 2004).

In Bangalore, water, electricity, telephone and other bills can be paid at kiosks set up in different parts of the city. Costing the state government Rs 10 crores, these centres bring under one roof the services of Bangalore Mahanagar Palike, Bangalore Electric Supply Company, BSNL, Bangalore Water Supply and Sewerage Board, City Police, Regional Passport Office, Commercial Taxes Department, Stamps and Registration and Regional Transport Offices. At these centres, applications can also be made for passport and telephone connections in an efficient manner (*The Hindu*, 1 April 2005) Under the National E-Governance Action Plan (NEGAP), an estimated six hundred kiosks operate in rural Tamil Nadu, run by self-employed people and NGOs.

A major step in the utilisation of information for identification of citizens entitled to various services is the establishment of the Unique Identification Authority of India with Nandan Nilekani at its head. At the first meeting of the board, the Prime Minister said that this was an attempt to remedy 'the lack of identity proof (which) resulted in harassment and denial of services to the poor, and led to leakages in various government programmes. UID [unique identity] will aid delivery of flagship schemes.' (Vinay Kumar, *The Hindu*, 13 August 2009).

Although identity cards were issued to voters as early as 1993, it has taken several years to move any further in that direction. The provision of clear identification to beneficiaries of services will assist the administration of the National Rural Employment Generation Scheme and the Public Distribution System. At registration, only basic information will be collected. Once an individual number is issued it can be used as proof to open a bank account, to obtain a passport and driving licence.

If successful, the implementation of the UID, which will depend on the adoption of a positive approach by dispensing agencies, will eliminate unnecessary forms with counter signatures, so common in the Indian bureaucratic system, and effect savings of up to Rs 20,000 crores by eliminating duplication.

Such programmes undoubtedly result in efficiency and transparency and reduce corruption. However, there is concern that the absence of institutional procedures and lack of expertise to develop electronic alternatives to complex government procedures may render such tasks difficult. In its recommendations to the Prime Minister, the National Knowledge Commission (NKC) advocated a re-design of government processes before undertaking any large-scale computerisation as digitalising at this stage is likely to add 'an additional layer of expense, complexity, delay and confusion'. As a start the NKC recommended that ten to twenty important processes such as birth and death certificates, proof of residence and so on be identified and hosted as web-based services (*The Hindu*, 9 May 2006). To assist the process, the Department of Information Technology decided to implement NeGP, a programme which will help to create an appropriate management structure with well-defined roles and responsibilities for each agency involved (Report, 2006–07).

Where e-governance has been introduced with inadequate research into needs or where implementation has been poor, the considerable expenditure incurred has brought no benefit to citizens. A case in point is the billing software developed by PriceWaterhouse for Kerala Electricity Board. To avoid costly errors being undertaken in engaging consultants for software projects, efforts have been made to develop standards to guide agencies when entering into contracts and for monitoring them. This brings to mind the Capabilities Management Model which was developed by IBM after it was sued by the New Zealand government over a project for the NZ Police (David Braue, 'Hard Rules for Software,' *The Age*, 24 June 2003).

Understandably, e-government in India 'faces an uphill task to reach interactivity and actual delivery of services' (*The Hindu*, 24 September 2004) with evidence suggesting that it is only reaching the economically and educationally well off who are accessing these services. Empowerment and transparency are unlikely to be achieved unless governments are committed to e-governance and are willing to adopt major restructuring (*The Hindu*, 21 March 2005). E-governance is not merely a case of providing resources for the purchase of hardware; its operability has to be tested in the context of citizen response. What is necessary is a clear government to government (G2G) interface and government to citizen (G2C) access, both of which should be effectively implemented. While some states have adopted e-governance, its impact, despite institutional support, has been negligible.

A major reason for this, not surprisingly, is the perception that the technology is complex and can be used only by educated people. More packages need to be produced in Indian languages. For some, the fees are too high (*The Hindu*, 12 April 2005). Public usage can be encouraged by simplifying operations and offering free training and demonstrations and lower fees.

6.3.3 Development

In an international survey conducted by the Economist Intelligence Unit and the IBM Institute for Business Value in 2006 on access to digital technologies for the vast majority, India was ranked 53rd among the sixty-eight countries surveyed (*The Hindu,* 7 June 2006).

In the area of education, a development of great significance is the satellite EDUSAT launched in March 2004 dedicated to distance learning in higher education (*The Hindu,* 4 March 2004). Delivering the Nayudamma Memorial Lecture, K. Kasturirangan, former Chairman, ISRO, declared that the role of space research as a 'tool of social upliftment' was being demonstrated in the areas of education and health reach, in the management of natural resources, more accurate prediction of weather patterns and quicker response to disaster (*The Hindu,* 17 June 2004). In addition to its vital role in the software industry, ISRO assists with access to health services to rural areas through telemedicine, provides weather forecasts for rural areas through its remote sensing, beams lessons and lectures through Edusat to primary schools, undergraduate and engineering colleges and has helped the spread of television in the country (see Chapter 5).

Microsoft India Private Limited, a subsidiary of the American parent, launched its Project Shiksha in 2002, designed to train secondary school teachers in several states including Karnataka. At its IT academies, teachers learn to use spreadsheets and other software applications to plan the teaching of their curricula and use the Internet to access material to supplement their teaching (*The Hindu,* 23 November 2004). Another large project to train high school teachers in the use of computer-based education was launched by INTEL. Likewise, Sun Microsystems launched a matching grants programme to provide hardware, software and web-based training material to institutions willing to share part of the investment (*The Hindu,* 27 April 2006).

A major breakthrough in the use of ICT as a tool of development is its contribution to democratic practices in India through the use of electronic voting machines (EVMs) (*The Hindu,* 30 July 2003). Described by Anand Parthasarathy as one of the ironies of the Internet Age, India's experience has been eagerly observed by other countries, including the UK, 'even as a technology leader such as the United States still agonises over whether to go in for e-voting'. Elections in India are, under normal circumstances, a massive undertaking. When called ahead of schedule in 2004, the supplier of EVMs, BEL, was under pressure to supply a further 60,000 units, following its initial supply of half a million units in December 2003. As the General Manager pointed out, this was indeed an environmentally friendly decision, sparing, as it did, thousands of trees which would otherwise have been chopped to produce the tonnes of ballot paper used in earlier elections (*The Hindu*, 27 February 2004). Rating the decision as bold and progressive, *The Hindu* wrote, 'It required courage and confidence in the country's technological as well as grassroots democratic capabilities to make the big jump in 2004.... A million-plus EVMs seem to have made an easy passage to India's hundreds of thousands of villages' (6 May 2004).

The success of electronic voting led the Election Commission to place orders for 1,37,000 EVMs worth Rs 130 crores. According to the Managing Director, these units will be improved in terms of design and will include an advanced display system and most important, a time stamping feature, which will enable officials to track voting patterns. Apart from reducing costs, EVMs, he added, are easy to operate, tamperproof and yield instantaneous results (*The Hindu*, 20 November 2006).

6.3.4 Manufacturing

Clearly, ICT is expected to have the greatest effect on activities related to information processing, such as banking and insurance, health care and education and general public administration. Most studies focus on the manufacturing sector, which was computerised decades ago (Boyer 2004). The widespread scepticism on the actual impact of ICT, the 'productivity paradox' attributed to Solow, overlooks the fact that it is only a general purpose technology. Effective utilisation, according to Foray, relies on building complementarities at many levels (institutional, organisational and technical) and in entirely replacing the old system.

The frequent upgrading of computers sometimes allows little time for organisations to adapt. One also has to recognise that business enterprises in India have to take into consideration the implications of adopting IT in an environment where computerisation is equated with reduction in employees. In states where unions are highly organised, introduction of new technology can occur only with the support of labour unions, which is very difficult. In fact until the mid-1980s the use of computers had to be approved by government (Joseph in Parayil 2006).

Assuming that a business has a distinct need for IT to improve its operations and the expertise to locate the right system, it is essential that it move cautiously towards adopting it. A case in point is that of Computerised Numerically Controlled (CNC) technology and programming which has become important for the manufacturing industry because of its quality standards, productivity, reliability and flexibility. These machines are highly sophisticated and there is an acute shortage of skills to operate them. Any enterprise planning a move from conventional to such high-tech machines needs to consider training for personnel before entering into huge commitments.

In making vital investments in IT one has to take a 'total cost of ownership (TCO)' approach, that is, incorporate essentials of IT—reliability, manageability, security and interoperability (*The Hindu*, 23 October 2006). Frequent reminders to firms on the need to protect themselves from incurring huge expenditures on IT are based on several cases that have come to light where vendors have installed systems that have not been easy to implement. To facilitate change, the Indian Machine Tool Manufacturers' Association organised a workshop in June 2004 for interested companies. Pioneer Computing Technologies offers a comprehensive IT-led solution called TPM-TRAK which replaces the guesswork and uncertainties with more informed assessments of the manufacturing system (*The Hindu*, 4 November 2004). To assist people to make appropriate choices, the Indian Institute of Hardware Technology (IIHT), Mysore, offers training programmes designed to facilitate use of free Linux operating system in computers. While programmes are designed specifically to assist organisational planners to use Linux in production settings, IIHT Red Hat Certified Engineers also offer necessary tool sets to system administrators to administer Red Hat Linux systems in various applications (*The Hindu*, 30 March 2006) (see Chapter 8 for a discussion on engineering training in Bangalore).

6.4 Lopsided Development: Export vs Domestic Market

India's export performance in the IT area has indeed been extraordinary. According to NASSCOM, the Indian ICT market overall has grown at an annual rate of 30 per cent from $1.73 billion in 1994–95 to $36 billion in 2005–06. Attributed by some to greater liberalisation and by others to active state intervention (Joseph 2003), the remarkable performance in software exports is explained by:

- quality low-cost manpower,
- the reverse flow of Indian entrepreneurship from the US,
- prevalence of the English language,
- advantage of time zone,
- focus on international business from the beginning, and
- government support in the form of special policies.

Poor IT growth in the domestic economy when compared with exports is a cause for concern and is attributable to India's long history of restricting competition through a system of licensing. Even if justified in some cases, this has had a distinct influence on the overall growth of the economy. While licensing allowed ECIL, a public sector company, to remain uncompetitive, it also placed limits on capacity and reservations for small-scale industries, allowing uncompetitive small industries to continue. In such an environment, the only way for computer companies to survive was, according to Heeks, to work around the rules (Heeks 1996, 132–133).

The current domestic market for industrial production is vast but, unless special incentives like those offered to software are offered in other areas, the growth of non-software products will always lag behind. Much of this is related to the context in which the two sectors developed. The origin of the computer hardware industry in the India of 1965 took place in an entirely different political and economic environment from that of software in 1985(see Chapters 4 and 5). That twenty-year gap and the restrictive environment in which it operated had a negative impact on the development of the hardware industry (Heeks, ibid.). Although dominated by the public sector with its limited competition, ECIL, CMC and BEL have played a significant role in meeting domestic demand and in creating a pool of skills which is crucial today (Greico 1984, Evans 1995). Liberalisation of the 1980s and 1990s favoured the software industry rather than the hardware industry and the former, because of its special characteristics, such as lower entry barriers, lower capital but greater labour intensity, lower rate of obsolescence and significant economies of scale (Heeks 1996, 24), were able to benefit from the favoured treatment.

While the growth of computer hardware faced a setback once software exports got priority, the crucial factor was the opening of the

TABLE 6-3 Annual Electronics Exports 2000–07 (in Rs crores)

Item	*2000–01*	*2001–02*	*2002–03*	*2003–04*	*2004–05*	*2005–06*	*2006–07*
Consumer electronics	648	700	750	825	1,150	2,000	NA
Industrial electronics	500	950	1,400	1,515	1,500	2,300	NA
Computers	1,250	1,800	550	1,440	1,200	1,025	NA
Communication and Broadcast Equipment	550	150	500	165	350	500	NA
Components	1,840	2,200	2,400	3,755	3,800	4,200	NA
Sub-total	4,788	5,800	5,600	7,700	8,000	9,625	11,500
Computer software	28,350	36,500	46,100	58,240	80,180	1,04,100	1,41,800
Total	33,138	42,300	51,700	65,940	88,180	1,13,725	1,53,300

Source: Department of Information Technology Annual Report, 2006–07.

market to imports, as well as the decline in demand for domestically produced goods. Despite opening of imports, the limited impact that such a vibrant ICT sector has had in improving productivity and competitiveness in other sectors is attributed by Joseph to the 'IT industry being locked up in low level design, coding and maintenance wherein linkages with the rest of the economy may be negligible' (in D'Costa and Sridharan 2003, 5). There was concern that the excessive focus on the export sector could eventuate into a 'Dutch Disease' (where too many resources are directed into one area at the expense of other sectors, with attendant effects on markets). When it comes to 'resource movement effect', however, Joseph notes the comments of the Task Force on Human Resources Development in IT which predicts a shortage of 10,000 teachers in software training. With mobility and substitutability of such skills, he feels that there should be a preference for software development at the cost of teaching and research as this could also have an effect on the goods producing sector such as hardware and communication. The adverse impact of resource movement fits in with the observation of the task force on IT which, in its report on hardware, noted a steady decline in that industry over the past seven to eight years. This trend has to be 'reversed into a growth path through the introduction of a set of policies conducive to growth and international competitiveness.... Thus today we have an IT revolution with a lagging hardware sector'. Joseph (2003, 14–15) concludes that the resource movement effect may have an impact on sectors that compete with IT for skilled manpower.

Undue emphasis on exports in Indian policy has unfortunately had negative effects on the development of the IT industry. Software developers tend to forego opportunities to test and perfect new products through interaction with end users. Saxenian therefore advocates closer working of the software industry with clients as a basis for developing expertise and new products (Saxenian, in D'Costa and Sridharan 2003, 185). While agreeing with her, D'Costa speaks of the need to diversify export markets from US to other Asian countries and bring about greater balance between domestic and export markets. Viewing the industry as being locked into a low level innovation trajectory (51–82), he advocates the development of inter-sectoral linkages in high-tech manufacture and sees the Simputer and HCL's uni-code PCs as positive signs (20). A reason offered by IT operators for their preference for export markets is the difference in margins between domestic and export markets. This short-sightedness ignores the importance of sound domestic markets as a springboard for exports (Porter 1990). The denial of special government support in the form of incentives and tax subsidies to domestic users of ICT have certainly not helped the situation.

Once castigated for their lack of innovative skills, Indian IT companies have with worldwide exposure taken on the challenge by setting up innovation laboratories. Key imperatives for such labs according to Shanthi Kannan (*The Hindu*, 17 November 2007) are (a) technology leadership; (b) taking such leadership across clients; (c) garnering support from academic and venture capital sources; (d) encouraging firms to take ownership of the technology; and (e) providing guidance and mentoring of core businesses. Innovation essentially boils down to the developing of new and improved value added products. TCS, Satyam and Cognizant have taken the lead and Chennai seems to be the favoured location for such labs. Illustrative of this is the cabin crew software management solution being developed by TCS Travel and Hospitality Innovation Lab in Chennai for British Airways. With this package, BA can monitor its 15,000-plus cabin crew located at Heathrow and Gatwick.

Of the nineteen labs in Chennai, TCS owns four, while Satyam has six including a digital car project and a future lab and Cognizant has five focused innovation labs. Concentrating on manufacturing and the automotive industry, Satyam decided to locate high-end research and design in Chennai and has entered into collaboration with international automobile manufacturers on design enabling it to work simultaneously with multiple R&D institutions across the world. Its lab 'provides research support services (all in digital form) in alternative fuels, hybrid engines, virtual test drive solutions and emerging infotainment' (ibid.). However, Satyam's thrust may have been impeded somewhat after its accounting scandal which has certainly affected the image of the company. At Cognizant's five focus labs, the approach to innovation is decentralised with coordination at the centre, ensuring that its innovation is relevant, i.e., results in business value.

Another successful collaborative effort is Heymath! Set up by an enterprising couple, Harish Rajan and Nirmala Sankaran in cooperation with Millennium Mathematics Project of Cambridge University, Heymath! uses computer animation to teach mathematics. Following the success of that project, a research lab has been set up at IIT Chennai and 'after perfecting the program, they first tested it in Singapore schools in this city state where they are innovative and ambitious and adopted Heymath! enthusiastically. After the success in Singapore, Heymath! was soon in demand in many other countries' (Rothermund 2008, 108).

As in most developed countries, a vibrant domestic market has to be cultivated to transform Indian IT from its excessive reliance on software to greater product innovation. The signs, though present, are sporadic and need to be sustained. With the gradual entry of ICT into various aspects of business and industry, and investments ranging from banking to insurance, transport, manufacturing, services and most important education and research, the wave of investments across sectors has made India the fastest growing country in IT spending registering 22.6 per cent in 2006 and an estimated 21.5 per cent in 2007 (Rs 75,891 crores). The domestic market was 'showing definite signs of breaking-out of the trend of hardware linked growth with the contribution of software and services exceeding that of hardware for the first time in FY 2005–06'. With a 21 per cent growth it was expected to cross USD 15.9 billion in 2005–06. While this segment is led largely by MNCs, Indian firms are gaining ground and should play a larger role as 'mid-sized firms increase their levels of IT adoption....Increasing adoption of IT in domestic industries is already beginning to reflect in their enhanced performance and competitiveness' which NASSCOM believes is to be encouraged (NASSCOM Strategic Review, 2007, 9). India's rising profile as a quality player in IT was hailed at an 'HP Asia–Pacific Enterprise Media Summit' held in Singapore, in May 2007. India showed strong budget growth for IT in the region. Indian firms were poised to spend 61 per cent of their budget on IT in 2007, a dramatic rise from just 6 per cent in 2006. The projection was that Indian IT firms would spend 41 per cent of their cumulative budgets on new initiatives in 2007, compared to 15 per cent in Japan and 33 per cent in North America (*The Hindu*, 24 May 2007).

The above trends, together with sound macroeconomic conditions and growth in usage by telecom, banking and financial services, education, retail, manufacturing and BPO/IT-related services and e-Governance initiatives of central and state governments, could result in good demand for sales of PCs, which were expected to touch 4.7 million in 2005–06. There was evidence of greater use of PCs by small and medium-sized enterprises located in towns and rural areas, a trend likely to increase with broadband access at one of the lowest costs in the world (Report of the Department of Information Technology, 2005–06).

While exports have had an effect on the diffusion of ICT in the domestic economy, one has also to examine the implications of foreign direct investment on the Indian software industry. With globalisation, companies are not entirely dependent on technological capabilities being available within the domestic environment. According to Prasada Reddy (1997), 'TNCs attempt to gain a competitive advantage by sensing needs in one country, responding with capabilities located in a second, and diffusing the resulting innovation to markets worldwide' (*World Development*, vol. 25, No 11, 1821–1837). Unlike conventional technologies where innovation required continuous interaction, from initial design to final marketing of product, 'new technologies can be geographically delinked from manufacturing and market' (ibid., 1832).

While critics seem to focus on India's lack of innovative capability, the unreported contribution of Indian designers through the large number of MNCs is difficult to assess without proper data. For example, design work carried out at the Intel India Design Centre (IIDC) at Bangalore was launched globally when its new quad core chips were used for both server and desktop platforms. IIDC has also contributed to some of Intel's other products. Likewise, much of TI's work is carried out by Indian designers (please refer Chapter 9). Design centres at Noida have notched up a few firsts: the first chips whose total design cycle has been completed in India and the 'first made in India chip for French-Italian semiconductor leader STMicro electronics—the Sti5107—a single chip solution to make a digital set-top box'. Two Bangalore-based firms have designed chips for Nforce 600I series multimedia boards followed by a chip-set for Intel's dual-core processor, leading Sridhar Manthani of nVidia's Bangalore Centre to claim: 'Our engineers developed this powerful chip in just 12 months—demonstrating that India's engineers rank among the best in the world' (*The Hindu*, 10 December 2006).

6.5 Digital Divide

Like other technological changes, IT has had an uneven impact varying between regions, groups and generations. When announcing a major milestone—the crossing of the ten-crore mark for telephones, the

Minister of Information Technology said that while India possessed the fifth largest telecom network after China, US, Japan and Germany, rural teledensity was only 1.7 per cent compared to 27 per cent in urban India, leading to fresh concerns about the growing digital divide (*The Hindu*, 14 April 2005).

Demand for ICT influenced by income levels and remoteness of rural areas suggest that policy should aim, as in the case of PCOs, at universal access rather than ownership. Such technological adaptations coming from indigenous sources can overcome technological dualism which is perpetuated with R&D originating in rich countries (James 2003). Boyer (2004) doubts if the digital divide is between developed and less developed countries and visualises a situation which 'might very possibly increase inequalities between, for example, Bangalore an emblematic figure of this new trend, and other Indian states, while at the same time reducing the difference between Bangalore and Silicon Valley' (108–09).

Kenneth Keniston (in Keniston and Kumar 2004) identifies the four digital divides that separate the information rich and poor: (1) those who are rich, educated and powerful and those who are not; (2) those who speak English and those who do not, i.e. dominance of the Anglo-Saxon culture; (3) rich and poor nations; and finally (4) the new elite labelled the 'digerati', i.e. the beneficiaries of the new technology and others who cannot or do not wish to use it. 'The critical question about the fourth digital divide, however, is whether the prosperity of this new digital elite spreads to the rest of the society, especially to urban poor and to rural villages, or whether it creates, an increasingly separate cosmopolitan, knowledge-based enclave' (18).

An interesting experiment in introducing computer use was conducted by Dr Sugata Mitra, Director, NIIT, who set up a computer in a slum at Kalkaji, New Delhi, where children could use it unsupervised. While this approach to learning was innovative, its social benefits were equally significant. Mitra observed that the children divided themselves into those who knew and those who did not and a child with the knowledge was more than willing to part with that knowledge in exchange for friendship—much to the joy of the adults, who felt that such gainful activity would keep their children away from petty crime (*The Hindu*, 10 February 2006). Two more followed—at Shivpuri, M.P., and Madantusi, U.P. Their success earned Mitra the Dewang Mehta Award from DIT, following which the World Bank, in collaboration with NIIT, set up Hole-in-the-Wall Education Limited to replicate this at over thirty locations in India (*The Hindu*, 13 April 2005).

Computer-based aids play a useful role in many areas. Fishermen in Kerala and Andhra Pradesh rely on satellite information about ocean temperatures from ISRO to locate good fishing areas. Cooperative milk dairies run by the National Dairy Development Board use computer-aided measuring equipment to combine volume of milk with fat content to calculate payment to members (Mascarenhas 1988).

Gyandoot, a project managed by the Indian Administrative Service in Madhya Pradesh, provides to villages for a small fee information on agricultural product prices, health, education, employment and access to district level officials. 'Use of this mechanism for citizen-government communication increased so much that district authorities were encouraged to redesign their management and response system... The use of low cost CorDECT Wireless in Local Loop technology for connectivity, together with the entrepreneurial business approach, has garnered praise for *Gyandoot* as a model of economic sustainability, earning for itself the Stockholm Challenge Award for 2000' (Abbot 2004, 72). Another program that has gained wide recognition is *e-choupal* (or village square in Hindi). Created by Indian Tobacco Company (ITC), which is now a diversified trading company, it is intended to provide farmers with information on crops, weather conditions and farming practices and to enable them to purchase grain and equipment. A total of 1,900 kiosks covering eleven thousand villages across fourteen states are manned by a lead farmer and the system is now used by more than three million farmers in north and central India (*New Scientist,* 19 February 2005, 53). Apart from eliminating middlemen, the scheme has helped to increase productivity, with ITC offering better prices at lower procurement costs (Greenspan 2004, 111–12).

Such innovative projects offer the people of rural India a range of opportunities to improve their lot. According to Greenspan, they signal a new attitude to the digital divide, a move from a fatalistic guilt-ridden approach to a more problem-solving one representing the possibility of moving from the digital divide to a 'digital dividend' (Greenspan 2004, 117).

Indian achievements to promote ICT in rural areas were showcased at the Information Society Summit held at Tunis in November 2005 and drew praise for its 'e-chaupal' rural e-biz solution, 'Hole in the Wall' experiment, and the joint Midas Communication Technologies and n-Logue ventures showing how broadband base station equipment can be used 'to fuel single PC kiosk and telemedicine patient data collection systems'. The biggest draw was the live link C-DAC telemedicine project where the patient was located at one end with the specialist at the other with a loudspeaker relaying audio from both locations (*The Hindu*, 6 November 2005).

The Karnataka Telemedicine Project set up in February 2004 as a joint venture of ISRO and the state government aims to provide expert medical advice to patients in rural areas through the use of satellite. It offers its services through a network of fifty-four hospitals and it is estimated that one lakh people have benefited from this programme, including the areas affected by the 2004 tsunami. Its services have even been accessed from Lahore, Pakistan, a gesture carrying great significance in the context of peace efforts between the two countries (*The Hindu*, 27 February 2005). ISRO signed a Memorandum of Understanding with government hospitals to introduce telemedicine connectivity linking it to all district hospitals. Such telemedicine linkages were also being introduced at Indian Air Force (IAF) Hospitals beginning with Bangalore and zonal hospitals at Jorhat (Assam) and Halwara (Punjab) (*The Hindu*, 7 October 2005).

During the December 2004 tsunami that wreaked havoc in the southern coastal regions of India, the village of Veerapattinam in Pondicherry was saved through the Infovillage programme developed and run by the M. S. Swaminathan Research Foundation (MSSRF).

The ISRO-MSSRF Village Resource Centre Programme launched by Dr M. S. Swaminathan focuses on assisting the Village Knowledge Centres (VKCs) run by MSSRF in Pondicherry. The Web is checked by volunteers for information on crop prices, weather forecasts and ocean wave reports for farmers and fishermen in addition to the times and location of roving medical clinics (Abbott 2004, 71) Following my study of veterinary clinics operating under 'Operation Flood', I had advocated roving medical clinics for rural areas (Mascarenhas 1988). *Mission 2007: every village a knowledge centre* was recognised by the International Telecommunication Union as the flagship of the 'Connect the World 2015' movement programme initiated at the 2005 World Summit on the Information Society (WSIS) held at Tunis. ISRO, MSSRF, the Tatas and other organisations were involved in a major programme to take the Internet and Space Age to six lakh villages by 15 August 2007. To achieve this, a national alliance of civil, industrial and academic organisations entered into partnership to make every village a knowledge centre. What started as a modest alliance in 2003 to provide multi-stakeholder partnership grew to a membership of twenty-two government organisations including the Ministry of Information Technology, ninety-four civil society organisations, thirty-four private sector ICT leaders and eighteen well known academic institutions. It also includes an international support group chaired by the Resident Representative of UNDP. Based on developments thus far, Dr Swaminathan was hopeful that the urban-rural digital divide could be substantially eroded. These developments include:

- the decision by the Department of Information Technology to establish 100,000 ICT-based community service centres to provide reliable broad-based connectivity to remote villages;
- the establishment of village resource centres at the block level by ISRO in collaboration with appropriate institutions to provide a range of services;
- the decision by the Ministry of Panchayat Raj to establish Internet-connected ICT centres in all the 240,000 panchayats and local bodies;
- BSNL's rural information society initiative which aims to set up 100,000 VKCs each covering a population of 2,000 or more;
- the establishment of public tele-information centres (PTICs) through the Universal Service Obligation Fund; and
- the inclusion of e-health facilities under the National Rural Health Mission by the Ministry of Health and Family Welfare (Swaminathan, *The Hindu*, 15 November 2005).

With assistance from Tata Trusts, a Jamsetji Tata National Virtual Academy for Rural Prosperity was established at MSSRF to train and elect one million rural men and women as Fellows of the Academy to act as torch bearers in the rural knowledge revolution and to help people meet their basic needs in education, health, nutrition, drinking water and agriculture (*The Hindu*, 18 October 2004).

The PURA (Providing Urban Facilities in Rural Areas) project aimed at bridging the urban-rural divide has been actively promoted by former President Dr Abdul Kalam. 'The project provides physical, electronic, knowledge and economic connectivity to rural areas so that life in villages becomes more comfortable and people from rural areas are not forced to migrate to urban areas.' It aims to improve transport, communication networks and education and provide better training, credit and banking facilities for effective economic activity. As of March 2006, PURA had been introduced in twenty-three districts of Karnataka (Minister for Rural Development and Panchayat Raj, *The Hindu*, 12 March 2006).

Yet another useful initiative in this area is the district-level Needs Identification survey created by Drishtee and electronically accessible to administrators. Information on government programmes and benefits is to be disseminated through fifty thousand information kiosks over a period of six years. Interestingly these are in states such as Bihar, UP, Orissa, Rajasthan which were not otherwise known for encouraging ICT (Thatchenkery and Stough 2005, 38–9).

While previously, fishermen in south India used information transmitted by ISRO on ocean temperatures to locate the best areas for fishing, they now have access to mobile telephones for information on relative prices for their catch in different markets. A mobile telephone enables a fisherman to call several markets to find out where his catch will fetch the highest price. Highlighting the importance of freely available information for competitive markets, Robert Jensen, a development economist from Harvard University, found that the proportion of fishermen who ventured beyond their home market to sell their catch jumped from zero to 35 per cent as soon as coverage became available in each region, eliminating wastage of fish and bringing about a dramatic fall in price variation (*The Economist*, 12 May 2007, 80).

The Karnataka government has, through the use of the Internet, set up Common Service Centres (CSCs) offering services in rural and semi-urban areas. Young men and women operate kiosks which offer services at convenient locations and at a lower cost. Once a name is fed into a computer, it stays forever, thus facilitating services such as the issuing of bus passes for the disabled. Funds have been allocated for five thousand such CSCs in rural areas for citizen-centric services, such as pensions and caste certificates. Such e-governance initiatives have helped to bridge the digital divide. Initiated two years ago in partnership with Comat technologies and 3i Infotech, there are now about 750 CSCs with plans to increase that number to four thousand. Government officials, dispensing such services from taluk offices, have felt the benefit in the course of their duties (*The Times of India*, 19 August 2008).

Cost or affordability of equipment acts as an obstacle in bridging the digital divide. Towards that end, the development of low cost computers has been encouraged in both the public and private sectors. The latest ultra low-cost computing-cum-access device that can revolutionise the dissemination of education was unveiled on 3 February 2009 by the Ministry of Human Resources Development. Estimated to cost between $20 and $30, '... the 10-inch long and 5-inch wide hand-held device, resembling a palmtop or a modem, helps e-learners access the Web easily. Priced versions of e-content available on the net can be accessed through this device'. In releasing the prototype to delegates attending the National Mission on Education through Information and Communication Technology, an official from the HRD Ministry claimed that it 'bore testimony to India's technological capability, with some of the components developed by engineering students themselves' (*The Hindu*, 4 February 2009).

6.6 Current Situation and Prospects

India's IT services were in 2003 considered second only to the US in terms of employment, with very promising prospects for growth in PCs, cable television subscribers and mobile telephones (Zaheer and Rajan 2003). Promoting the idea of 'IT for all by 2008', the National Democratic Alliance government reduced excise duty on IT hardware from 16 per cent to 8 per cent and abolished the special additional duty (SAD) of 4 per cent. However, that regime of tax incentives changed in the March 2006 budget when Finance Minister P. Chidambaram introduced an 8 per cent excise duty on packaged software and 12 per cent on computer products, a move seen as unhelpful in achieving the declared objectives of increasing access to Internet and computer ownership. Retrograde as the measure appears, it will, in all likelihood, force indigenous and international vendors to push prices upward.

Lacking access to telephone or computers, the large majority of the rural population is missing out on the gains of the information revolution. Although the big companies are bypassing them, India's research institutes, the IIT in Chennai and the IISc in Bangalore have come up with inexpensive solutions to meet rural needs.

The low-cost Simputer, a joint product of local company Encore Software and scientists from IISc, is one affordable option. Being manufactured at BEL for the Karnataka government, Ammu Joseph describes the Simputer as India's 'indigenous, open source, low cost, hand-held, multi-lingual, multi-purpose computing device ... specifically designed to take information technology to people on the have-not side of the notorious digital divide...' (*The Hindu*, 7 December 2003). Indeed, as noted by Saxenian, such collaboration between an academic institution and business in India is rare. 'It is based on free software (the Linux operating system), designed to be open and modular, and offers multiple connectivity options. It also includes a Smart Card reader/writer, which provides a delivery vehicle for financial transactions on the internet and for e-commerce....Some of the potential applications include using the Simputer as a platform for micro-banking, for data collection, for internet access, for dissemination of agricultural information, and as a laboratory for experiments in rural schools' (Saxenian 2002, 87). One of its earliest uses was by traffic police in Bangalore who can now book offenders on the spot! Unlike rival machines, the Simputer 'can be used by those who cannot read or write. Speech-synthesis software developed at the IISc converts text in downloaded pages into spoken words in three Indian languages—Hindi, Kannada and Tamil. Commands can be inputted by tapping icons on the screen and listening to the Simputer'. IISc scientists who donated their time to the task did so with the aim of developing not just 'an end product but ... an evolving platform for social change' (Jayaraman, 'India Online', *Nature*, vol. 415, 24 January 2002, 359). Other affordable PC options are the CSIR-supported Encore-IISc Mobilis (*The Hindu*, 22 June 2005) or the Lakshman Rekha priced at Rs 10,000.

The most recent indigenous low-cost computer on the scene is Jagruti (awakening), the Community PC developed by Intel to bridge the urban-rural divide. Rural communities will be provided with opportunities to work with leaders in education, business, government and online and Internet service providers, with Internet kiosks based on the new Intel-powered 'Community PC' to be set up in rural areas. Designed to provide access to those who desire technology but are unable to access it owing to unreliable power sources or weather conditions, the Jagruti is described by Intel as 'a highly reliable, manageable system that supports remote "diagnostics and control" features at low power'. Apart from its ability to handle high temperatures and humidity, it is equipped with a customised power supply (*The Hindu*, 1 April 2006).

A crucial development in the bid to increase accessibility of ICT is the Vasantha Braille Cube developed by Vidya Vrikshah. A simple and easy tool, the cube uses a universal Braille dot matrix as a language learning device for the visually challenged. Its ease of use has encouraged two hundred schools to seek supply. In reporting issues that came up at the International Telecommunication Union seminar held in March 2006 at Doha, Anand Parthasarathy commented on India's insensitivity to its own physically challenged. While the cube is seen as a step forward in reducing the digital disadvantage, he asks if India has done enough to assist disadvantaged people in gaining access to ATMs and other electronic devices (*The Hindu,* 16 March 2006).

If the discussion thus far in this chapter suggests Indian software development has been lopsided, that is export-oriented, that situation is showing some signs of change. Satellite communication, broadband and Internet access have led to a shift from onsite to offshore work, encouraging a large number of international companies to set up operations in India, using local design and advanced software skills. Observers predict that India can become the global hub of embedded software cornering a share of the $21 billion world market. Already there are over a hundred multinational and domestic companies focusing on embedded software, and these include MNCs like Delphi, Texas Instruments, ST Microelectronics, Motorola, Intel and Cadence which have set up large development centres, and leading Indian IT companies like TCS, Infosys, Wipro and HCL Technologies. Together they have brought about significant change from what existed until recently. 'Driven by huge investments across all sectors, India's domestic IT market is expected to grow at 21.5 per cent this year to Rs 75,891 crore, making it the fastest growing segment in the Asia-Pacific region' (*The Hindu,* 28 January 2007).

Zaheer and Rajan categorise IT firms into three types. The first covers traditional software IT service houses such as TCS, Wipro, Infosys and Satyam which are moving up the value chain and becoming global providers of software and services worldwide. The second refers to the brick and mortar firms, in particular financial services such as Citicorp and GE Capital, which seek the benefit of remote services. The third type are the new generation Silicon Valley-style entrepreneurs, Farbmart-com and Mindtree-com, which provide B2B with ties to US business and venture capital. Associating their technological development with their origin, the authors consider that such 'technological imprinting' (which evolutionary economists call path dependent) has shaped their mindset and accordingly categorise them into:

- ethnocentric: older firms with India-based operations for exports,
- polycentric: firms with investments in several countries, and
- geocentric: global operators with employees and owners of different nationalities (Zaheer and Rajan 2003, 217).

Software developers see the need to move up the value chain demanding specific competencies such as digital signal processing software (DSP). 'India has the highest concentration of DSP-literate programmers in the world, a consequence of companies such as Texas Instruments, Motorola and Analogue Devices lobbying India's technical institutes to add DSP courses to their curricula' (ibid., 221). 'Just about any embedded product application that involves rapid numeric processing is a candidate for DSP. And the market is booming in fact' (Sofia Tippoo, *The Times of India Educational Supplement*, 15 April 2002, vol. 1, Issue 44).

Indian software companies like Wipro and HCL are service companies which develop products jointly with their clients. The intellectual property in such cases rests with the clients while the producers are paid for their resources and time. Although product development is far more lucrative, Indian firms are reluctant to enter that field on their own because of the high investment and the fear of failure. However Ittiam, (an acronym for the Cartesian *I think therefore I am*), a new entrant, is doing things differently. As the first technology firm in India which is 100 per cent driven by intellectual property (IP) licensing, Ittiam licenses its intellectual property for which it earns royalty and provides DSP systems for embedded applications, reference boards and customised solutions for customers worldwide. (Zaheer and Rajan 2003, 221).

The new multinational development centres in India have encouraged the return to India of a large number of Indians as entrepreneurs, a reverse brain drain viewed by Zaheer and Rajan as a 'seamless integration' between Silicon Valley and some of the new firms in the Hyderabad–Bangalore axis of the Silicon Plateau (215). Saxenian (2006) calls it a process of 'brain circulation' which has created the 'New Argonauts ... a community of technically skilled immigrants with work experience and connections to Silicon Valley and related American technical centers' who are critical components of regions whose growth is based on entrepreneurship and experimentation (4). A case in point is i2 Technologies. 'The move to India initiative undertaken by i2 Technologies to relocate many of its personnel from the U.S. to its Indian development centre is a reflection of how the world perceives India and has helped the Indian IT industry move towards maturity' (*The Hindu,* 3 December 2003). Evidence of this is a new model of IT-enabled services offered by Mumbai-based Omnitech Infosolutions. It is an adaptation of the Build, Operate and Transfer (BOT) model used largely to finance bridges and roads and to operate IT-services. Omnitech Infosolutions builds the facility, hires employees and operates it for a period after which it hands it over to its clients. During the building and operational phases, both parties work closely, with the client monitoring the operation but not handling day-to-day operations. According to the Chairman of Omnitech, this is the 'next wave in business process outsourcing' (*The Hindu,* 23 March 2006).

6.7 The Backlash

While Indian software developers have put India on the IT world map, they have unwittingly become the target of critics who question the undue emphasis given by government to the export of software (Information Technology Action Plan) (Saxenian 2002, Joseph 2003). With its advanced technology, easy access to telecommunication through satellite links, time advantage which allows for round-the-clock operations and its highly-skilled English-speaking workforce, India can offer efficient services on a competitive basis. However such outsourcing has produced a backlash particularly in the US. While its economics gurus preach to the rest of the world advising them to close down inefficient operations and outsource them to more efficient operators, the US itself appears to be pursuing the opposite course. Any attempt to withdraw from such a market will damage not only the US stand (ideological) on free open markets but also its own economy by rendering services uncompetitive.

It should be pointed out, too, that India, under pressure from developed economies like the US, reluctantly adopted economic liberalisation after a long history of state support for education and industrial development and should not now be denied global access to business opportunities on purely competitive terms. It is fair to point out that some of the outsourcing and IT-related services are directed to India by US-based Indians. Brain drain, encouraged by the offer of a special type of US visa, has been especially beneficial to the US economy, with no investment on its part. While their contribution to the US economy continues to be immeasurable, India, which is now receiving some of the benefits from that investment, should not now be penalised. As this debate heats up, its reverberations are heard in India too, although the tone here is one of confidence rather than concern (Jagannathan, *The Hindu,* 29 February 2004).

Viewing the outsourcing issue in a historical context, Timeri Murari commented, tongue in cheek, 'In one way, we should be grateful to the British for having colonised us. That's what I mean about history: it slyly repays the wrongs committed centuries ago. The British forced us to adopt their ways and insisted we learn their language. History just did the rest. English became the lingua franca of the world and our popularity today is entirely due to the fact that we write, read and speak English fluently'. However, he warned that this may change as one never knows what MNCs may do next. (*The Hindu,* 2 November 2003).

When outsourcing gets clouded with other issues like security or secrecy of data for economic or privacy reasons, business transactions become difficult. Competitors can use real or trumped up accusations which are not easily verifiable. In 2005, some employees of an Indian ITES firm were accused in the British media of disclosing account numbers of their clients. It is a prospect that no client can ignore irrespective of the authenticity of the complaint. While the technical capabilities of Indian ITES/BPO firms are accepted worldwide, there is no way to safeguard against charges of security whether true or malicious. (*The Hindu,* 8 February 2006). Bangalore police unearthed a fake credit card racket involving data thieves, electronic professionals and non-resident Indians. Police arrested three persons who with accomplices from abroad had created 123 fake credit cards of thirty-five banks. The police recovered Rs 7 lakhs worth of electronic goods which the accused had purchased using fake cards (*The Hindu,* 23 June 2007) Both industry and governments are seriously concerned about protecting security and maintaining secrecy. That Indian firms are concerned about the issue of data security is reflected in the collaboration entered into between TCS and Stanford University to work on joint projects in the area of data privacy (*The Hindu,* 14 February 2006).

The IT-BPO sector is currently engaged in a four-pronged programme to achieve the following objectives:

- engaging key stakeholders in building a common understanding of issues relating to information security,

- educating them in developments in information security policies and practices,
- enactment of policy reform required to ensure compliance, and
- assisting in enforcement by cooperating with enforcement agencies (NASSCOM Strategic Review, 2007).

6.8 The Social Consequences

Technology is a two-edged weapon; while it offers opportunities, such opportunities come with social consequences. As the industry gains prominence, other issues have come to the fore. The prolonged use of computers which can result in RSI (repetitive stress injury) or OOS (occupational overuse syndrome) or Carpal Tunnel Syndrome needs to be handled both at the industry and government levels. Crucial to employee well-being are factors like ergonomic furniture and the need to micro-pause (i.e., take small breaks) and exercise while seated at a computer station. A research study at Bangalore revealed that at least 75 per cent of two thousand IT professionals surveyed had mental stress disease (MSD).

Brunda Amruthraj claims that IT professionals go through 'anxiety, depression and loneliness because of their work environment and often exhibit feelings of inadequacy, lowered self-esteem and dissatisfaction. This reflects itself in the form of social, marital and sexual problems'. According to Dr Padmini Prasad of the Institute of Sexual Medicine, '40 per cent of the couples visiting infertility clinics are computer professionals ...long working hours, stress and pressure at work, night shifts, and lack of sleep can lead to various sexual problems' (*The Hindu*, 31 January 2005). Other problems include nervous breakdowns, impaired eyesight and an increased rate of divorce. Much of this is a result of long working hours, being away from home for up to twelve hours with little time for family and worst of all, the all-night or 'graveyard' shifts. 'No doubt, IT companies pay them handsomely, but the work extracted from a single employee is treble that of a normal output'. To overcome work-related hazards, Jyothirlata Girija advocates a work code for IT companies restricting hours of work, employing more staff at lower salaries, the formation of a union of IT employees and the introduction of regular labour laws regarding working conditions (*The Hindu*, 2 November 2004).

Those long night shifts at call centres have even become the subject of a best-selling novel by Chetan Bhagat (*One Night @ the*

Call Center)—a parody on the way call centre workers think and act. Such work is seen by some as destroying the energies and talent of young Indians responding to international customers (Shashi Tharoor, *The Hindu*, 26 February 2006). Studies on call centre employees in Bangalore undertaken by Tata Institute of Social Sciences revealed that 73 per cent of employees had hyperacidity, 78 per cent suffered from backache, 71 per cent reported loss of appetite and 88 per cent were smokers and much of this had been caused by stress (*The Hindu*, 27 April 2006).

Apart from security, secrecy, working conditions and urban infrastructure, other issues such as hazards to health and the environment caused by the sudden explosion in ICT need to be urgently addressed. That the issue of safe disposal of computer waste is causing concern among environmentalists in Bangalore was revealed in an interview on BBC (Whittaker, 8 November 2004). Karnataka Pollution Board estimates that Bangalore generates over ten thousand tonnes of e-waste every month. Rag-pickers attempt to retrieve metals like lead and copper used in computers. Apart from the risk involved in such extraction processes by ill-qualified people, environmentalists have called for the enactment of government regulations on the handling of wastes as well as the import of used computer material. In its leader, *The Hindu* (28 December 2004) said that the situation was serious, and regulation was urgently needed to stop illegal imports and to set in place institutional structures for the safe disposal of domestic scrap. Medical experts have expressed concern that exposure to such hazardous substances on a regular basis can damage the brain and nervous system, lungs, kidneys and the reproductive system of women and children employed by scrap dealers. Legislation is urgently needed to deal with the problem (*The Hindu*, 20 March 2006). In response, a bill drafted by the Central Pollution Board was to be introduced on a trial basis in Bangalore.

With the rapid growth of mobile technology in India, it is also necessary to study the health hazards of transmission towers in urban centres. The issue was brought to public attention in 2000 by research carried out in Scandinavia and Britain, the results of which were quickly refuted by telecommunication equipment producers. Research on the issue is confusing as a Swedish study established a link between prolonged use of mobile phones and the risk of a brain tumour (*The Hindu*, 2 April 2006). The need for the problem to be addressed was highlighted at the Electromagnetic Interference Compatibility conference held at Bangalore in March 2006 where the norms established by international organisations on the safe levels of radiation were discussed. Following the example of several countries with high cellular phone usage which have promulgated standards for safe limits of electromagnetic radiation, Indian participants called for urgent judicial and legislative action (*The Hindu*, 5 March 2006).

6.9 Conclusion

India's IT policies covering a period of forty years are bearing fruit, less dramatic perhaps in hardware where it all began, but certainly in software. Beginning with IBM's controversial exit in the 1970s, government encouragement and private sector initiative led to rapid growth, resulting in the establishment of over 230 MNCs in Bangalore by the early years of the new millennium. While business communication was facilitated by the Internet through India's telecommunications and satellite network, a simultaneous boom occurred in software exports with Indian professionals being able to work offshore (in India) instead of having to be sent to clients' premises (onsite). Although the type of work undertaken was predominantly at the lower end of the value chain with concern expressed about the use of higher qualified personnel for low skilled assignments, the long-term payoff from such assignments was realised later with the drive by Indian firms for CMM certification. Today, India has the largest number of CMM Level 5 certification software firms.

Overall, India's success in software exports is tempered by questions as to whether this may eventually turn out to be a case of Dutch disease. The other issue that is of concern is the failure of software to penetrate into the domestic economy. To encourage growth, the domestic market needs to be stimulated by the adoption of a collaborative approach along the lines adopted by Central Machine Tools Institute (CMTI), HMT and Processor Systems Incorporated (PSI) who worked together in the development of CNC machines (Mascarenhas 1982). Such an approach would lead to optimal use of resources. It would require establishing partnership with local industry by encouraging clusters and for IT industry to develop solutions that meet real needs of users. The base of IT consumers has to be extended to incorporate medium and small enterprises covering small towns and even rural areas. The manpower for this has to rely on reviving vocational training such as

Industrial Training Institutes (ITIs) whose products would overcome shortage of skills. Another strategy is to encourage commercialisation of Indian IT products through collaboration with research institutes. Generally, a successful export sector builds on a thriving domestic sector, but in this case, stagnation of the latter was caused by excessive restrictions imposed on the domestic computer industry until the 1980s and the high cost of imports arising from duties. An area that needs to be urgently addressed is low PC and Internet usage resulting from low ownership of PCs. Although Internet cafes are booming, they are no substitute to PC ownership and the answer to this lies in the affordability of PCs. The situation has been improving dramatically in the last few years with domestic users increasingly adopting IT in business operations.

As India becomes the sought-after destination for outsourcing of telecom and financial services, known as BPO, that market could reach a point of a worldwide backlash. It is crucial therefore that some foresight and planning be directed towards this, should such a scenario come about.

Two other concerns crucial to the development of IT in India are greater promotion of e-governance, whose record to date has not been significant, and the need to overcome the digital divide. While the southern states have advanced considerably in promoting e-governance, its progress in the rest of the country has been minimal. As for the digital divide, in the context of existing poverty, uneven levels of education and population size, it would be naive to wish away such divisions rapidly. Human societies have since time immemorial been distinguished along lines of ethnicity, religion, income and education and have grown to adjust and cope with such distinctions. May we hope that the digital divide will be different and may perhaps help to even out other aspects? While one cannot be complacent about the present situation, it is only realistic to accept and understand that in a vast and diverse nation like India the achievement of such goals will take time, competing as they will with demands for resources to meet other basic needs.

7

Foundations of a Modern Industrial State

7.1 Introduction

In the introduction to this study, I noted the attempts made by the Indian Government to promote industrial development. Although unintended, certain states, owing to resources or historical advantages, have benefited more than others. Generally, a national development strategy is arrived at through a process of democratic consensus and it is expected that planned allocation of resources will promote both growth and income distribution. While that is a desired objective, one cannot ensure that the financial resources invested will result in expected outcomes. Through fifty years of post-Independence development experience, there is enough evidence to support this contention. As the introductory chapter indicates, further inequalities between states appear to be emerging with the growth of ICT.

Mysore state, formed in 1956, and renamed Karnataka in 1973, was, for reasons of security and prior industrial record, regarded as a 'model state', favoured by the central government when setting up defence industries. Deriving its name from *Mahishasura*, the buffalo-headed monster said to have been slain by the goddess *Chamundi*, the tutelary goddess of the Mysore royal family (Hayavadana Rao 1936, 73–4), Mysore has a long and illustrious history that goes back to the great Vijayanagar empire and beyond. Between 1761 and 1799, the daring exploits of Hyder Ali and Tipu Sultan raised the ire of neighbouring rulers and the British East India Company, resulting in warfare, the subsequent entry of the British into the area and the eventual restoration of the Wadeyars.

Apart from a rich cultural and political heritage, Mysore has been blessed with abundant natural resources, minerals such as gold, iron, manganese and mica, large river systems such as the Cauvery and the Bhadra, forest wealth such as teak, sandalwood and rosewood, and much exciting wildlife. Native to the area is one of India's best known cattle breeds, the *Amrut Mahal,* used by Hyder Ali in his military exploits in the Deccan and sought after by cattle breeders all over India. Mysore's location in the Deccan plateau and its average elevation of three thousand feet ensures an equable climate all year round. Such a favourable climate, a bounteous red lateritic soil and plentiful water supply enable the growth of flora from both tropical and temperate zones, irrespective of seasons (Ismail 1954, 41, Hayavadana Rao 1929). Mysore was ruled by Maharajas who encouraged the setting up of representative institutions and the development of the infrastructure through hydro-electricity and irrigation projects and a range of industrial undertakings.

In this chapter, I attempt a broad canvas of Mysore's past, hoping to identify historical linkages to explain why the Mysore region of Karnataka emerged as the 'Silicon Plateau' in the 1990s. The boom in information and communication technology attributed to both the quality of human power and the environment renders it interesting to examine where the reasons of this success are rooted. The head start in technological capability goes back to at least a hundred years when Bangalore was one of the first cities in India to have electricity. That initiated an era of several pioneering ventures associated with the state, both in education and industrial development, spearheaded by the prestigious IISc guiding Mysore to the forefront of industrial and technological development.

Following this introduction, in Section 7.2 I discuss attempts to enlist public participation through institutions such as the Representative Assembly, the Legislative Council and the novel Economic Conference. Section 7.3 covers particular policy innovations such as compulsory primary education, schools for the deaf and blind, and *shishu vihar* or pre-school education, all seen as being well ahead of the times. Section 7.4 deals with the cultural openness that prevailed in the early twentieth century in Mysore, which remains a distinctive feature of the region. Section 7.5 covers pre-Independence development. Section 7.6 presents a comparative view of industry and agriculture. Section 7.7 gives an account of major projects. Section 7.8 focuses on the role of government, followed by a conclusion.

7.2 Public Involvement in Issues of Public Interest

As early as the late nineteenth century, when the greater part of India was under British rule, Mysore set up deliberative institutions, such as a Representative Assembly (1881), Legislative Council (1907) and an Economic Conference (1911).

The Representative Assembly first set up in 1881 with limited powers of petitioning was, during the *dewan*ship of Sir M. Visvesvaraya, vested with enhanced powers of legislation, taxation, discussion of the budget, interpellation (in the sense of the right of parliament to submit formal questions to government), the moving of resolutions and the submission of representations on matters of public interest (Hayavadana Rao 1929, Vol. IV, 91). It was the only 'representative institution of its size on the sub-continent and hence an important element in the development of Mysore's progressive reputation' (Manor 1977, 12).

The Legislative Council established in 1907 included among its powers the passing of resolutions, legislation, questions and answers and debates on important issues connected with general administration (Visvesvaraya, Speech to the Legislative Council, 3 February 1914, 333).

Despite their limited power and the general perception of them as mere debating societies, the Assembly and the Council nevertheless offered opportunities for the emergence of a cohesive opposition to princely authority (Manor 1977, 25–26).

Of the deliberative bodies, the Economic Conference, regarded as unique for the period, was established in June 1911 with the following objectives:

- to associate men of enlightenment, public spirited citizens, prominent agriculturists, merchants, etc., with the officers of government in deliberation concerned with economic programmes in Mysore,
- to keep alive public interest in numerous questions claiming attention by expression of views and discussion,
- to stimulate the capacity for effort among people by a series of conferences and to suggest the adoption of practical measures by government wherever it could render assistance, and
- to hold an annual conference to discuss the more important questions that affect the material prosperity of the state (Hayavadana Rao 1929, Vol. III, Economic, 1).

The aim of the Economic Conference was to bring together officials and non-officials to gather information on different subjects, investigate them through discussion and analysis and thus generate ideas which would yield practical results. During the fifteen years of its existence, nearly four hundred subjects were discussed resulting in 150 decisions being taken by government. The key ones implemented were compulsory primary education and the establishment of Mysore University and the Bank of Mysore. All government activity was subject to an Efficiency Audit to ensure both discipline and efficiency.

7.3 Innovative Policies

Mysore's reputation as a model state arose from the innovative policies introduced under an enlightened administration. As early as September 1913, Mysore state had passed a bill making primary education compulsory for children between the ages of seven and thirteen. *Shishu Vihar* (early childhood education centre), started by Professor and Mrs M. V. Gopalaswamy in the 1930s, was an educational concept well ahead of its time internationally. '*Shishu Vihar's* founder had a well-defined philosophy of early education'—a philosophy expounded by novelist R. K. Narayan in *The English Teacher*. Krishna, the main character in the novel and friend of the headmaster, is told by the latter, 'This is the meaning of the word joy—in its purest sense ... that adults could learn a great deal by watching and playing with the children here'. He added that his observations of children at play had given him 'a glimpse of some purpose in existence and creation'. When Krishna asked this extraordinary man when precisely the children did their study, he was told that 'study is a part and parcel of play'. Through his characters, it appears that Narayan was suggesting that the aim of education is the 'preserving as long as possible the original vision of childhood' (Susan Ram and N. Ram 1996, 392–93).

To complement early childhood education, the State government set up health centres in certain well-populated areas of the state. Mothers were encouraged to bring their infants to be checked by a health nurse and were given free milk. These facilities were in addition to local dispensaries which had a qualified doctor, supported by male and female nurses. The state's emphasis on health led to a proposal in 1908–09 that the local medical officer should undertake medical examination of school students fortnightly and recommend treatment at the dispensary if necessary. This scheme was formalised in 1916 on the recommendation of the Economic Conference and regular medical examination of students was instituted (Hayavadana Rao 1929). In keeping with this tradition of innovation, Mysore state was the first to set up a birth control clinic, at Mandya in 1931 (Cadene and Holmstrom 1998, 170).

In the 1920s, government turned its attention to providing education for the disabled by setting up schools for the speech impaired, the visually impaired and the hearing impaired. 'The institution [school for the deaf and dumb] has earned for itself a very wide reputation and attracted pupils from various parts of India' (Hayavadana Rao 1929, vol. IV, 590).

Another significant innovation of the time was Akashvani, a broadcasting venture started in 1936 by Professor Gopalaswamy which covered Mysore city and surrounding districts before the advent of All India Radio.

The Mental Hospital at Bangalore, founded in 1847, was regarded as the finest in the country. Described by Lord Lothian as a picnic place and by a professor of mental health as a monument to the vision and wisdom of those responsible for mental health (Ismail 1954, 53–54), the hospital, under Dr M. V. Govindaswamy, introduced 'technological innovations on par with advances in psychiatry elsewhere in the world'. Professor E. Maudsley of Maudsley Hospital, New York, notable in the field of mental care, during his visit to Bangalore, had been full of praise for the 'pavilion system, open spaces, well established laboratories and recreational facilities' (*The Hindu*, 20 March 2005), and suggested the establishment of a post-graduate school. Following Independence, that suggestion led to the establishment of the All India Institute of Mental Health in 1954 with Dr Govindaswamy as its first director. Renamed the National Institute of Mental Health and Neurological Sciences (NIMHANS) in 1974, it continues to be at the forefront of mental health education and treatment in the country.

Animal welfare featured prominently in the state. In 1937–38, Sri Jayachamarajendra Wadeyar started the Mysore Pinjrapole Society, the equivalent of the Society for the Prevention of Cruelty to Animals (SPCA). Currently Pinjrapole is staffed by fifty employees, including trained veterinarians. While cattle constitute the majority, it also houses horses, dogs and birds that are sick, injured or neglected (Shivkumar, *Deccan Herald*, 5 January 2001).

7.4 Cultural Openness

The perception of Bangalore as a centre of technological diversity and innovation can be explained in terms of the 'multiple cultures' perspective, according to which challenge from external stimuli tends to stimulate innovative activity. Most software companies that have invested in Bangalore have done so not merely in recognition of the region's high-tech infrastructure and qualified manpower but also because they regard it as a cosmopolitan area where one can integrate comfortably with local people who combine what is best in East and West—as reflected in its traditional music and dance, its lifestyle, its clubs, its suburbs named after past British residents and its blend of architectural styles (*The Hindu*, 30 May 1993). During his reign, Sri Krishnaraja Wadeyar IV (1902–1941) adopted an open policy with regard to senior positions in his administration. In 1911, he appointed M. Visvesvaraya, Chief Engineer of the state, to the position of Dewan (State Premier), a position which until then had been generally held by a member of the Mysore Civil Service. If Visvesvaraya's appointment as Dewan was a departure from convention, the appointment to that position in 1928 of his Private Secretary and former classmate, Mirza Ismail, who happened to be the grandson of an immigrant of Persian origin who had settled in Bangalore as an importer of Arabian horses, was a cause for even more surprise! Both Visvesvaraya and Ismail turned out to be outstanding administrators and their appointments were a reflection of His Highness's standards of leadership and openness. A similar appointment was that of Dr Brajendranath Seal as the first Vice-Chancellor of Mysore University. Under him, the university attracted scholars such as A. R. Wadia, K. T. Shah, Radhakumud and Radhakamal Mukherjee, and even Dr S. Radhakrishnan from Oxford. Significantly, all hailed from outside the state. Together, these scholars created an educational environment which produced graduates who went on to make very valuable contributions to the country. Reviewing the film 'The Gentle Knight of Music', produced by M. Y. Krishnaswamy about his classmate, Veena Doraiswamy Iyengar, with a script by H. Y. Sharada Prasad (all contemporaries at Maharaja's College along with R. K. Narayan, R. K. Laxman and T. S. Satyan, noted photojournalist) Vatsala Vedantam writes that 'it will long be remembered as a gracious tribute to one of the great masters. It will also be remembered as the catalyst which brought together three outstanding alumni of Maharaja's College Mysore, better known as the Oxford of India' (*The Hindu*, 1 July 2007; for an insight of those years, see Satyan 2005).

R. K. Narayan, creator of the fictional town of Malgudi, never disclosed if it was intended to be a depiction of his favourite city, Mysore. He did however say, 'Every time I go back to Mysore ... I feel thankful to the Heavens for placing me there... The quality of life Mysore offers is unique. The atmosphere is placid and poetic, and one is constantly tempted to enjoy the moment setting aside all other thoughts' (Susan and N. Ram 1996, 92).

The all-encompassing feeling that one associates with Mysore is best exemplified in the annual festival of *Dasara* or *Navratri*. It involves offering of puja over nine nights and ends on the tenth day, *Vijayadasami*, with celebration of victory. Celebrated in great splendour annually by the Wadeyars of Mysore, the festival is of mythical significance as it commemorates the victory of goddess Chamundeswari over Mahishasura, and traces its origin to the Vijayanagar kings of the seventeenth century (Hayavadana Rao 1936).

During the reign of Krishnaraja Wadeyar IV, Dasara had 'come to be known as the most magnificent festival celebrated in South India' (ibid., 146–49). Today, the festival continues with a different perspective. Closely associated with the Wadeyar dynasty in pre-Independence times when the annual celebration and durbar were rather exclusive and attended mainly by invited guests, today the democratically elected government has introduced a populist element.

That different religions and faiths can live in harmony is best exemplified at Baba Budengiri in Chikamagalur, where the tomb of a Muslim seer, credited with the introduction of coffee into India, is venerated by both Hindus and Muslims. Further evidence of the harmony and religious tolerance of this region is revealed in the historic car festival of Sri Chennakeshavaswamy temple in Belur. According to local people, it symbolises the century-old notion of communal harmony in the town. A *maulvi* from Modoor reads passages from the Koran before the start of the *rathothsava* (*The Hindu*, 21 April 2005).

Mysore's record of religious tolerance was highlighted in 2001 at the bi-centennial of the historic Abbe Dubois church at Ganjam, a village not far from the city. Abbe Dubois arrived at Mysore to enquire into the state of the 1,800-strong Christian community following the war between the British and Tipu Sultan. The French established the Catholic Church at Mysore on a permanent basis and enjoyed the protection of the Wadeyar family. French missionaries established several religious and educational institutions and continued to work in Mysore until the 1970s.

During a drive through Melkote on Indian Independence Day (15 August), historian Ramachandra Guha observed the celebrations at a school. Taking centre stage were three children dressed as Mahatma Gandhi, Sir M. Visvesvaraya and Dr Ambedkar. Pointing out that the inclusion of Dr Ambedkar in itself was a reflection of changing perceptions in Karnataka since the 1980s, he writes, 'In past times, they [the downtrodden] and their leaders were mocked both by Brahmins and by the peasant castes, the Vokkaligas. That school children can now openly pay tribute to Ambedkar is a sign of how much this has changed' (Guha 2003).

Analysing this further, Guha writes, 'If indeed, these are the three Indians most revered in modern Mysore, then the curious thing is that not one is a native of the region. ... I like to think that the anointing of these three "outsiders" as heroes is characteristic of the inclusive spirit of the Carnatic plateau. This is a soil that has proved inhospitable to chauvinism. Consider that Melkote, my ultimate destination that day, was a village rescued from obscurity by the migration there of the 11th century saint-teacher Ramunajacharya, fleeing persecution by Saivite rulers in what is now Tamil Nadu. The locals gave him refuge and honour. Ramanuja repaid this by showing some broadmindedness of his own, notably by admitting Dalits to his temple' (ibid.).

That inclusiveness that Guha observes in Karnataka can be extended to its unique blend in social life, its architecture, scholarship and, interestingly, its music. If different parts of India can boast of their history and natural beauty, what marks Karnataka, according to Guha, is 'its culture of capaciousness, the ability, manifested down the ages, to harmoniously incorporate elements from other parts of India and the world'. While Karnataka with other states in south India is the home of Carnatic music, it also boasts of well-known exponents of the Hindustani style of classical music in Bhimsen Joshi, Basvaraj Rajguru, Gangubhai Hangal, Kumar Gandharv, Mallikarjun Mansoor and Ramakanth Kaikini. Although the two styles rarely co-exist in other parts of India, with either Carnatic or Hindustani being dominant, performances in either style are appreciated all over the country. Karnataka, perhaps for historical or cultural reasons, has encouraged both styles of music. In January 2006, the Union Minister for Information and Broadcasting singled out All India Radio, Bangalore, as the only station to broadcast four hours daily of Hindustani and Carnatic music.

Mysore's rich music tradition owes much to the Wadeyars and their inheritance from the Vijayanagar kings. During the reign of Krishnaraja Wadiyar IV, music flourished with eminent artists such as Ariyakudi Ramanuja Iyengar, Vardachar, Fiaz Khan and Abdul Karim Khan, the last two being exponents of the Hindustani style. To encourage Western music, Krishnaraja Wadeyar set up a palace band with a German conductor which performed on ceremonial occasions and during the Dasara celebrations. His successor, Sri Jayachamaraja Wadiyar, was a talented composer in both Carnatic and Western classical music, and was Founder President of the British Philharmonic Society. A visitor to the region in the 1970s wrote, 'During its final princely period, Mysore attracted many scientists, artists and musicians. The Maharajas, fine scholars themselves, were generous and perceptive patrons of every form of creative endeavour and Jayachamaraja Wadeyar, the last Maharaja, is a composer of distinction' (Dervla Murphy 1976, 68). The Wadeyars' patronage of the arts extended to the fostering of India's ancient learning with the establishment of the Oriental Institute which houses ancient manuscripts.

Comparative studies have established that the history and culture of a people and a country tend to be reflected in their attitude to machines and equipment. Karl Deutsch writes about the Ford tractor given to the Havasupai Indians, a tribe of Native Americans mainly found in Arizona, USA, who used it for one season and, lacking the culture, knowhow and discipline, allowed it to rust after that! (Deutsch 1971, 32). Cultural influences explain differences in approach to techniques and artefacts between people and regions and this can be extended to understand how certain spiritual and ritualistic practices influence individual attitudes and behaviour.

One such ritual is the practice of the annual cleaning and worship of machines, instruments, equipment, vehicles, bicycles and working animals on *Ayudhya Puja* day during Dasara festivities. In his *Hindu Manners, Customs and Ceremonies,* Abbe Dubois characterised the puja as 'entirely military; no native belonging to the profession of arms, be he Pagan, Mohemedan or Christian makes any scruples of joining in it' (Hayavadana Rao 1936, 198–99). Identified initially with armoury and household animals when warriors attended to the tools of warfare, these were taken in procession to Banimantap where the Maharaja offered puja at the Bani tree. The Maharaja's puja at Banimantap on Vijayadasami became a state-wide celebration with workers and households venerating their tools of trade on Ayudhya Puja on the eve of Vijayadasami (Hayavadana Rao 1936, 7).

When laying the foundation of the building of the Mythic Society on 7 August 1916, Sir M. Visvesvaraya recalled that Mysore had been the scene of some of the exploits depicted in the epic poems Ramayana and Mahabharata and had produced great preachers of religion and dynasties of kings who had wrought mighty deeds. Its people 'possessed a high degree of artistic skill and talent as evidenced by the superb specimens of sculptural art, such as, the rock temples of Halebid and Belur, the great stone statues at Sravanabelgola, and the fine stone bull on Chamundi Hills; known as Mysore's Nandi bull, it was described by Mark Wilks in his *History of Mysore* as 'probably the largest and the most skilfully executed figure of this kind in the south of India' (Hammish 1930, 42). 'These monuments of a bygone age are the best of their kind and have no rivals in any other part of the world (Visvesvaraya's speeches, vol. I, 1911–18, 365).

Father Tabard urged Mysoreans 'to study Mysore, [for] Mysore is a country which, in every way, is worthy of our devotion and love' (ibid., 365). To which, Sir Mirza Ismail added, 'those who have travelled the world over agree that this is one of the fairest lands in the world, full of nature's loveliness, delectable in climate, rich in resources, above all, in patient and kindly human character, a land fit for the devotion of true men' (1954, 31). Such an idyllic land was developed by a dynasty of benevolent rulers and enlightened Dewans into what was described as *Ramarajya,* a kingdom ruled by the gods, by Mahatma Gandhi.

7.5 Pre-independence Development of Mysore

Richly endowed with natural resources, Mysore adopted a deliberate policy of industrialisation in order to process its agricultural and mineral resources, earning for itself the label of a 'model state'. To implement its policy, government adopted state intervention and, in so doing, acquired considerable entrepreneurial and technological experience. For example, while exploiting the iron ore resources of Kemmangundi at the Bhadravathi Iron and Steel Works, a method for the distillation of wood oils was developed as an adjunct to the making of iron and steel.

Slag, a by-product of the iron and steel making process, was converted into cement. In providing the infrastructure for private companies such as Kolar Gold Mining Co. to operate effectively, the government offered both incentives and concessions and also started undertakings, which, either because of large capital requirement or at the risk of being unremunerative in the short term, were beyond the resources of the private sector.

7.5.1 Industrialisation as a Strategy of Development

In an approach that is reminiscent of Japan's strategy of industrialization based on imported technology during the Meiji era, assimilation of new ideas and technology was central in the administration of the Dewans who were at the helm of power during 1890–1947. In pursuit of his vision ('industrialise or perish'), Visvesvaraya advocated a strategy of import substitution in areas such as sericulture and sandalwood oil. Export of raw cocoons and sandalwood ceased and instead both were further processed to the final stage, creating employment and benefiting 28,000 families of cultivators and eight thousand families of weavers.

The sericulture industry in Mysore dates back to the days of Tipu Sultan, who is reported to have had silkworms brought from Bengal and reared at several centres. However, the industry later fell into decline and was revived by Jamsetji Tata (Lala, *Business Line*, 14 May 2004) who had studied the cottage industry in France and Japan and thought that the temperate climate of Mysore would be suitable as he had earlier observed mulberry trees there. In line with his philanthropic leanings, his interest was in creating a livelihood for the poor and, eventually, a new industry for India. With the grant of rent-free land and an annual subsidy of Rs 3000 from the Mysore government and help from the Salvation Army, Jamsetji rejuvenated the industry.

Silkworm rearing and silk reeling were seen as profitable occupations for agriculturists in a region blessed with an ideal climate and a favourable economic environment. Several years later, however, competition from Chinese and Japanese silk producers sent the Mysore industry into decline. The weakness of the industry was attributed to relative cost differences and inefficiencies in production (Balakrishna 1940, 38). To assist the industry, government set up the Sericulture Institute and Sericulture Department to provide improved varieties of silk worms for producers.

With that firm foundation and further support from the central government in the form of a Central Silk Board, Mysore's silk industry has, despite a brief slump a few years ago, continued to grow from strength to strength as a major domestic and export earner. Karnataka's current output is estimated at nine thousand tonnes, and in recent years, Karnataka Silk Industries Corporation has, in a move to protect the quality of the silk sari produced, obtained a Geographic Indication Registry (GIR) notification and restricted availability of its products to certain outlets only (*The Hindu*, 17 December 2004).

Another of Mysore's famous products is sandalwood. The sandal tree is a small evergreen, flourishing in the elevated regions of Mysore. Its products, particularly oil, are highly valued for medical and cosmetic purposes. Until 1916, sandalwood grown in Mysore was auctioned by the Forest Department and exported to France and Germany. However, the government's policy to process the raw material locally led Visvesvaraya to ask his Director of Industries to explore the prospects of conducting experiments for the extraction of the oil at the IISc. Led by Professors J. J. Sadborough and H. E. Watson, the search for the process was successful and resulted in the establishment of the Sandalwood Oil Factory at Mysore in 1916 with capital of Rs 7 lakhs. As the plant for the factory could not be imported due to the war, the entire machinery was manufactured in India. Two factories were set up, one at Mysore and the other at Bangalore, with a total capacity of 26,000 lbs of oil per month. According to Balakrishna (1940), the factories were established at an opportune time, because the price of sandalwood oil rose from 21 shillings per lb in 1914 to 50 shillings in 1917. As the market changed with the war, the two factories were amalgamated at Mysore with an annual output of 120,000 lbs. To promote its products, the pre-Independence Mysore government set up a Trade Commissioner's Office in London.

Noted for its purity and its essential organic properties, Mysore sandalwood oil 'satisfies the requirements of the pharmacopoeia' (Balakrishnan 1940, 80) and is used in Europe for the manufacture of high grade toilet soaps and for various other medicinal purposes. Mysore sandal soap is reputed worldwide for its consistent quality and is easily recognisable in stores by its original packaging which has been retained to this day. Mysore sandal shaving soap, marketed in Europe by Crabtree and Evelyn, London, proved to be a gift which brought this writer much joy, when my daughter purchased a cake of it in Paris in 1994.

By 1960, Mysore's share of the world's sandalwood production had touched 75 per cent, earning almost a crore of rupees in foreign exchange. As the first commercial venture of the Mysore government, the performance of the sandalwood factory is now seen as 'a vindication of the enlightened and successful industrial policy pursued by the government and bears an excellent testimony to its vision and foresight' (Balakrishna 1940, 11).

As a successful model of import substitution, both ventures of the early years of the twentieth century, one in sericulture and the other in sandalwood oil, demonstrate Sir Visvesvaraya's vision. He believed that, 'Imports inflict double injury; it [*sic*] drains capital and denies jobs to locals' (Rao 1973, 210) and bemoaned the fact that 'many of the articles in common use for the manufacture of which raw materials are available in the country, or were being manufactured here at one time or another, are being obtained from abroad, showing that the country has been following policies which have made her dependent on foreign countries for some of her barest necessities' (Visvesvaraya 1934, 63).

7.5.2 Education and Expertise in the Development Process

In the pursuit of industrial development that occurred during the period of Sri Krishnaraja Wadeyar's reign, the training of personnel and induction of expertise from other parts of India and abroad were greatly encouraged. Visvesvaraya was persuaded to return from Bombay to Mysore to take up the position of Chief Engineer in 1909, and he was appointed Dewan in 1912, holding that position until 1918. Prior to taking up the Dewanship, he embarked on an extensive journey, visiting Japan, Britain, Europe and the United States of America to see for himself the developments that had taken place in those countries.

As an admirer of Western technology, and the Westerners' values of discipline and hard work, Sir M. Visvesvaraya believed that education and the acquisition of skills were critical to the development of the state. That view, enunciated early in the twentieth century, reminds one of the 'entitlements and capabilities' theory advocated by Amartya Sen in the 1980s (Sen 1984). The essence of Visvesvaraya's economic philosophy was to rid people of fatalism and to show them that the only way out was to change circumstances. In Marx's words, quoted by Sen (1984), this meant 'replacing the domination of circumstances and chance over individuals by the domination of individuals over chance and circumstances' (497). The solution, according to Visvesvaraya, lay in improving the capability of every citizen through education and vocational training, (1943, 11–12).

When necessary, experts were invited from abroad to impart training in skills. To assist Mysore's sericulture industry, Signor Washington Mori, an Italian expert, was invited along with Japanese experts. Following establishment of the Sericulture Farm at Channapatna, Signor Mori returned to Italy but was invited back when disease threatened the industry. His recommendation that disease-free cocoons be imported and that silk yarn be extracted elsewhere and brought back to Mysore to be woven into fabrics was rejected on grounds of cost. Instead, the department decided to rear disease-free eggs and to continue with the extraction process locally. When differences between the expert and the department were referred to Visvesvaraya, he accepted the department's point of view. (Rao 1973, 288). Despite his admiration for Western S&T, Visvesvaraya could quite firmly dispense with foreign experts if he considered their advice or attitude inappropriate to the needs of the state.

Several other experts were employed to assist in the development of the state. The services of Mr Rait, a Government of India cellulose expert, were secured to explore the possibility of using bamboo for the manufacture of paper with the hope that it could eventually replace 'sabai grass'. A protective tariff imposed by the Tariff Board provided the impetus and the state with its immense bamboo resources went ahead with the establishment of the Mysore Paper Mills in 1936 (Balakrishna 1940, 91–93).

A key principle in all of Visvesvaraya's commercial undertakings was that local skills and talent should be encouraged and trained. While relying on foreign technical expertise at the start of a venture, he stipulated that local people be trained to take their place at the end of a contract. Such a stipulation in the agreement with an American firm to build an acetate plant in Mysore prevented the venture from going ahead because the firm was unwilling to train Indian workers to take their place (Rao 1973, 253)

As a pioneer in technical education, Mysore established a School of Engineering in 1862 to train staff for the subordinate engineering services. Following this, several industrial schools were set up in the districts, in addition to the two at Mysore and Bangalore. By 1921–22, there were twenty-four such schools attended by 1,057 students, and four industrial schools for girls with a total of 149 students. A feature of education policy in Mysore state was the grant of liberal scholarships for education at all levels within the state, as well as outside the state if such facilities were unavailable (Hayavadana Rao 1929, 618). To meet its industrial needs, the state government sent young scientists and engineers to Britain and other countries to obtain practical training.

With regard to the technical schools established at Bangalore and Mysore, Sir M. Visvesvaraya noted that the objective of such institutions was to create an incentive for manual work in the younger generation and to provide the means of earning a livelihood by following an independent profession (Speech to the Mysore Representative Assembly, 11 October 1913). When admission for higher levels of technical education in Madras and Bombay for candidates from Mysore became restricted, an engineering college was established at Bangalore in 1922 which offered courses in civil and mechanical engineering. That college was later named the Visvesvaraya University of Technology.

Noting the inordinate emphasis on theory and the consequent lack of attention given to application in the Indian system of education, Sir M. Visvesvaraya advocated the importance of imparting practical education. In a speech at Central College, Bangalore, he expressed his preference for the Japanese system and stated, 'It is not in the glory of Bangalore as a seat of learning that we are interested. What immediately concerns us is the equipment of the city for developing the intellectual ability and the executive power of our citizens and for the training it should afford to prepare future manufacturers, merchants, businessmen, economists, lawyers, engineers, statesmen, etc.' (Speeches, vol. II, 16 March 1912, 27). A fact-finding mission was sent to the United States, Britain, Japan and Australia, upon the return of which a university was established at Mysore in July 1916.

7.5.2.1 The Indian Institute of Science (IISc)

If the Maharaja and the annual Dasara celebrations earned Mysore worldwide attention, none could have imagined that the laying of the corner stone of the IISc at Bangalore by His Highness on 1 February 1911 would lead to the emergence of such a renowned centre for research and teaching in Theoretical and Applied Science and Engineering. Despite the odds and the opposition to its location, the combined efforts of J. N. Tata, the government of India and Mysore government led to its establishment at Bangalore. While acknowledging the role of Tata in establishing the Institute, the Maharaja also acknowledged the contribution of his mother, who, as Maharani Regent, had donated 371 acres of land, a portion of the building grant and an assured annual income for its upkeep. (Krishnaraja Wadeyar's *Speeches*, 84).

In deciding to locate the Institute at Bangalore, those early planners were influenced by the fact that Mysore had pioneered the generation of hydro-electricity as early as 1900, established a range of innovative industries and encouraged technical education among its youth. Beginning with the successful extraction of sandal oil, the close working relationship between the Institute and industry was gradually extended to other areas like obtaining scientific data regarding yields of charcoal, tar, acetic acid and wood spirit from other types of trees. As a result, investigations on wood distillation undertaken by students led to a substitute for coal when the iron and steel venture was launched at Bhadravati. By 1917 it was associated with the Sandalwood Factory (Mysore), Soap Factory (Bangalore) and straw board manufacture from bamboo in Bangalore (Subbarayappa 1992).

Following the establishment of an aircraft factory at Bangalore, a department of Aeronautical Engineering was set up. The Mysore government provided substantial funding for research and teaching in Aeronautical and Automobile engineering, with the condition that 30 per cent of seats be reserved for Mysore candidates. The Institute's emphasis on industrial research is evident from the electrical engineering work undertaken for the Sivasamudram Power Station, Hindustan Aircraft and Bhadravati Iron and Steel Works.

Prior to Independence, 'the Indian Institute of Science had developed a character and tradition of its own... Above all, it was emerging as a "mother institution", as several bright students began to occupy key positions in various scientific and technical institutions making important contributions to national development' (ibid., 174–5). Homi J. Bhabha and Vikram Sarabhai, graduates of the Institute, were founders of two of India's outstanding scientific institutions. The former headed the TIFR where the AEC was set up, while the latter established ISRO whose administrative centre, DOS, is located at the IISc, with several agencies linked to it located all over India. Although both died relatively young, Bhabha at fifty-six and Sarabhai at fifty-two, during the period of their stewardship they left indelible marks on those institutions. Present-day ICT owes its beginnings to them and to several others associated with the Institute.

An interesting observation made by Maddox and Rich is the differentiation of graduates of the IISc from IIT graduates. Referring to the former, they write that the complaint that 'graduates leave for overseas once the ink is dry on their certificates is almost non-existent, perhaps because those concerned have been given not merely a saleable education but a degree of engagement in the practice of science and technology in India' (1984, 593). In its efforts to constantly upgrade its academic offerings, the Institute, in cooperation with ISRO, has developed a degree programme combined with seminars on subjects such as orbital mechanics, remote sensing, satellite meteorology and propulsion of rocket vehicles.

The National Conference on Electronics organised by Vikram Sarabhai in 1970 provided momentum for the development of electronic and computer engineering in the country. It was followed by the establishment of a Centre for Electronic Design in cooperation with the Swiss Federal Institute of Technology and the Department of Electronics. UGC funded centres in Microprocess Application Lab, IISc-ISRO Space Technology Cell and the Computer-Aided Design Lab have had a significant impact on Bangalore's capability in the field of electronics. In the context of renewable energy, a crucial contribution is the IISC's work on silicon-based materials vital to the electronics industry and for the development of photovoltaic cells in harnessing solar energy. As Subbarayappa claims, '...nowhere else in the country is research of such quality being done over such a wide range of subjects' (ibid., 288–89).

7.6 Industry versus Agriculture

The impression that the Mysore government was geared more towards industry than agriculture is a conclusion that one could draw if one took at face value Sir M. Visvesvaraya's call, 'industrialise or perish'. In actual fact, however, he advocated a broad-based development strategy. To encourage agriculture, an Agricultural School was set up at Hebbal and a demonstration farm at Rayankere. The school was later upgraded to a college and has now grown into the University of Agricultural Sciences. While pursuing a policy of industrialisation, the Mysore government also encouraged animal husbandry, agriculture and horticulture.

In the area of animal husbandry, Mysore is well known for the Amrut Mahal, an indigenous breed of cattle for whose development a special department was created. Land was alloted at Rayankere for the purpose of grazing this breed which is peculiar to Mysore and has attracted the attention of cattle breeders in India and abroad. 'In November 1907, an application was received, through the Inspector-General Civil Veterinary Department, Calcutta, for two good specimen bulls and three cows to be sent to England for breeding purposes to meet the wishes of His Grace, the Duke of Bedford' (Hayavadana Rao, vol. IV, 1929, 732). Over the years, Mysoreans have developed mixed-breeds particularly from Holstein, Jersey and Red Dane strains imported by the Rayankere farm. Local cattle breeders acquired the skills of rearing such animals and were offered supplies of green fodder grown at the farm at a reasonable price. For many low income households, this offered secondary income, mainly in the towns and cities. Free veterinary services were provided by the government, including the servicing of stud bulls for a nominal fee. The introduction of artificial insemination in the 1960s increased the demand for such services. The broad institutional foundation and reasonable cattle rearing skills combined with moderate climate led to an explosion of the bovine population under the White Revolution (Mascarenhas 1988).

Leslie Colman, the Canadian head of Mysore's Agriculture Department hoped to increase the state's agricultural output by developing a new plough which had to be cheap and simple for the ordinary villager to break the soil when it was hard and dry, instead of waiting for the arrival of the monsoons. Then, when the rain did come, the water would soak into the earth immediately, instead of running off and being largely lost (Slater 1926, 249–50). Apparently, Colman was unaware that Mysore farmers were already using an advanced plough which had attracted the attention of Major Wilks whose description of farming is worth quoting:

> On the first shower of rain after harvest the homefields are again turned up with the plough, and this operation, as showers occur, is repeated six successive times during the dry season, at once destroying the weeds and opening the ground to the influence of the sun, the decomposition of water and air, and the formation of new compounds. The manure of the village, which is carefully and skillfully prepared, is then spread out on the land, and incorporated with it by a seventh ploughing, and the harrowing with an instrument nearly resembling a large rake, drawn by oxen and guided by a boy: when the field is completely pulverised, a drill plough, of admirable and simple contrivance, performs the operation of sowing twelve

> rows at once by means of twelve hollow bamboos (reeds) at the lower end .... This laborious process rewards the husbandman in good seasons with a crop of eighty fold from the best land. ...the whole world does not, perhaps exhibit a cleaner system of husbandry than that of the cultivation of Ragee ... in the homefields of Mysore (Hammish 1930, vol. I, 224).

Historically, Mysore's climate, quality of soil and level of humidity had been recognised as suited to horticulture at least as early as the days of Hyder Ali and Tipu Sultan. Known for their contribution in laying out Bangalore's famous Lal Bagh, they encouraged the grafting of mangoes and the cultivation of figs at Ganjam. A German expert, Krumbeigal, was invited to further develop Lal Bagh and public gardens elsewhere in the state. Sir Mirza Ismail as Dewan was especially keen on the development of horticulture. He notes, 'For those whose tastes lie in horticulture there are attractions equalled in very few places in India. The combination of an equable climate all the year round with a good soil and plentiful water supply makes it possible to grow plants of the tropical and temperate zones side by side and in almost any season of the year' (1954, 41).

Orchards were set up under the supervision of the agriculture department across the state and their produce sold at local markets. Another visitor to the state, Baba Buden, brought coffee seeds, reportedly from Arabia, and these were successfully planted at Chikamagalur, starting a totally new coffee belt. Spices like cardamom and pepper were grown alongside coffee shrubs in coffee estates. Flue-Cured Virginia (FCV) variety of tobacco grown in Mysore is in international demand because of its superior quality and low nicotine and tar content. The Tobacco Board set a quota of eighty-four million kg for 2005.

Mysore's rosewood, sandalwood and teak forests were not just sources of forest wealth; they were home to an abundance of wildlife, namely elephants, tigers, panthers, cheetahs and bison. Unfortunately, inadequate conservation policies have resulted in decline in both forest and wildlife wealth. An incidental outcome of this, albeit negative in the context of present-day conservation thinking (and rightly so), was the taxidermy business developed into an art form by the Dutch family firm of Van Ingen and Van Ingen, which has recently closed its world-renowned establishment at Mysore.

Mysore's luxuriant forests have, since time immemorial, been home to large elephant herds. To prevent overgrazing, a conservation policy was adopted early. This was done through a process of capturing adult animals which were then tamed and sold for a variety of uses. Known as the *Khedda,* that process of a stockade trap for wild elephants is unique to this region and was carried out once in a period of eight to ten years.

Canal and tank irrigation was a crucial aspect of agricultural development in Mysore. In a speech to the Legislative Council (7 July 1914), Sir Visvesvaraya reminded the members that a large percentage of the population depended on agriculture and were forced to rely on a fitful monsoon. 'If water which would otherwise go to waste is collected in large reservoirs, it will be available for growing crops throughout the year. Such works will provide occupation to the people in all seasons and are the best form of protection against famine that we can provide in the country' (*Speeches,* 163). By this time, Visvesvaraya had already established a reputation as an irrigation engineer having advocated the Block Irrigation System that was endorsed by the Irrigation Commission. The scheme envisaged that one third of a block should be provided with irrigation for a perennial crop (sugar cane) while the rest of the block would be used for the rabi or monsoon crop. Thus each block would undergo a triennial crop rotation (1951, 12–13). According to the Irrigation Commission Report, the objective of the system was to distribute the benefits of irrigation in each village within blocks of specified units and in selected soils and situations and to conserve water. However efforts to introduce the system met with resistance from cultivators and some government departments.

A major contribution to water conservation was the development of sluice gates by Visvesvaraya while working as an engineer in the Bombay government. They were first used at Khadakvasla and later at the Krishnarajasagara dam in the Cauvery to prevent water flowing over the reservoir above the storage level. Automatic closure of the gates when water exceeded the level resulted in increased storage of about 25 per cent. A demonstration of the integrity and ethical values of this great statesman was that, while taking out a patent for this invention, Visvesvaraya declined any claim to royalty, declaring that his work had been done as a government servant (Visvesvaraya 1951, 14, see Mascarenhas 2004).

7.7 Major Projects

Induction of technology and expertise became vital to the programme of industrialisation adopted by Mysore during 1900–1940. It was in the area of hydro-electricity generation and distribution and the iron and steel works that Mysore state proved to be a true pioneer and an innovator. Three major projects, the Sivasamudram hydro-electricity project, the Cauvery River scheme and the Bhadravati Iron and Steel Works, are examined in this section.

7.7.1 Sivasamudram Hydro-Electricity Project

The Sivasamudram project was intended to harness the river Cauvery for irrigation and power generation although the latter was not explored until the late nineteenth century.. Following a study tour of Canada and the United States by Deputy Chief Engineer Captain A. J. De Lotbiniere (Chandrasekhar 1981, 146) which deemed the proposal of generating power at Sivasamudram and transmitting it ninety-two miles to the Kolar Gold Fields feasible, there were protracted negotiations with the governments of Madras and India and opposition to be overcome regarding the enormous cost. The project was undertaken by the General Electric Company with electrical plant from the USA, hydraulic plant from Switzerland, penstock pipes from Scotland, insulators from Italy and timber from Australia—truly international in terms of supplies! Once it was harnessed, the river transformed Mandya in Mysore and Tanjore in Madras presidency into granaries.

Challenging as its construction was, its successful completion in 1902 at a cost of £340,000 or about Rs 50,000,000 with a labour force of five thousand when the project was in full swing, established Mysore's reputation in the field of power generation. As the largest power project in India at the time, Sivasamudram 'represented the pinnacle of Karnataka's technological achievements' (*Deccan Herald,* 10 May 2002) and its completion will always remain a tribute to the vision and farsightedness of Sir Seshadri Iyer (Chandrasekhar 1981, 150).

7.7.2 Cauvery Reservoir Scheme

This involved building a masonry dam with a height of 124 ft capable of holding forty-eight billion cubic feet of water to irrigate 150,000 acres of land and generate eighty thousand horse power of electricity to meet both the contractual commitment to supply power to Kolar Gold Fields and for electrification of the state. The design included a lake with a masonry dam 8,600 ft long and 130 ft high above the river bed and 140 ft above the lowest foundation. The width of the bed at the foundation was to be 111 ft with a catchment area above the dam site of 4,100 square miles and an average annual flow of water through the river gorge at the dam site estimated at 220,000 million cubic ft (Visvesvaraya 1951, 43–44). Estimated to cost around Rs 91 lakhs, the sum was questioned by the Finance Department. When faced with objections, Visveswaraya sought direct intervention from the Maharaja claiming that 'a reservoir on the Cauvery is an absolute necessity for the future prosperity of the state' (Rao 1973, 64). After personally studying the proposals, His Highness approved it in its entirety (ibid., 65).

The project had to overcome one more hurdle, that is, the agreement of the Madras government which happened to be in the process of planning a dam at Mettur. After protracted negotiations with both Madras and the Government of India, the project was allowed to proceed. Initial plans for the dam were for 124 ft in two stages, one for power and the other for irrigation. The Government of India agreed to the first stage—a 80 ft high dam. At the construction of the foundation, it had to be assumed that permission for the initial plan of a 124-ft dam would be given, Mysore's case being based on the fact that the benefits it was deriving were not in keeping with the total water flow through its area. The argument was upheld by the Arbitration Committee but Madras refused to accept the decision, resulting in delay in construction of the project. 'But foundations for the two stages had, for important technical reasons, to be simultaneous and could not be laid at different periods...The problem was a grave one, but with rare courage and without a moment's hesitation, Sir M. Visvesvaraya took the risk and decreed that the foundations should be laid as for the higher dam and the works begin. As we know, events have fully justified the robust confidence and optimism of the Dewan' (in *M. Visvesvaraya: by Contemporaries and Admirers*, 15 September 1960, 220). When finally completed in 1931 at a cost of Rs 10.5 crores, government received annual revenue of one and a half crore of rupees and the overall benefit to the population was estimated at Rs 15 crores (Visvesvaraya 1951, 46–48). It was the largest reservoir built in India till then and possibly the largest irrigation canal as well.

The reservoir submerged 1,800 acres of land. About thirty million cubic feet of masonry was used in its construction. It has 161 sluice gates constructed at different levels, of which 136 were manufactured at the Bhadravati Iron and Steel works; the rest were imported. These gates developed and patented by Visvesvaraya operate on electricity and 'automatically close when the water level is below 124 ft. When the level of the lake rises above 124 ft, the gates automatically rise and allow excess water to flow out' (Rao 1973, 61). A feature of the masonry dam is that it was built without any cement. In its place a local variant called 'surki', 'a mortar prepared by mixing lime, brick and sand in different proportions and ground firmly together', was used. The entire excavation was carried out with human labour, employing ten thousand workers (ibid., 60).

Although capable of irrigating three lakh acres of land, the scheme was restricted by agreement to irrigate only 175,000 acres of land. Through the bountiful supply of water, Mandya district became ideal for growing paddy and sugar cane. The sugar cane grown there led to the setting up of the Mysore Sugar Company which annually produces forty thousand tons of sugar valued at Rs 3.5 crores. In addition, spirits were distilled and rectified and converted into fuel grade ethanol. According to Balakrishna (1940), the rectified spirits were utilised for the factory lorries (24). Mr Rangunatha Rao, Chief Chemist at the Mandya Sugar Factory during 1935–38, set up the new distillery which produced industrial and potable alcohol. In 1944, he designed, constructed and set up a new ethanol plant at Symbhaoli with a capacity of 15,000 litres a day. His efforts were finally rewarded with a patent for *petrohol* in 2003 (*Deccan Herald*, 25 February 2003). The total power generated from the Cauvery amounts to 79,000 h.p. and that generated with the aid of stored water amounts to 83,000 h.p. As a result, the power revenue of the government increased from Rs 16.65 lakhs to Rs 1.33 crores in 1948–49.

7.7.3 Bhadravati Iron and Steel Works

The Bhadravati Iron and Steel Works, according to Rao (1973), is 'one of the great industrial and engineering enterprises that perpetuates the name of its founder Visvesvaraya [who] fought against heavy odds and gave this country a great national basic industry of paramount importance' (74). Kemmangundi near Bhadravati had iron ore resources in abundance but the state lacked coking coal generally used in iron ore smelting. However, there were other factors favouring the location of the works such as the availability of limestone used as flux and water from the river Bhadra for both the works and the township (Balakrishna 1940, 67). A natural substitute that was considered for coal was wood charcoal which could be easily obtained from the forests around Bhadravati to manufacture pig iron on the model of charcoal iron factories in the United States and Sweden. Initial investigation on the proposed project began in 1915–16 and was undertaken by C. P. Perrin, an American steel expert based at Tata Iron and Steel Works, Jamshedpur (Rao 1973, 75). Taking into consideration the availability of wood, the cost of transporting it by tramways and the sale of by-products like calcium carbide, Perrin concluded that pig iron could be produced at the cost of Rs 30 a ton.

The two central issues on which government advisors differed were, one, whether it should be pursued by government or handed to a private sector firm, and two, whether consultants from within India or from abroad should be appointed. Concluding what proved to be a constructive debate, the government decided that it would undertake the task with Tata Iron and Steel company as the managing agents. An agreement to this effect was signed in May 1918 (Rao 1973, 79). The project 'envisaged a blast iron furnace for producing 57 tons of charcoal pig iron per day, a wood distillation plant capable of carbonising 200 tons of wood per day, producing in its wake by-products calcium acetate, acetic acid, methanol, acetone, wood tar, etc.' (ibid., 80). Estimated to cost Rs 94 lakhs, the final figure owing to delays and price escalation was Rs 211 lakhs on completion in 1922.

Declining market prices for steel and pig iron and the increased capitalisation caused by construction delays led the American consultants to suggest a temporary closing down of the steel works. Before taking a decision, His Highness sought the assistance of Sir M. Visvesvaraya, then based at Bombay, who accepted the task on condition that he would be allowed complete authority. Foremost in his plan was the decision to keep the Works in operation if the declining price was the only reason for its suggested closure, as well as a request to bring back Perrin. Returning from the United States with some staff, Perrin and his assistants set to work and got the Works back into efficient operation again. Once complete, Visvesvaraya agreed to take over the management of the plant and formed a Board of Management with himself as Chairman. Bringing his engineering and administrative skills to bear, he streamlined the entire operations including the accounting and reporting systems, with all sections of the Works now having to report directly to the Board. While continuing to be based at Bombay, he kept a close tab on operational matters and was able to achieve a dramatic turnaround in the fortunes of the company. Later, unforeseen flooding of the works led the Chief Engineer (who had come with Perrin) to suggest its closure for six months. Undeterred, Visvesvaraya held the American Superintending Engineer V. G. Gudkov responsible and recommended his removal. In his place, he appointed N. Madhava Rau, then a Government director, as General Manager and secured the services of young civilian officers on secondment. 'What was more important, by example and precept he infused into them the spirit of self-respect and self-confidence. He did not spare himself in making the Works self-supporting' (Rao 1973, 88–91).

Having achieved a remarkable transformation against the worst odds, Visvesvaraya recorded it thus in his memoirs (1951): 'The operations have been reduced to a system, the cost of production reduced, local staff trained for various positions, methods of modern administration introduced and the Works have gradually been made to pay their way'. He also notes the letter he received from His Highness, who recalled his meeting with Mr Perrin, the American consultant. He (Perrin) 'was particularly struck by the fact that you were able to dispense with all American labour, and were managing entirely with our own men. It is an achievement the state should be proud of' (letter dated 12 February 1927, 87–88). In a centenary volume celebrating Sir M. Visvesvaraya's birthday, N. Madhava Rau recalls: 'The speed with which the work was carried out and completed within the stipulated time was a revelation, even to me, of the soundness of Sir M. Visvesvaraya's instincts in such matters and his driving force and also of the capabilities of the staff roused to the highest pitch of effort by his inspiring guidance and optimism' (in *Visvesvaraya: by Contemporaries and Admirers*, 15 September 1964, 54).

Following its completion in 1923, subsequent additions of auxiliary plant such as Pipe Foundry and Machine Shop were made in 1926. A Steel Plant with a Rolling Mill was added in 1934. However, the Tariff Board, without giving due consideration to the special circumstances of the aftermath of the war and the particular characteristics of the Bhadravati plant, found that the plant was over capitalised in comparison with other steel producers and therefore less successful. Responding to the comments of the Tariff Board, Balakrishna (1940) argues that the Bhadravati Iron and Steel Works was a product of special regional considerations and, in the absence of coke, the wood distillation plant had become a necessity, even though it worked below rated capacity in the 1930s. As it was the only wood distillation plant at that time, it was difficult to argue for its dismantling because the acetate of lime it produced was vital for national defence. In that context, Balakrishna considered the comparison with other Indian coke iron plants unwarranted (69–71). Notwithstanding the Tariff Board's negative view of the performance of the plant, Husain (1960) commended Visvesvaraya for his ability in 1927 to 'sell Mysore charcoal pig iron in the coastal regions of America, after paying freight charges by rail and steamer, at prices lower than it could be manufactured in that country, upon which the authorities in Washington threatened to raise tariff on exports, if the sale of steel exceeded 5,000 tons a year' (77).

7.8 Role of Government in Development

Government initiative and finance were instrumental in establishing Bhadravathi Iron and Steel Works, the Sandalwood Oil Factory and the Government Soap Factory. Addressing the Representative Assembly on 11 October 1913, Sir M. Visvesvaraya clarified government policy on investment for public works such as the hydro-electricity, railway network and other projects. 'A forward policy in this respect is subject to two essential limitations, viz., (1) that the investments in each case be remunerative and constitute a fresh asset, and (2) under no conceivable circumstances, should the finances of the state suffer embarrassment' (*Speeches,* 1917, 117). Within these broad parameters, the state adopted a broader role in industrialisation leading Sri Krishnaraja Wadeyar to claim that government had learnt a lesson in a 'new political economy'. 'There was a time when we hesitated to undertake a work unless it promised a return on the capital invested of six per cent. In these days we take a somewhat different view. We look for our interest, not only in the return to the treasury but also in the wealth and happiness of the *ryot,* and if we can assure ourselves that the work of this nature is going to bring prosperity to the countryside, that fact in itself affords a generous return' (Sri Krishnaraja Wadeyar, *Speeches,* 1940, 49–50).

That vision dictated the actions of men like Sir Seshadri Iyer, Visvesvaraya and Ismail and led the government to enter into partnership with the private sector to set up undertakings like the Mysore Sugar Factory, Mandya Paper Mills and the Spun Silk Mills. Such financial and administrative cooperation between government and the private sector, according to Balakrishna, was fully justified and twofold: 'to inculcate a spirit of enterprise among entrepreneurs of the state by enlisting private cooperation from the outset and educate private capitalists in the art of industrial management' (1940, 210). In 1915, even before government's investment of Rs 220 lakhs on Bhadravati

Iron and Steel Works, the Mysore government had already invested nearly a crore and a half rupees on various projects. Visvesvaraya considered these a worthwhile investment, capable of bringing a return to the state in the long run. In proclaiming this achievement in a speech to the Mysore Economic Conference (27 July 1915), he stated that 'it is a matter of satisfaction that we have been able to carry out, from accumulated balances and current savings, works of this magnitude and character which, in other countries, would ordinarily be constructed from borrowed funds' (*Speeches*, 1917, 263).

Observing the extraordinary development in the generation of hydro-electric power, Chandrasekhar (1940) listed the mighty irrigation schemes, the vast hydro-electricity undertakings, both generation and distribution, the major iron and steel works, the large sugar factory, the railway network in addition to the vast amount of shares in semi-private industrial undertakings, as the properties of the state and the assets of the people (81) and acclaimed Mysore not merely a technician's paradise but a vast experiment in state socialism. Other prominent industries wholly state-owned, partially owned and purely private seemed to gradually develop in the state. These include Mysore Industrial and Testing Laboratary (1931), Amco Batteries Ltd. (1934), Mysore Lamp Works (1936), Mysore Tobacco Company (1938), Mysore Stoneware Pipes and Potteries Ltd. (1938), Mysore Vegetable Oil Products (1938) and Mysore Glass and Enamel Works Limited. In addition to Kolar Gold Mines which became government owned, other prominent undertakings were Government Porcelain Factory, Government Soap Factory and Government Electric Factory adding to the existing portfolio in spun silk, sandalwood, sugar and paper.

Large private sector establishments in textiles included Bangalore Woollen, Silk and Cotton (Binny's), Minerva, Lakshmi and Swastik in Bangalore, Davangere Woollen and Textiles, Krishnarajendra Mills in Mysore, and large industrial enterprises such as REMCO, MICO and Kirloskars. Despite the growth of private sector industries, the state continued to play a prominent role until the 1990s (Heitzman 2004, Nair 2005). It was this promising industrial base that led the central government to set up major public undertakings following independence.

While this sounds like a comprehensive tribute to the successful role of the state in the economy, the issue has been and remains debatable if not controversial today (see Chapter 3). However, in the Mysore of the early twentieth century, as the state remained the only major source of capital, as well as expertise, it adopted a pragmatic policy of industrialisation. The government deemed it necessary to exercise monopoly control over certain industries such as generation and distribution of power and that of public utilities and special resources such as sandalwood. In areas where the private sector was capable of taking initiative, the government worked in partnership either by managing or holding some share in such undertakings. To assist the private sector, the government developed hydro-electrical power and built a transmission line over ninety-two miles to provide it for the Kolar Gold Mining Company. Likewise, the Bank of Mysore popularly known as Mysore Bank provided capital to entrepreneurs.

While paying glowing tributes to the contribution of Sir M. Visvesvaraya in the development of irrigation, power and industries in Mysore, Sir Mirza Ismail countered critics thus: '... here in India, where private enterprise is proverbially unenterprising and private capital notoriously shy, governments have perforce to take more active industrial promotional interest in the problems of trade and industry than by merely passing legislative measures regulating the hours of work here or amending the company law there. Indeed in the peculiar circumstances prevailing in this country, a certain amount of state socialism is necessary if the pace of industrialisation is to be accelerated' (Ismail 1954, 34).

The broad-based nature of industrial development almost led to a point when Mysoreans could talk of various products that they had become accustomed to and regard them virtually as 'entitlements' (Sen 1984). In this vein, Sir Mirza Ismail exhorted Mysoreans to 'wash themselves with Mysore soap, dry themselves with Mysore towels, clothe themselves in Mysore silks, ride Mysore horses, eat the abundant Mysore food, drink Mysore coffee with Mysore sugar, equip their houses with Mysore furniture, light them with Mysore lamps and write their letters on Mysore paper' (1954, 38).

Of the major policies that emerged from the Economic Conference, a significant role in industrial development of the state was played by the Mysore Bank. Referring to the initiative taken by the Economic Conference in 1911 to establish a state-aided bank, the Dewan in his address to the Representative Assembly informed members that the bank had been open for business as of 2 October 1913 (Visvesvaraya's *Speeches*, 1917, 106). The Bank of Mysore operated as an independent institution and the state government, while instrumental in its establishment, did not have any share in its capital nor any interest in its financial operations. However, to ensure that the bank operated on sound lines, the government required that the appointment of the General Manager be submitted to it for approval. The Bank financed trade and commerce in a big way and rendered signal service in promoting the economic and social development of the state.

7.9 Conclusion

Although it is difficult to establish any direct links to the present-day success of Karnataka (old state of Mysore) in IT, this account of the historical foundations of the development of Mysore during the reign of Sri Krishnaraja Wadeyar helps to explain the region's current position as India's IT capital and offers some clues as to why it is favoured by multinational investors.

Under its benevolent monarchy and farsighted dewans, Mysore in the early twentieth century was generally regarded as progressive and, was, in fact, a pioneer in many areas. Its many innovative policies and, in particular, its industrial policies of state intervention accelerated its economic development.

Historically, the state was renowned for its political institutions, its novel methods in enlisting support for new ventures through the Economic Conference, its openness to outsiders with talent (a feature that is present even today), its cosmopolitan character and its pride in the positive cultural aspects of its past, encouraging all religions, faiths and cultures to co-exist in harmony. The state was a pioneer in compulsory primary education and early childhood education, unknown in most parts of the world until then. It set up schools for the physically impaired, advanced mental health facilities, a family planning clinic, child welfare centres, municipal dispensaries, medical examination of school students, broadcasting and compulsory insurance for public employees.

Independence in 1947 brought with it further opportunities for a state with such a solid industrial foundation and a culture of openness and enterprise which had been nurtured by those in power. Research and industry flourished during the period 1950–80. The 1980s saw the generation of multiple resources and skills within the region resulting from central government investments and that, combined with the state's positive policies and generous incentives, accelerated the development of high technology contributing to the ICT boom that one sees in the region today.

8

Bangalore—Software Capital of India

8.1 Introduction

In the 1990s, ICT emerged as an important field for exports from India. This sudden growth, particularly that of computer software in Bangalore, led commentators to refer to the region as the 'Silicon Plateau' (Saxenian 2002). In the previous chapter, I have traced the pre-Independence historical and technological legacies of the region and the development of the region's potential following Independence, first through central government investment and later through state government policies which encouraged domestic and multinational investment. In recent years, the region's high-quality human resources, its renowned S&T infrastructure, its thriving engineering industries, the impact of ISRO, C-DAC, C-DOT and the IISc and Bangalore's open and cosmopolitan culture have together contributed towards its development into a knowledge-based economy. This has encouraged scholarly interest in the region's development resulting in several major studies (ILO 1998, Heitzman 2004, Nair 2005, Hamm 2006).

This study adopts an institutional comparative political economy approach to explore the configuration of various public, semi-public and private organisations involved in Bangalore's transformation into India's software capital and attempts to understand the political and socio-economic relationships in the development of ICT in India, and Bangalore in particular. The basic foundation for industrial transformation was laid by harnessing the natural resources of the region and establishing an institutional foundation for education in engineering and technological research (see Chapter 7). Those early advantages were further consolidated after Independence with central government investment in S&T and expenditure on defence establishments and public undertakings (see Chapters 2 and 3).

In Section 8.2, I examine some unique characteristics of the region. Section 8.3 analyses the role of the state government in promoting information technology in the region. Section 8.4 discusses the growth of second tier destinations in an attempt to overcome congestion in Bangalore; Section 8.5 examines factors that have facilitated the development of IT and Section 8.6 examines why Bangalore is the centre of IT. Section 8.7 discusses investment in research and training and Section 8.8, the growth of software companies in Bangalore, followed by a conclusion.

8.2 The Mysore Region

Bangalore, the unofficial software capital of India, is the political capital of Karnataka state. Karnataka was formed in 1956 with state reorganisation following demands to restructure state boundaries on a linguistic basis. When the country's state boundaries were redrawn, Mysore state acquired Kannada-speaking regions from Bombay, Madras and Hyderabad and the centrally administered territory of Coorg. Known in earlier years as India's garden city, Bangalore, with its well laid out roads and salubrious climate, was seen by many Indians as an ideal place to raise their families as well as to settle in following retirement. Its climatic conditions had, in the nineteenth century, led to its popularity with the British, who set up a cantonment there to house its military establishment. In line with other states which changed place names to Chennai (for Madras), Kolkata (Calcutta) and Mumbai (Bombay), among others, in November 2006 a coalition government constituting two populist groups in the legislature succumbed to sectional pressures to adopt the vernacular version *'Bengaluru'*. I have preferred to use 'Bangalore' in this study (see Nair 2005).

Its dust free environment and its mild weather owing to its elevation (980 metres) and more importantly the availability of highly skilled engineers attracted Texas Instruments, which, in 1986, established a design centre for computer-aided chips (Dore 1989).

Dubbed by Holmstrom as India's Cheltenham (the English town of that name in Gloucestershire is a health and holiday spa resort), this once sleepy garrison town and pensioner's paradise, has, according to him, now acquired the image of India's industrial success story, being the leading contender for the title of India's Silicon Valley (Cadene and Holmstrom 1998, 169–229, see Section 8.6). Bangalore's many central government undertakings and national research institutes attract world-class professionals giving it a cosmopolitan character. For the younger set, there is the appeal of the city's pub culture. '...Bangalore is the locus for the semi-serious BAIT (Beer Drinkers Association of Information Technology) which regularly brings together senior IT industry managers to discuss strategy, on the condition that they drink a minimum of six mugs of beer during the evening' (Heeks 1996, 104). Quality of life is certainly an important factor when decisions on location are made for a knowledge-based industry in which 'entrepreneurs and managers belong or aspire to belong to a culture which is consciously modern, meritocratic, cosmopolitan, used to foreign travel, entertaining each other in fine restaurants for which Bangalore is justly famous. These are settings in which ideas are exchanged,... business contacts and friendships formed' (Cadene and Holmstrom 1998, 203).

8.3 Role of Government

In identifying factors that influence decisions on the location of software companies, Heeks (1996) cites labour availability, infrastructure, proximity to customers, proximity to previous employer and residence and quality of life. However, a crucial factor that he overlooks is the role of government policy (91). More specific studies of Bangalore's software industry (ILO 1998, Venkatesan and Malvea in Yue and Lim eds. 2003, Heitzman 2004, Nair 2005) clearly identify that role, and this study certainly endorses the notion that state intervention is vital to the industrial transformation of TW countries. In tracing the development of Bangalore into a metropolis, Nair (2005) demonstrates that Bangalore pursued a path that differed from the older cities of Calcutta and Bombay and predicts that it may indeed be the city of the future. This is reflected in the way the city has grown. In 1941, it covered an area of sixty-six sq km with a population of 410,967. Sixty years later, in 2001, the city had extended to 531 sq km with a population of 5,686,844 (ibid., 79).

Government is a crucial segment of the triple helix and is vital to a knowledge-based economy. Yet another factor that is crucial in encouraging investments in high-tech industries is the relationship between the state government and the private sector, which, in Karnataka, has been both stable and consistent. Following the choice of Bangalore by Texas Instruments, which attracted the attention of other foreign investors, too, the state government proceeded to develop Bangalore as a software industrial centre via its 'Package of Incentives and Concessions for New Industrial Investments in Karnataka 1993–1998' (*The Hindu*, 26 January 2003).

Although not directly linked to the dramatic growth of ICT of the 1990s in Bangalore, the foundations for that growth had been laid by government as early as the beginning of the last century. Building on the strong S&T base that had evolved through the IISc and various engineering colleges, Bangalore developed into a centre of high-tech industries in the post-Independence era, moving to a higher plane with the establishment of C-DOT, C-DAC and ISRO (see Chapter 6). Further growth followed in 1976 when the Karnataka state government sought to promote the electronics industry with the establishment of the Karnataka Electronics Development Corporation (KEONICS).

Initially, the main objective of KEONICS was to promote the electronics industry which it did by launching into production ventures, joint or otherwise, for the manufacture of TV sets. The move into development work came later with the establishment of Electronics City. Although its entry into the manufacture of TV sets turned out to be a disaster, its joint ventures with M/s Krone Communications Limited and Yokogana Blue Star Limited continue to perform well (*Vijaya Times*, 21 July 2004). However, its uncertain performance has on occasion attracted threats of possible closure by government. Undaunted, KEONICS has followed other options and appears since 2000 to have turned the corner by redirecting its focus to computer training and consultancy services. Its other contracts include the establishment of technical collaboration with Tata Telecom for the production of EPABX-500 plus exchange for the defence sector and with CMS technologies for the production of road traffic signals (KEONICS, *Annual Report*, 2002–2003).

KEONICS's major contribution to Bangalore's IT industry is Electronics City, an industrial park which attracts IT entrepreneurs by offering land developed for this purpose and concessions such as subsidies on fixed assets, term loans and working capital. Acknowledgement of KEONICS's contribution to Bangalore's current status as the centre of Indian electronics industry came when DOE set up STPIs as an autonomous agency of the Government of India at Electronics City, offering communications and infrastructure facilities to software companies (see Chapter 6).

As STPI's major centre, the Bangalore unit located at Electronics City provides quality services to 1322 companies registered under it, a 45 per cent increase from 2002–2003. Approximately 200 IT buildings in the city are connected through microwave or territorial links with its international gateway, an integrated Network Operations Centre (NOC), rendering Bangalore the largest data communication network in the country (STPI *Evolve: Stay Connected,* 2004). According to B. V. Naidu of STPI-Bangalore, growth of foreign investments in IT in Bangalore has averaged four companies a week in 2002. Of the new IT companies starting business in Bangalore between March and September 2002, fifty-six were 100 per cent foreign equity firms bringing in investment of Rs 1125 crores while twenty-three were business process outsourcing companies. In 2003, 168 software exporting companies and five new electronic hardware exporting companies registered with STPI. In 2004, there were almost 230 multinationals, some with development centres, operating in Bangalore (Kripalani 2002). Of these, the majority are Fortune 500, and 60 per cent of these are 'SEI level 5' certified companies, making Bangalore a quality hub for the IT world. With the intention of spreading IT to other parts of the state, STPI has established earth stations at Manipal and Mysore and has plans to set up one at Hubli. An Export-Promotion Industrial Park has also been set up by the government at Bangalore, exclusively for export-oriented industries.

Facilities provided by STPI-Bangalore boosted Karnataka's software exports in 2005–06 over $8.5 billion or Rs 37,600 crores, from Rs 27,600 crores a year back. Mr Naidu of STPI claims that, despite Bangalore's infrastructure hassles, Karnataka with 1,600 IT companies heads the list in software exports, accounting for 36 per cent of the country's exports which stood at $23 billion in 2005–06, with Karnataka's export growth being above the national average of 30 per cent. Hardware exports for 2005–06 jumped by 40 per cent to Rs 2,481 crores from Rs 1,768 crores a year earlier. There were 201 new software units and the employment of seventy thousand people in IT, ITES and BPO sectors during that year (as against 198 units in 2004–05) (*The Hindu,* 4 May 2006). The NASSCOM–Mckinsey Report 2005 estimated a 25 per cent annual growth from this sector in Karnataka with exports reaching $18 billion by 2010.

The global economic recession has had an effect on IT exports in Karnataka with the growth rate declining from 24 per cent in 2007–08 to 15 per cent in 2008–09. The state accounts for almost a third of India's IT exports. In the three years commencing from 2005–06, IT exports from the state increased by 34 per cent, 28 per cent and 24 per cent, respectively. The downward trend was attributed by the Secretary to the Department of IT, Karnataka government, to the recession. To cope with this pressure, IT companies have shifted their focus from the US to Asian markets and are exploring opportunities in e-governance projects in Union and state governments (*The Hindu*, 24 June 2009).

At the Confederation of Indian Industry summit in January 2007, the focus was on Bangalore's software industry, considered the fourth largest technology cluster in the world, after Silicon Valley, Boston and London. Its rapid expansion (*The Hindu*, 21 January 2007) and apparently unstoppable growth are causing concern especially with regard to future shortages of human resources to support the software sector. Of the nine lakh people who work in the Indian software sector, three lakhs work in Karnataka. Estimating India's requirement at 2.5 million and Karnataka's at one million, the Executive Director of STPI estimates that there will be a shortfall of at least half a million by 2010 (*The Hindu*, 19 March 006). To pre-empt the impending shortage of talent, the McKinsey Quarterly 2005 advocates improving the quality up to the level required by multinationals, adding that 'policymakers can play an important part in raising standards by framing curricula that reflect current and future demand in employment' (Farrel et al., *Deccan Herald*, 3 October 2005).

Significant areas of growth are call centres (that respond to customers seeking information or making complaints), medical transcription centres and Business Process Outsourcing (BPO) centres (which outsource business via the Internet). Such work is growing at the rate of 50 per cent annually and is likely to have grown to $25 billion by 2008 (*The Age*, 12 July 2003). While call centre work pays well, it does involve shifts around the clock and is generally unexciting. The next level up is the BPO area. However, BPO firms in Bangalore face the threat of losing close to 25 per cent of annual revenue owing to employee attrition caused by dissatisfaction with existing management practices or poaching by other firms. To remedy this, companies such as America Online (AOL), which employs 1500 at its facility located at the International Technology Park near Whitefield, provide opportunities for training and development. Wipro, Infosys and TCS send their employees for training to their clients' offices, giving them the opportunity to travel, learn and meet other social needs. Other inducements include leasing flats to staff at low rents, attractive housing schemes, low interest loans, quality cafeterias, transport facilities and scholarships to undertake further studies.

At a recent conference of BPO firms held at Bangalore to discuss trends and developments in the sector, a major concern expressed was the transition currently occurring from BPO to KPO (Knowledge Process Outsourcing) caused by the negative perception of BPO. Delegates spoke of the need to address the image of BPO as mere telephonic communication with international clients in acquired accents at odd times. This negative view of the industry has resulted in BPO being seen as short-term employment at best and not a career option (*Times Ascent*, 7 December 2005). While BPO employment offers attractive salaries, 'employees cease to be social beings and often get isolated from their families and friends. BOSS—the Burn-Out Stress Syndrome—is a common condition among BPO employees and includes chronic fatigue and insomnia due to the alteration of the twenty-four-hour biological rhythm of the body' (*The Hindu*, 10 January 2006).

Marshallian 'knowledge spillovers' or localised external effects arising from agglomeration of economic activities are basically a recognition of the role of the triple helix (firms, universities and research institutes, and technology parks) and its contribution to regional development. However, a key factor in regional innovation and growth is the presence of social capital, which basically is 'the expression of norms of reciprocity and trust between individuals and organisations that are embedded in a system of cooperation' (Cooke 2002).

In 1997, Karnataka became the first state to announce a Millennium IT policy. Its objectives were:

- to utilise the power of IT to eradicate poverty and empower women;
- to reduce unemployment by absorbing educated youth into the IT industry;
- to establish 225 training centres all over the state to train educated unemployed youth in IT skills;
- to promote the usage of Kannada in IT;
- to use e-governance as a tool and deliver a government which is proactive and responsive to its citizens;

- to unleash Karnataka's engine of incubation by opening up to other multinationals who had applied for international patents;
- to encourage business with countries where English is not the principal language—links have since been established with Denmark, France, Germany, Italy, Israel, Japan and the Netherlands; and
- to maintain Bangalore's and Karnataka's pre-eminent position in the field of IT as well to maintain the former's rating among the top ten technical cities in the world.

Since March 2000, IT in Karnataka has been taxed at the lowest level in India—0.25 per cent on computers and computer peripherals. A 4 per cent work contract tax on annual maintenance contract on hardware has been waived. Firms have been given a five-year exemption from purchase tax on computer hardware, peripherals and other capital goods including captive power generators and a ten-year exemption from sales tax. Those using captive generator sets enjoy exemption from payment of electricity tax and sales tax on fuel and generators.

Other components of government policy include:

- the hosting of the annual IT Com at Bangalore, one of the largest software conventions,
- support for CLICKTRONICA, the annual hardware event,
- the setting up of a venture capital fund of Rs 30 crores, and
- the establishment of the IIIT at Bangalore in 1999 (IIIT-B) based on public-private partnership.

The annual IT Com offers Indian and international software companies a venue to display their products, to exchange information and to develop business contacts. Highly reputed in the IT field, such renown has been gained in a short time and is revealed by the extent of interest shown by well-known companies for whom participation at the event has become a part of the software business calendar.

The electronic and hardware version of IT Com is CLICKTRONICA which participates in international exhibitions, promotes exports and publishes the magazine *CLIKNET*. CLIK, the Consortium of Electronic Industries in Karnataka, established in 1982 with 250 members to promote the electronics industry, has set itself the following goals:

- to produce $160 billion worth of hardware by 2008 to meet the software target of $87 billion,

- to generate 1.2 million employment opportunities by 2010,
- to direct its research towards finding uniquely Indian solutions for India's problems, and
- to keep up the focus on hardware to ensure continued competitiveness in IT (*The Hindu,* 4 August 2005).

STPI was instrumental in assisting the state government of Karnataka in developing 'Khajane', a software e-governance program for the Treasury. The first of its kind in the country, Khajane was the culmination of the search for a Treasury Management System and was introduced in 2003. It computerises all twenty-six district and sub-treasuries in the state, linking them to a central server through V-SAT. 'Thanks to "Khajane", systemic deficiencies have been eliminated and speedy disposal of claims has become a reality... there is better budget monitoring and cash management ... and there is greater transparency of transactions' (*The Hindu,* 15 February 2006). Its successful operation earned an award for exemplary initiatives in e-governance from the Department of Administrative Reforms and Public Grievances of the Government of India. It also received the Silver Icon in the 'Outstanding performance in service delivery—professional category' at the National Conference on e-Governance held at Kochi in February 2006 (ibid.). *Bhoomi,* a system developed to provide information to land owners and acclaimed by the World Bank, has been discussed in Chapter 6. Other developments include the computerisation of the state's road transport corporation and the development of an IT Backbone by connecting 140 of the 175 taluks with fibre optic network.

The close association of the IT industry with the Karnataka government seen by analysts as a shift from predominantly state-directed industrial development towards a more private sector-directed development became pronounced with the elevation of S. M. Krishna, a friend of N. R. Narayana Murthy (then CEO of Infosys Technologies) and of the IT sector, as Chief Minister in 1999. At the Bangalore Summit of 24 January at which many new plans for the city were unveiled, Nair observed that '... the corporates were in command: the elected coporators, all of whom showed up, were mere witnesses to the spectacle of power' (Nair 2005, 123). That relationship was also highlighted at the inauguration of the Indian Institute of Information Technology–B campus, when Narayana Murthy commended Karnataka's business friendly bureaucrats for their significant role in promoting IT in the state. IIIT-B, a joint venture between the state government and some MNCs, offers a broad-based education at master's and doctoral levels in computers, communication and related technologies. Innovative features at this institute include a 'think tank' and a focus on entrepreneurship (Naidu in Jasswalla and Taylor 2003, 126–27). To keep abreast of both growth and the increasing complexity of ICT, the Indian government has set up a further six Institutes of Information Technology. A beneficial outcome of government policy is the standardising of the IT syllabus in the state's engineering colleges, rendering Karnataka the first state to have a separate IT syllabus.

Karnataka encourages IT enterprises with a range of venture capital for start-ups. Apart from the state-promoted venture fund of Rs 30 crores (KITVEN), financial assistance is also available from Karnataka State Industrial Investment and Development Corporation, Karnataka State Financial Corporation and several private sector venture capital agencies (see Section 8.4.3).

In 1997, Karnataka set up another pioneering venture—the International Technology Park Limited (ITPL). Established with an investment of $665 million comprising 40 per cent from Tata, 40 per cent from a consortium of Singapore companies and 20 per cent from KIADB, the IT Park, situated on 1.2 million sq ft near Whitefield, is the largest in the country, possessing world-class facilities. Three massive glass buildings named Creator, Innovator and Discoverer accommodate 928 software companies which are involved in integrated circuit design, communication software and related areas. Similar parks have been set up at Bangalore, Mysore, Mangalore and Gulbarga. The 288-acre Export Promotion International Park located near ITPL exclusively for export-oriented industries has been provided with dedicated water, electricity and communication facilities. General Electric's development centre located there is staffed by over seven hundred scientists in multidisciplinary technological development activities. Another large joint venture project is the Carnegie Centre for Software Engineering established by the Karnataka government with Carnegie Global Technologies Inc, the Indian Institute of Science and LG.

Software India Limited offered services in consulting, training and education in the entire Asia-Pacific region (Naidu in Jasswalla and Taylor 2003). The knowledge corridor covering an area of 12,000 acres between Electronics City on Hosur Road and the Information Technology Park near Whitefield was to be serviced by an eight-lane highway and world-class infrastructure at a cost of Rs 4000 crores (*The Hindu*, 20 February 2004).

Bangalore's success in attracting high-tech investments can be attributed to the stable relationship between the state government and the private sector. Despite changes in government, industry policy has remained fairly consistent. 'Industry leaders have come to expect that any changes vis–à–vis industry would be planned and could be anticipated' (ILO 1998, 3). Efforts by the Karnataka government to spread IT to other parts of the state include the setting up of training centres with assistance from NIIT and Aptech in smaller towns and government-run schools and providing internet access points in rural areas (Zaheer and Rajan 2003, 207).

Following close on Bangalore's heels, some Mysore companies have developed software with distinctive features. The thirty-two IT companies registered with STPI were poised to export software worth Rs 500 crores during 2005–2006. With wireless fidelity (Wi-Fi) covering the entire city, Mysore, spread over 138 square kms, was the first city in the country and among the few in the world to become wireless Internet-enabled ('Mysore gets WiFi for wireless Internet access', *The Hindu*, 15 October 2004).

In February 2005, Mysore received a tremendous boost with the inauguration of the Infosys Leadership Institute (ILI) with a proposed annual intake of 400. Built on 700 acres of land on the outskirts of Mysore, the Institute adjoins Infosys Global Education Centre which will train engineering graduates. Considered to be the largest such centre in the world, it includes an education research block, a food court, an employee care centre and hostel accommodation. With Bangalore facing infrastructure-related problems, Mysore is set to become the next best destination for multinational companies (*The Hindu*, 13 October 2004). Wipro announced the setting up of a state-of-the-art Global Service Management Centre (GSMC) at Mysore 'to provide integrated remote service delivery across applications and infrastructure for its clients in India, West Asia and Asia Pacific' (*The Hindu*, 17 March 2006).

At the opening of the mega IT complex Software Paradigm India (SPI) City, Mr Naidu, head of STPI, spoke of the need to bring Mysore and Bangalore 'closer' by improving the connectivity between the two. At the same occasion, Mr Shankarlinge Gowda, Secretary, Department of Information Technology, announced that the government had approved IT projects worth Rs 2,000 crores to be set up in Mysore under a single–window agency which will eventually employ 40,000 people. In addition to many Bangalore-based firms which intend to establish operations at Mysore, several MNCs have also set their sights on Mysore.

The unplanned growth of industries in Bangalore has placed unprecedented demands on the region's physical infrastructure. If these problems are not handled properly with appropriate planning, Bangalore, which is already under pressure for water, power and transport, is likely to break down. Heitzman in a lecture to Citizens Voluntary Initiative for the City (CIVIC) in Bangalore warned his listeners on the dangerous pattern of urban development, i.e., becoming a Silicon Valley 'may only be a product of imagination about the city and may encourage a dangerous pattern of urban development (*The Hindu,* 5 January 2004).

While Bangalore has apparently replaced Mumbai as an industrial centre (Heeks 1996), the Karnataka government has failed to keep pace with the development of infrastructure. Economic agglomeration certainly has advantages for the development of industry, but city planners have not anticipated the transportation congestion, environmental pollution and housing shortages that have occurred (Heitzman 2004, Nair 2005). Bangalore's airport designed for the 1950s and 1960s was experiencing serious congestion problems, receiving about 2.45 lakh passengers arriving on 4200 aircraft each month. A new international airport constructed at Devanhalli twenty-five kilometres from the city opened for operations in early 2008. The long-overdue Bangalore Metro Rail project, patterned on Delhi's metro rail and intended to facilitate movement of daily commuters and reduce the multitude of two and three-wheelers, is expected to be completed by 2012.

The fear that Bangalore could become another 'mega city slum' is very real. In recent years, the attraction of the IT scene in Bangalore has been such that it has drawn an estimated 1.8 million young people to the city. While the migration to the city is depleting the hinterland, Bangalore appears to be bursting at the seams (*Deccan Herald,* 23 March 2003). To overcome the effects of clustering of ICT companies in Bangalore, the Karnataka government has adopted a regional strategy by extending the industry to second-tier cities like Mysore and Mangalore. STPI has set up earth stations at Mysore, Manipal and

Mangalore to provide facilities to the software companies that have set up development centres. NASSCOM's suggestion that integrated knowledge townships be set up on the lines of those set up for the manufacturing sector in the 1950s is worthy of consideration (*The Hindu*, 19 May 2006). For a comparison of Bangalore's response to the growth of industries in the 1950s, which was the establishment of planned industrial colonies (townships), to the sporadic growth of software enterprises, which is 'occurring within enclaves across the city, spilling beyond the designated IT corridor', see Nair 2005 (92).

Between the various perceptions of the city ranging from 'the pensioners' paradise' to the city of the future, the risks and uncertainties have contributed to an environment of growing schism between privilege and the lack of it. The emergence in the 1980s of various social and language *sanghas* (groups like Rajkumar Abhimanigala, Kannada Ranadherra Padhe, etc.) reflected the growing resentment against immigrants, particularly those from Tamil Nadu and was aggravated by the long-standing Cauvery water dispute and Tamil assertiveness. Such mobilisation on parochial issues while being disruptive and, in some cases dangerous to life and property, is a strong indication 'of democratic order asserting itself in very visual ways, and the conflicts a sign of the lack of consensus among the citizens' (Nair 2005, 272–3). 'Political interventions may be the only available recourse for large sections of urban society who cannot participate in the visions of "silicon valleys" and "biotech capitals", and who are ill served by both the legal machinery and the processes of policy making' (ibid., 344).

A case in point is the student agitation against the re-allocation of land belonging to the University of Agricultural Sciences GKVK campus to the development of a biotech park which was intended to help develop links between that campus and the IISc and simulate conditions as at Stanford University and the University of California. Although the 'critical mass'(Ramesh Hariharan of Strand Genomics in Nair 2005, 341) for the successful outcome of such a venture does not exist in that area, a development such as this would have been beneficial to the students themselves in the long run. However, government was forced to drop the project and have it shifted to the IT corridor instead.

While this is certainly not the image that the government and the IT sector want to project to the outside world, such occurrences are a reflection of 'the growing pains' incurred in the passage from a mere city to a metropolis. The model visualised by the term 'Silicon Valley' is based on the concept of a highly advanced information society and is clearly not the situation in India as it fails to take into consideration relevant ecology and economic distribution. According to Heitzman, this image of Bangalore as the new Silicon Valley was projected by US business and government, and unconsciously adopted by Indians. 'Thus Silicon Valley became the dream of the technologists in Bangalore as it had become the dream of technologists throughout the world' (ibid., 211). While Saxenian (2003, 2006) and Kogut (2003) view Bangalore as the 'Silicon Plateau', Heitzman (2004) holds a different view, suggesting that the Karnataka government has used the Silicon Valley image as a game of regional advantage with competitors at a global level as well as within India (201). He portrays it as an image projected by US business and government and unconsciously adopted by India; an image that has remained at an intellectual level, containing nothing of substance, used as 'a brand name, a marketing logo in the promotion of which the state allied with private interests to promote a new identity for a garden city that, unfortunately, had lost many of its gardens' (211). Bangalore, he concludes, 'has been living on its dreams. In its modernist vision of the industrial city and the science city, the future lies in research, development, applied technology and planning' (ibid., 212).

Saxenian (2002) who initiated the use of that image however feels that comparisons with Silicon Valley are misleading as they give the impression that Bangalore should replicate the US model (see Section 8.5.2 for connection between Bangalore and Silicon Valley). Evidence suggests you need not create a Silicon Valley in Bangalore but you should gain insights into its working to evolve an indigenous version appropriate to Bangalore's economy (see Mascarenhas 1988 to understand how the 'Anand Model' of a dairy cooperative was replicated in Karnataka). On the contrary, as the origins of IT and the infrastructure at the two places vary, Bangalore, she feels should follow its own path of development and cites the example of the Simputer (189), a product designed for the Indian market which could be viewed as an important model for replication across India. 'It is low cost, applies leading edge technologies. It is based on free software (the Linux operating system), designed to be open and modular, and it offers multiple connectivity options. It also includes a smart card and reader/writer which provides a delivery vehicle for financial transactions on the Internet and for e-commerce' (87).

The new economy, which evolved as a result of the development of the Internet and globalisation 'was also marked by the transport of an economic model, often called the 'Silicon Valley' model, to countries that had long been shown by researchers as inhospitable to these institutions' (Kogut 2003, x). Different economies, including India, 'a classic dual economy', were challenged in different ways as compared to the US which is distinctive because of the role played by Silicon Valley. The Silicon Valley model is supported by institutions/situations such as (1) venture capital, (2) equity markets, (3) a fluid labour market for global talent, (4) fiscal policies that lower the costs of starting and operating business, and (5) proximity of university and research institutes within a region. While Kogut admits that the above model underestimates the influence of government, military and industrial policies, Leslie Stuart (2001) went so far as to say that the US government is the '... biggest Angel of all' where an angel refers to initial investors backing an entrepreneur. '... More importantly, a list of institutions distracts from the arenas of discourse and coordination that are embedded in social and professional communities. Whether we call this a network, or social capital, a community of practices, or simply connections, the business transaction is a strand within a greater social fabric' (5–6).

Comparisons with Silicon Valley filter down to difficulties of replication. 'Spreading practices is not easy, and spreading practices is the key to spreading actionable knowledge' (Brown and Diguid 2000, 23). Acknowledging the difficulties in replicating Silicon Valley, Brown and Diguid explain that such 'knowledge ecosystems develop over time, building connections between participants until they reach a critical mass and take on a collective dynamic all their own.... Our point, rather, is that these collective competencies are grown organically, not simply implemented mechanically... because local factors (culture, institutional forms) contribute critically to localisation, it's a mistake to imitate established ones' (ibid., 38).

Similarly, Dossani and Kenney, while discussing the prospect of developing venture capital acknowledge the difficulties of cross-national transfer of institutions (2002). While 'Bangalore is the "one region in India that could have encouraged the development and the production of specialized software", the overwhelming dependence of the industry on the global, rather than the domestic market and the fundamental "lack of domain specific knowledge" set limits to the visions of Bangalore as a "silicon valley"' (Balaji Parthasarathy in Nair 2005, 341).

Efforts by the S. M. Krishna government to project Bangalore as a 'city state' on the lines of Singapore (or San Jose, 'capital of Silicon Valley') by funding major projects were essentially in keeping with Mysorean tradition. However, according to Nair (2005), there was a significant difference. 'Such policies come not at a time when the market needs to be coaxed into playing a determining role in industrial and city development, but when it has already gained dominance. At no previous stage in the economic history of the city has industry aspired to redefine the image of the city, manage its services, and streamline its finances with as much confidence as the captains of the new economy, represented by BATF [Bangalore Agenda Task Force] and its subsidiary Janaagraha' (334).

BATF, a private-public partnership led by the CEO of Infosys, N. R. Narayana Murthy, was set up in 1999 to address the problems caused by Bangalore's extraordinary growth. With the support of Chief Minister Krishna, and local businesses and professionals, BATF took an interest in development schemes and attempted to resolve a wide range of problems covering traffic congestion, roads, bus shelters, solid-waste management, public health and sanitation and property taxes. 'Civic entrepreneurs', as Cooke (2002) terms them, can be effective catalysts in the creation of a regional economy and in building constructive community relationships (102). However, Nair describes their civic interests as middle class. 'Roads, rather than public transport; garbage and pollution, rather than public housing; mosquitoes and public toilets, rather than public health' (2005, 336). For other sections of the community, the priorities were 'job opportunities in poor neighbourhoods, and an overwhelming anxiety to claim citizenship and voting rights by getting on to the voters list' and, of course, the availability of water (ibid.). However, BATF was unable to inculcate any discipline in the construction area. 'Perhaps nothing emphasizes the triumph of unbridled market forces as clearly as the impunity with which telephone and cable companies have scarred Bangalore's road surfaces' (ibid., 339). Such blatant disregard is, in my opinion, a broader symptom of growing corporate arrogance previously unknown to this region.

The corporate sector which gained ascendancy through its access to the corridors of power shows little concern for ordinary citizens. While its young employees receive salaries that are not available to employees in other sectors, the former indulge in conspicuous consumption in a city known for its sobriety. *The Economist* (3 January 2004) commented, 'Bangalore, known as the hub of India's information technology industry, also claims to be the capital of its pub culture. The two boasts, of course, are linked. The explosion of the IT business and its offshoots has helped to produce a new breed of young professionals with money in their pockets and their own ideas of how to spend it. Imported malt whisky at 500 rupees ($11) a shot—about what an agricultural labourer earns in a week—is one option'. Described by Suhel Seth as 'yuppification', today's IT professionals positively relish conspicuous consumption and certainly do not share the qualms felt by their parents, who were brought up in a climate that mixed Nehruvian socialism with ancient Hindu ideals of renunciation. 'Rolex', says Mr Seth, with his profession's knack for pithy hyperbole, 'has replaced religion' (ibid., 17). Unfortunately, this culture has spread to less affluent sections of the community, who tend to purchase modern conveniences while borrowing to the hilt.

Following the defeat of Krishna, which was seen as a rejection of his government's IT and urban-centred policies, BATF lost its momentum. When the brief term of the next Congress party-led coalition government ended in 2006, it was replaced by the Janata Dal (Secular)–BJP coalition which set up eight Special Economic Zones (SEZs) with a budget of Rs 27,000 crores for the purpose of promoting IT and other areas (*The Hindu*, 25 March 2006). However, the activity of the SEZs has not been without contention. A case in point is the incorporation of the successful Ittasandra Producers Cooperative Society into an SEZ.

With this change in the political environment, the cosy relationship between the IT sector and the government was replaced with a businesslike relationship. This however did not discourage the industry from continuing to seek incentives and concessions to which they had got accustomed over the past two decades. Further, there was the suggestion that the state, while reducing its regulatory role in urban areas and encouraging private investment in schools, housing and fibre optic cable installations, should attempt to delink the rural from the urban and free the city 'from the preoccupation and problems of the Indian village' (Nair 2005, 338).

Two recent studies of Bangalore reveal different perspectives. While Heitzman (2004) claims that the IT sector is not as significant as it is made out to be, claiming that the textile sector has a larger workforce, Nair (2005) attributes Bangalore's growth to the IT and IT-enabled industries. Contrasting this with the growth of public sector industries of the 1970s in planned enclaves on the outskirts of the city, she analyses the city's development in three phases with each phase corresponding to changes in the role of the state and concluding that the current phase has shifted the 'affairs of the city in favour of the corporate sector from an otherwise strong public sector role' (123).

8.4 Why Bangalore is The Centre of Information Technology

Being a knowledge-based undertaking, IT relies for its success on an appropriate configuration of supportive political, economic, scientific and technological institutions. Apart from public policies which have already been discussed (see Chapters 4 and 5, and Section 8.3), the two other segments essential to its development are the S&T infrastructure vital for the generation of new ideas and innovative techniques, and the availability of skilled and trained people. Within the global economy, the recognition of Bangalore as a source of high-quality design capability has facilitated the transmission by multinational corporations (MNCs) of firm-based knowledge. Such regional focus has increased as companies move particular production processes rather than entire firms, explaining why regions retain their importance in a global economy. While regional knowledge is generally tied to place and context, today's centres of innovation are no longer based entirely on natural endowments or large factories, but rely more on the linkage between university research and development, entrepreneurship and venture capital. 'It is networks of knowledge and people-—the creative connections, so to speak—that ... (are) the motor force of regional economic growth' (Florida 2005, 163).

In attempting to understand the apparently sudden transformation of Bangalore into India's software capital, I have elaborated on the city's historical background and its post-Independence development in S&T and industry. While this may explain the region's post-liberalisation success in attracting foreign investments, its strong Silicon Valley link is attributable to economic forces. In the 1970s, graduates from India's prestigious engineering schools failed to get employment opportunities commensurate with their qualifications and left the country in droves heading mainly for the US where they pursued graduate studies and gained experience in the ICT area. During the 1990s boom, many of them became entrepreneurs in Silicon Valley. The other catalyst was the skill shortage experienced by the US particularly during the Y2K scare which led that country to attract more Indians, offering H1B visa to short-circuit their entry. Their presence in the US encouraged companies like Texas Instruments, Hewlett Packard and Motorola to establish operations in Bangalore. While their pre-liberalisation experience in dealing with local organisations had not been quite so encouraging, they did however persist, confident that the region was a source of quality engineering talent. 'Such cross-regional start-ups with headquarters in the United States and development centres in India contributed to a deepening of the ecosystem for entrepreneurship in regions like Bangalore' (Saxenian 2006, 276).

While a favourable environment appears to be the prime factor in attracting IT entrepreneurs and human creative capital, genuine success is, according to Florida (2005), dependent on the presence of the three Ts—talent, technology and tolerance. A tolerant open environment attracts varied talent, and the mobilisation of innovative creative capital creates wealth (53). Generally, technical communities in regions such as Bangalore are built on collaboration between firms, between firms and financial institutions and between firms and universities. However, Saxenian (2006) notes the absence of collaboration between industries, and the lack of industry–university interaction in the Bangalore region. While collaboration is natural to some cultures, Singhal and Rogers (1989) state that such collaboration is not valued in India, citing the apocryphal case of an international conference of crab experts where each participating country displayed a sample of its crabs in a glass jar, sealed with a lid. The exception was the Indian jar which lacked a lid. When asked the reason, an observer was told that the jar did not need a lid because whenever a crab tried to climb out of the jar, the other crabs would pull it down again (154–55)! HMT's failure to enlist the support of DOE in entering into collaboration with Citizen for the manufacture of electronic watches is illustrative of this attitude. However, successful cases of collaboration include the design and development of CNC machines with PSI and CMTI (Mascarenhas 1982) and, more recently, that between Encore, IISc and BEL in the development and production of the Simputer.

To encourage greater industry involvement in education and training, the government has set up IIITs at Bangalore and six other locations which are affiliated with leading software firms such as IBM, Microsoft, Oracle and Sathyam (NASSCOM 2001). At the completion of Project Invite (Initiative to Nurture and Vibrant Information Technology Ecosystem), an initiative of IBM with BITES and the state Department of IT and Communication, the Director of BITES declared that 'Project Invite had proved industry-institute interface was not only possible, but also successful' (*The Hindu*, 27 November 2006).

As more examples of such positive experience are publicised, we can expect increased interaction and the development of a cooperative culture, building on local linkages as well as Bangalore's close connections with Silicon Valley. Noting several promising ventures in Bangalore, one of the most significant of which is the Simputer, Saxenian (2003) envisions prospects for NRIs (non–resident Indians) particularly those in Silicon Valley as international collaborators.

For analytical purposes it would help to focus on three factors that are significant to Bangalore's IT boom: (1) role of science and technology, (2) entrepreneurship and (3) venture capital.

8.4.1 Science and Technology

The success of Bangalore's Software Technology Park in attracting major foreign investment and in contributing directly or indirectly to over 50 per cent of software exports proves Preer's (1992) assertion that science parks in regions with prior concentration of research and development activity are the ones likely to succeed. Amid the 'central dynamic of the technopolis; the interaction of science and industry to produce new commercial products and processes.... the most important characteristic of a technopolis is entrepreneurship' (Preer, 56). Clearly Bangalore has emerged as a technopolis and as a 'region that generates sustained and propulsive economic activity through the creation and commercialisation of new knowledge' (ibid., 55).

As a result of the farsighted policies adopted by the Indian government in the 1960s and the 1970s, there are thirty R&D organisations of the central and state governments in Karnataka, of which twenty-eight are located at Bangalore. In addition, 115 industrial units in Karnataka have in-house R&D facilities recognised by the CSIR, and account for 10 per cent of all CSIR-recognised R&D centres in the country. In terms of scientific and technical personnel, Karnataka leads with 151,000, accounting for 9.2 per cent of the national total (Naidu in Jasswalla and Taylor 2003). As early as 1989, Singhal and

Rogers emphatically claimed: 'This city is the science and technology capital of India, with the highest concentration of scientific institutions and technical personnel' (1989, 163). Certainly a far cry from 'the time when IISc ... existed in splendid isolation' (Nair 2005, 82).

From its inception, IISc has played a vital role by setting up new departments in response to developments in the field, as well as catering to the demands of the aeronautics and electronics industry (Subbarayappa 1998, see Chapter 7, Section 7.5.2.1). From this concentration of S&T institutions emerged an agglomeration of high-tech firms which received further promotion from state and central governments with the setting up of Electronics City, STPI and International Technology Park (ITP).

During the last decade, over 350 medium-sized units have been established at Bangalore with small-scale units increasing in number from 800 to 10,500. Bangalore has several industrial parks, of which Peenya Industrial Estate is the largest in India. Undertakings like ITI and BEL have encouraged the establishment of several ancillary industries, most of which are based at Bangalore.

8.4.2 Entrepreneurship

Bangalore's emergence as an internationally recognised technopolis is due in large measure to its strong entrepreneurial culture and to the presence of IT-focused venture capitalists. The former, as Saxenian (2002) points out, is necessarily dependent on the wide availability of venture capital which can support 'multiple experiments with new products, new services and new applications'. Of far more importance is the other lesson from Silicon Valley—that 'entrepreneurship is a collective, not an individual process. It depends on a wider process of collective learning, typically within a localised community'. Such a technical community is built on collaboration between different firms, firms and universities, and firms and financial institutions. However, a serious drawback to entrepreneurship in India is the tendency for banks to fund business as collateral against assets or shares and not against finished goods. In addition, excessive bureaucratic procedures and poor infrastructure pose serious obstacles as experienced by Radha Basu of Hewlett Packard and Kailash Joshi of IBM (Saxenian 2006).

Evolving transportation and communication technologies, while allowing small businesses to enter into partnerships with foreign producers, will eventually blur the distinction between multinationals and entrepreneurial firms (Saxenian 2003) and create enormous scope for transnational communities to take on a role played thus far by MNCs. 'By becoming transnational entrepreneurs, these immigrants can provide the critical contacts, information and cultural know-how that links dynamic but distant regions in the global economy' (167). That this is already taking place is demonstrated by the professional success of Indians at Silicon Valley. 'By 2000, Indian engineers were at the helm of 972 Silicon Valley-based technology companies, which accounted for approximately $5 billion in sales and 25,811 jobs' (ibid., 181). Such links between US and Indian software programmers have been effective enough on occasion to influence Indian government policy. 'Thus while reversal of the "brain drain" is not yet on the horizon, there is a small but fast-growing professional community linking Silicon Valley and regions like Bangalore, and one that could play an important role in upgrading the Indian IT sector in the future' (Saxenian 2003, 183). And this, according to her, includes the potential for localized technical communities in India's hitherto veiled aerospace and defence research outfits in Bangalore.

Collaboration between Silicon Valley and Bangalore in IC design has grown considerably since the move to Bangalore of companies like Intel and Texas Instruments (TI) in the late 1980s. Evidence of this is reflected in the quality of design work done at companies like Oracle, Intel and TI. The latter recruits graduates through a rigorous screening process from IITs and the IISc. Such research requires strong synergy between departments of chip designing and chip-related software development and is carried out at TI's Bangalore unit (Patibandla and Petersen 2002). 'Engineers at TI's chip design unit in Bangalore have earned 225 US patents and developed a digital signal processing chip that was commercialised worldwide. Recognition of the growing sophistication of the research and engineering work done in India for well-known corporations has not only increased the confidence of the Indian community but has also provided domestic Indian software companies with an alternative model to low-end on-site outsourcing' (Saxenian 2006, 287).

From software development, a natural progression for Indian engineers is chip design. Vinod Dham, one of India's best known chip designers, believes that 'such quality resources should not be wasted in mundane jobs, and should be challenged to innovate, develop, and deliver superior products that come with the pride of ownership... We will see a lot more engineers who are "chip heads" and not "software geeks"'. A casual count of chip designers in Bangalore in 2005 brought up an estimate of 6,000 to 10,000. Realising that a joint effort would 'help India achieve leadership as an electronic product design hub' (Saxenian 2006), some companies in Bangalore have created a non-profit IP Exchange Forum (ibid., 317). Initially intended to encourage the development of technical talent, provide methodologies for evaluation, create standards, disseminate information on technical trends and markets and reduce duplication in IP development, its primary goal is to enhance the credibility of Indian product design (316–17). Such coordination by software companies is a healthy sign that cooperative effort is gradually creeping into the Indian software industry.

When the IT boom of the 1990s in the US caused a skills shortage, Indians were recruited to fill the gap by the offer of temporary visas. In 2000, 124,697 Indians received H1B visas. Alerted to the possibilities, Indians working in Silicon Valley ventured into cross-regional start-ups between the Valley and India. Thus began a beneficial exchange between the US and India. As stock market valuations of Indian software companies moved up, venture capitalists were drawn towards India with many successful Indian entrepreneurs playing key roles. Once resented, NRIs were now welcomed. Bangalore was described in 2000 as 'a gold rush town... There are headhunters outside the office complexes, waiting to jump (chip) designers when they leave work' (Saxenian 2006, 309–10); the return movement was directed largely to Bangalore.

Rating Bangalore with Silicon Valley as 'dream places for hi-tech entrepreneurs', Murthy and Raju (in Saxenian 2002) conclude that because the IT professional in Bangalore is 'much more easily satisfied than his or her counterpart in the Valley ..., the motivation for entrepreneurship is not as high in Bangalore as in the Valley' (199). Despite this, India's top computer companies continue to perform well, with Wipro, TCS and Infosys Technologies enjoying a fair share of the global market. Of these, Infosys is unique as it was started solely as a software company. Established in 1981 at Pune by N. R. Narayana Murthy and others and moved to Bangalore the following year, its real growth began in the 1990s when it exploited the time difference between the US and India to move from onsite work to offsite contracts. Aided by improvements in telecommunication services such as the digitalisation and deregulation of telecom in 1991 and the availability of satellite communication, Infosys made rapid growth, with its employee strength reaching 7500 and its revenues touching the Rs 9214.6 million mark in 2000 (Bhatnagar and Dixit in D'Costa and Sridharan 2003, 246–51). That year the company received the Government of India's award for Excellence in Corporate Governance. According to Greenspan (2004), the success of Infosys is built on precise systems, processes and routines that monitor and measure all aspects of every project and a reputation for meeting its targets (87).

Infosys's registration as a US tech stock company on NASDAQ in 1999 was significant not merely because it was the first Indian company to do so, nor because this was a crucial step in its efforts to become global. In fact, it was the generation of 70 per cent of its revenue in the US where it needed to gain recognition (Maitra, *Deccan Herald-Economy & Business*, 5 April 2002). In addition to being the first Indian company to adopt international accounting standards for reporting, it has also inculcated better management practices on American lines, offering stock options to its employees.

Despite setbacks in 2003 with the worldwide decline in IT stocks, Infosys managed to retain its position in the market through internal efficiencies and diversification into other areas of the IT business such as system integration solutions. Such vision and forward strategies have helped Infosys to grow from $100 million in 1999 to $500 million in 2001 and cross the $1 billion mark in 2004 (*The Age*, 20 April 2004). Following its successful performance in 2007 of 60 per cent compounded annual rate, *The Hindu* declared, 'That is remarkable by any standards and it seems highly unlikely there is a comparable record of achievement in the history of corporate India' (17 January 2007). Its performance was maintained with 21.1 growth in the first quarter of 2007–08 despite a weakening US dollar. During that quarter, the company added thirty-five new clients and 7004 employees with a total of 75,971 from sixty-five countries; a further twenty-six thousand were to be recruited in 2008–09. Today, Infosys Technologies is a multinational operating in seventy-two countries (*The Hindu*, 12 July 2007). Its campus, built on forty-four acres of land twenty miles outside Bangalore, is probably the world's largest such facility, equipped with 4500 PCs and its own power generation plant (David Stephen, *India Today*, 1 January 2001, 54). A visit here is a 'must' for most dignitaries who call in at Bangalore. Yes, a shrine it certainly is, founded by a visionary whose personal values are epitomised by his simple life, a sense of dedication and a concern for employees (ibid.).

In his role as Chairman and Chief Mentor, Narayana Murthy continued to guide the company, albeit from afar, while his successor, Nandan Nilekani, who played an active day-to-day role, has also moved on. Anticipating the demands of a fast changing global business which needs high-quality leaders, Infosys has set up a Leadership Institute at Mysore. To meet the demand for staff and cater to its international requirements, Infosys in 2006 hired three hundred graduates from institutions like MIT and Harvard to undergo a six-month course at their training centre at Mysore, before starting full-time jobs in Infosys's US offices (*The Age*, 6 June 2006). A business is measured not merely by its returns for its shareholders or payment to its employees in the form of bonuses. Following the Tata philanthropic tradition of the early twentieth century in helping to set up the IISc, the Infosys Foundation funds various civic and heritage projects.

8.4.3 Venture Capital

The success of high-technology firms in the US has been associated with the role of venture capital (VC). In the first half of 1999, VC funds in the US invested more than $2.5 billion in early-stage companies with decisions on successful recipients playing a critical role in the development of high-tech industries. Interestingly, such industries tend to operate in close-knit networks, and new firms tend to locate themselves near existing firms of the same type to establish markets for scarce inputs. Such tendencies have implications for regional economic development policies (Sorenson and Stuart 2001, 1546–88). Observing VC's vital role in the growth of Silicon Valley, Saxenian (2002) and others would like to see it adopted in Bangalore which has a similar concentration of high-tech firms. However, transferring a particular practice from one environment to another is often fraught with difficulty and in this case there are economic and cultural obstacles as well (Murthy and Raju, in Saxenian 2002). Dossani and Kenney (2002) state that, as in other countries, 'the Indian venture capital industry is the result of an iterative process, and is still in its infancy. If it is to be successful it will be necessary not only for it to grow, but also for its institutional context to evolve' (228).

India's first venture capital organisation was the Technology Development and Information Company of India (TDICI), a subsidiary of Industrial Credit and Investment Corporation of India (ICICI). While its location at Bangalore was an acknowledgement of the Government of India's recognition of that city as the national centre of high technology, its move away from the parent body presented an opportunity to build a distinct new culture. Despite some errors in funding import substitution ventures or in allowing lower level staff to take vital decisions and thus overlook some high-quality opportunities, TDICI achieved a 27 per cent rate of return from its inception in 1986 to 1994 and is considered the most successful of the early government-related venture capital operations.

A major reason for increased venture capital in Bangalore is the lower cost of failure as compared to Silicon Valley. While initial investment in Bangalore costs around $700,000, in the US this would be closer to $2 million. A group of venture capitalists with experience of working in both Silicon Valley and Bangalore set up the JumpStartUp Venture Fund of $45 million. Following this, Ashok Narasimhan, formerly of Wipro, and entrepreneur Raj Reddy set up July Systems based in Silicon Valley and Global Product Centre at Bangalore. Saxenian considers that July Systems with the many high-profile entrepreneurial spin-offs from India's Wipro has become 'a managerial training ground for Bangalore, playing a spawning role similar to that of Fairchild in Silicon Valley and Acer in Taiwan' (2006, 313). Entrepreneurs arriving from the US are provided with basic infrastructure by Global Technical Ventures, a company set up by a group of venture capitalists.

Bangalore's failure hitherto to produce any world-class software package is attributed to the lack of a vibrant VC culture willing to front up with funds for development. Willingness to take risks among Bangalore entrepreneurs is much lower as Indians generally prefer a steady career to one with a huge income at high risk. 'Though Bangalore has attracted several high-quality technology-focused venture capitalists, it has a long way to go before matching the hands-on approach, commitment, relationships, and risk appetites of some of the leading VC funds in the Valley' (Murthy and Raju in Saxenian 2002). Ojha and Krishnan (2003) agree that entrepreneurship is not as well developed in India and feel that a supportive context with adequate VC is crucial for Indian entrepreneurs to move to the higher end of the value chain and produce high quality 'originative software' as against the current 'derivative' software (220–222).

8.5 Role of Investment in Research and Training

Bangalore is known for its distinctive educational, cultural, industrial and scientific institutions, among which the IISc takes pride of place. While not playing a direct role like Stanford in Silicon Valley, IISc's contribution to Bangalore's scientific and engineering landscape, since its start in the early twentieth century, is immeasurable. As a centre of advanced S&T learning, it offers quality education and research, influencing other institutions where its graduates are employed in teaching, research or in industry. Its earliest impact on the region was the research it undertook on the extraction of sandal oil for the Mysore government, developing a product which earned the state worldwide recognition as well as a sizable income which continues to contribute to the region's economy. IISc is also the headquarters of the space agency ISRO which has extensive sub-contracting links with the Peenya Industrial Estate. In recent years, it has become involved with the C-DAC development centre for the production of supercomputers as well as the development of the Simputer. Its next venture as of 2003 was to set up a Mini-Fab for the research, design and development of micro electromechanical sensors (MEMS), which has wide application in automotive, biomedical and aerospace industries. A larger unit was built at Bangalore in collaboration with the private sector for the purpose of commercialising the product, replacing the Chandigarh based Semiconductor Complex Limited (SCL) that was destroyed by fire (*The Hindu*, 22 March 2003).

Prior to Independence, Mysore state had established a tradition of technical training by setting up institutes in each district followed later by engineering colleges. The Small Industries Services Institute, which was instrumental in building industrial estates for the purpose of undertaking work for large public undertakings, has institutes all over India offering courses for school leavers. Other training institutes which are publicly funded include the Foreman Training Institute, Government Toolroom and Training Institute and the Electronics Test and Development Centre which provide both training and consultancy services. In order to offer advice to SMEs about new technology, the Karnataka government has set up the Technical Consultancy Services Organisation of Karnataka (Tecsok). The Centre for Electronic Development and Technology (CEDT) of the IISc, with Swiss assistance, also offers training and advice. The Nettur Technical

Training Foundation (NTTF), also funded by the Swiss, in the 1950s, now has seventeen centres, many of which are in Bangalore, training over 3000 students. Of the 120 candidates for its Four-Year Diploma in tool and die making, half that number hailed from rural areas and received free tuition and subsidised or free hostel accommodation. NTTF offers a post-graduate course in tool engineering and its Electronics Centre offers programmes in CNC programming and CAD (Cadene and Holmstrom 1998, 216–17). Peenya centre, now the hub of NTTF operations, includes an assembly unit where physically challenged women produce switches for cars manufactured by Maruti Udyog Limited (*The Hindu*, 28 June 2004).

In addition to the wide range of research and training services on offer, the impact of the Central Mechanical Training Institute (CMTI) in Bangalore is discernible in the many innovative and successful engineering firms set up by its designers. In collaboration with HMT and Process Systems Incorporated (PSI), CMTI was the first in India to design and develop CNC machines. 'The NC lathe is the first Indian attempt at a completely indigenous NC machine with CNC system. A micro-processor-based CNC system offered with this machine is completely Indian in design and execution and employs the latest technique in semi-conductor technology, the micro-processor' (Mascarenhas 1982, 121).

Independent of the variety of factors that have influenced location decisions, a known element here is the reputation of the region for a skilled labour force, quality science and technical education and a cosmopolitan environment. Such an environment generated a qualified workforce and stimulated the growth of ancillary industries which were established to meet the demands for a range of inputs required by the large public undertakings (Mascarenhas 1982). One can hypothesise that within a period of fifty years, a new generation of scientists and engineers has grown up in an environment that today forms the backbone of the software industry.

It has to be acknowledged that Bangalore's emergence as the centre of high technology rests on the contribution of the public sector to the region, the development of which is comparable with southern California where a thriving aerospace industry and defence-related contracts played a crucial role similar to the aerospace research and manufacturing complex around Bangalore (also see Heitzman 2004; Nair 2005, see Chapter 3). Three important public sector undertakings, namely HAL, ITI and BEL which have had an influence on the IT sector, are discussed below.

8.5.1 Hindustan Aeronautics (HAL)

Hindustan Aeronautics has emerged as a major aircraft manufacturer supplying the latest versions of MIG 21s, Jaguar strike aircraft, helicopters and trainer aircraft and is in the final stages of testing a Light Combat Aircraft (LCA). Listed in its *Annual Report* (2003–04) as the first of an upgraded series, the Jaguars were built incorporating a nav-attack system with a new mission computer. HAL was assigned the responsibility to develop aircraft engine components for Sukhoi and Boeing-led consortiums as a risk-sharing partner (*The Hindu,* 18 June 2004). With its emergence as the focal organisation for aircraft manufacture, other related research and development agencies were set up, thus contributing to Bangalore's growth into a major centre for aerospace design, engineering and manufacturing.

Building on this, that area was chosen to develop the LCA to replace the ageing MIG-21. In 2001, HAL developed the Technology Demonstration Aircraft (TDA) powered by GE-404 engines with plans to replace them with Kaveri, an indigenous engine to be developed by Gas Turbine Research Establishment (GRTE).

In 2004, after witnessing a test flight, the Prime Minister named the LCA 'Tejas'.

However, even after several years, GRTE has been unable to come up with a suitable engine to power the LCA. Since 2005, it has been holding talks with the Russians and the French, seeking co-development in the production of an engine. This was expected to take four years to develop, and, when brought up to performance level, the engine was expected to be superior to the GE-404. When fitted with it, the LCA is expected to be comparable to the Mirage 2000 and, in many respects, even superior, although it was only meant to replace the MIG-21 (Parthasarathy and Puri, *The Hindu,* 9 March 2008). Disagreements have arisen between National Aeronautic Development Agency (NADA), which is responsible for the design and development of the LCA, and HAL, which is responsible for its manufacture. 'Dual control has resulted in mutual blame game.' While HAL sources have criticised NADA for not providing HAL with the blueprints of the aircraft, scientists at NADA have responded by saying that talk of blueprints is 'passe' (Ravi Sharma, 'IAF reluctant to place orders for LCA', *The Hindu,* 10 July 2005).

When flown in 2001, the LCA as Technology Demonstration Aircraft (TDA) was not weaponised. When air–to-air missiles are accommodated, extensive design changes will be necessary. With its networking capabilities it will be more than comparable to anything 'the IAF had and possibly would have, even after it acquires the 126 Multi-Role Combat Aircraft (MRCA) now under consideration...' (ibid.).

'As for network-centric capability, which intrinsically needs indigenous systems for secrecy, security and inter-operability, it is superior in the LCA compared to any aircraft in the IAF's inventory' (ibid).

According to Parthasarathy and Puri (2008), 'It is a fallacy to think we can continue the importing spree and still have such network-centric capability... At Rs 120 crore to Rs 140 crore a plane, compared to at least double that amount for any of the aircraft types now bidding for the 126 MRCA, is not the LCA a highly cost-effective fighter for volume introduction into the IAF?'

This view was expressed by Air Chief Marshall S. P. Tyagi who had urged the Indian government to formulate an aeronautics policy and create an Aerospace Commission 'to coordinate research and development efforts of aerospace related industries and thus help to reduce cost and duplication of effort in a sector that is cost-intensive'. Acknowledging that many of India's projects rank among the best, he said that the sector's dependence on imports will force India to accept 'outdated equipment and technology because of politico-economic compulsions of the seller nations'.

8.5.2 Indian Telecommunication Industries (ITI)

Until the telecom equipment manufacturing sector was opened to the private sector, India's only source of equipment was Indian Telephone Industries (as it was previously known) set up at Bangalore in 1952. Emerging five decades later as a major telecommunication equipment manufacturer with facilities for design and manufacture, today it is also the major outlet for products designed by its French collaborator, Alcatel, for whom it manufactures large capacity switches. The other major player in the field is C-DOT, which manufactures digital switches and switchgear equipment for small and medium-sized telephone exchanges. However until the push for digitalisation initiated by Pitroda, ITI produced exchanges with outdated technology based largely on technical collaboration negotiated by Posts and Telegraphs, its controlling department. Both systems chosen by the department proved unsuitable—Strowgear at high cost with 'un-learnable' technology and the Pentacosta with its cross-bar technology which proved unsuitable for the Indian network.

Sridharan (1996) draws attention to 'the pattern of policy incoherence and missed opportunities' in telecom. (181). He writes, 'India had a head start with the existence of ITI, with its production of electromechanical crossbar exchanges, and the Telecom Research Centre (TRC) indigenous design of a small (1000-line) electronic exchange, the SPC-1, which was fabricated by ITI and BEL and had completed field trials by 1979' (Sridharan 1996, 181). Much time was lost in attempts to modify the unsuitable Pentacosta crossbar exchange to suit Indian conditions, thus delaying the move towards digitilisation (ibid., 182). Pitroda's perseverance shook the telecommunication establishment and it yielded to both digitalisation and its subsequent restructuring under his leadership. The establishment of C-DOT in 1984 represents a transformation in thinking and attitude within the telecommunication equipment manufacturing sector.

Mani (1995, 2003) attributes the continued dependence on imported technology in TW countries to the lack of technological dynamism. Under departmental control, ITI took some ill-advised decisions, a crucial one being the location of two manufacturing units of electronic switching system away from ITI where the R&D unit was located. Ultimately, errors such as this affected training costs, the development of skills and the development of the telecommunication industry in India. Even the extraordinary performance of C-DOT (discussed in Chapter 6) has been undermined by exaggerating its failures, instead of highlighting its successes. This successful indigenous effort was in danger of being destroyed by government for political reasons (Mani 1995, 119–120). The continuously evolving environment of telecommunications with its huge market and profits is an attraction for multinationals who are likely to bring pressure on wavering governments.

8.5.3 Bharat Electronics (BEL)

Established in 1954 to meet the needs of the Ministry of Defence in terms of radars, communications, telecommunication and semiconductors, BEL's exclusive status as a defence supplier has changed recently with opportunities for competition being opened to private sector firms.

Unlike many other public undertakings, BEL earned some profit during its fifty years of existence including an average growth rate of 10 per cent over the last five years. For the financial year 2001–2002, it showed a turnover of Rs 20299.8 million, a 14 per cent increase over the previous year. While developing expertise and displaying a good record in R&D and exports, BEL, like many high-tech public sector firms, has served as a training ground for engineers. 'BEL serves as the mother hen for the Indian electronics industry. Every year 10 to 15 per cent of BEL engineers leave the company to join other electronic firms' (Singhal and Rogers 1989, 164). Its presence in Bangalore with a workforce of 20,000 in the 1980s, according to Evans (1995), 'helped to lay the groundwork to make India's "silicon plateau" the country's most promising technopolis' (130). Two areas vital to IT are the cooperative efforts between BEL & ISRO for the manufacture of Satellite Electronic Payload (Transponders) and Computer Mother Boards with INTEL chips. BEL's Central Research Laboratory has brought out smart cards for use in security and exports PCB test software to Switzerland, power devices to UK, and defence sub-systems and solar products to Singapore among others (*Annual Report* 2001–2002). Celebrating its fifty years, the Managing Director expressed the company's aspirations to become a world-class organisation in the near future (*The Hindu*, 22 April 2004). Two other significant contributions are its collaboration with the IISc and Encore for the manufacture of Amida Simputer and the development of the EVM used in the last Indian elections (see Chapter 7).

In the context of IT, BEL made a major contribution by collaborating with C-DOT for the manufacture of Rural Automatic Exchanges, a product that ushered in the communications revolution in the country. In a study of Top Performing Companies by the *Journal of Aviation and Space Technology*, BEL was ranked first out of forty-two in the medium-sized category (*The Hindu*, 9 September 2004). Other indigenous products which are in an advanced state of completion include the hand-held and frequency-hopping radios, upgraded L-70 and ZU-23 guns and Rajendra variant radars.

In its efforts to progress further into areas of rocketry and robotics, BEL set up a fund in July 2009 in collaboration with IISc to establish a chair in the field which will be open to established academics worldwide. BEL has continued to develop more powerful missiles that can travel over long distances such as Agni and Brahmos. The Advanced

Air Defence (AAD) missile, successfully tested at an altitude of fifteen kilometres over the Bay of Bengal, is an endo-atmospheric interceptor missile. As part of the development of a two-layered Ballistic Missile Defence, it is a single-stage solid rocket-propelled missile equipped with a navigation system, a high-speed computer and an electro-mechanical activator, and has performed manoeuvres based on the data uplinked from the radars to the interceptor(Mallikarjun Y, 'Interceptor destroys simulated missile', *The Hindu*, 3 December 2007).

At its peak in the 1970s, the industrial workforce employed in HAL, ITI and BEL was probably around a quarter of a million, many of whom had come from rural areas in search of employment. Such concentration of skills created an industrial milieu which then generated an environment fostering innovative behaviour and the desire for an improved life style. Skilled technicians, after several years' service, earned enough to afford a good education for their children, of whom many attended university and quite probably followed the engineering line.

In answer to the current cry (from the IT sector) about the quality of graduates and more particularly the poor infrastructure, Narendra Pani points out that during the boom of the public sector in Bangalore in the 1950s and 1960s 'strategies were never confined to the workplace—townships and mass transportation networks were created that minimised the use of existing infrastructure... It is an imagination that confines itself to [a] few glamorous workplaces and projects that is at the root of Bangalore's information crisis' ('Bangalore turns against itself: IT industry undermines city's educational infrastructure', *Times of India*, 28 November 2005). He traces Bangalore's numerous English medium schools and its institutions of technical education to a series of historical accidents. English medium schools were started in the 1850s by Reverend Possett to educate Anglo-Indians who at the time faced discrimination. Technical education emerged at the initiative of Sri Krishnaraja Wadeyar. While laying the corner stone of the IISc in 1911, he urged that scholarships be offered to poor but worthy students. Pani comments that the availability of technical education was fully exploited by the public sector units. 'The unionised working class at these units ensured that even the lowest paid among them had access to these institutions. By the 1960s, Bangalore had a large body of technical manpower ... Instead of recognising this history, Bangalore's dominant IT imagination chips away at the very basis of its success. Access to engineering education has become expensive. The preoccupation with IT also reduces the scope for bringing the poor into the organised working class. They cannot then hope to provide technical education for their children as the public sector workers once did. Once Bangalore loses its manpower advantage it is left competing on the basis of physical infrastructure with much richer urban centres' Concluding that it is time for Bangalore to regain its industrial base and the technical education that helped to create its IT manpower, he laments, 'at one time Bangalore had the intellectual giants who could wonder with T. S. Eliot "where is the wisdom we have lost in knowledge? Where is the knowledge we have lost in information?" Today, the city is wondering where is the information we have lost in information technology'.

8.6 Growth of Software Companies in Bangalore

Bangalore's IT boom is a recognition of the particular importance of human capital that is abundant in the region. Clearly, transnational corporations like Texas Instruments or Hewlett Packard decided to invest after assessing the value of human capital and the technological capabilities of local research and educational institutions (Patibandla and Petersen 2002). While eliminating the need for multinational companies to secure control over another entity through branches located in other countries, structural changes in the world economy have made it possible for firms to work in joint ownership (Kogut 2004). The diffusion of new IT and telecom technology is rapid and is relatively inexpensive if use is made of free operating systems such as Linux.

Foray (2004) relates such 'openness' to the peculiar features of software as a technology, and concludes: (1) software is a complex system that generates unbounded learning processes as thousands of developers work on the same software to generate increasing returns; (2) being a highly codified technology, it can be used as a collective learning process by exploiting the potential of the new electronics infrastructure; and (3) software belongs to a certain class of technology that brings consumers and knowledge producers together. In other words, users can become developers (178). Software also differs from manufacturing in that a software engineer is constantly learning while he works (Patibandla and Petersen 2002).

While the entry of multinationals is likely to enhance existing capabilities through both backward and forward linkages, such growth can also increase through agglomeration economies. 'Agglomeration, or external economies... accrue to firms that locate close to one another. They exist when the net benefit to being in a location with other firms increases with the number of firms in the location' (McKendrick 2004). The result can be seen in the concentration of high-end R&D work at Bangalore which currently has about 230 MNC development centres and over sixty thousand IT professionals. Linkages between research institutions and universities and collaboration with large Indian firms have gradually helped the cluster to achieve high levels of technological capabilities (Patibandla and Petersen 2002, 1572–73).

Beginning in 1986 with the entry of Texas Instruments which established a computer-aided design centre in Bangalore at a time when Rajiv Gandhi, India's tech-savvy Prime Minister, was keen on liberalising imports and exports, particularly information technology, IT growth at Bangalore has continued unabated. Drawn to Bangalore by its weather, its dust-free environment and its skilled manpower, TI's entry was assisted by DOE, which by-passed existing regulations to accommodate the company. Satellite links enabled the Bangalore design centre to work in close communication with TI's headquarters at Dallas. Its entry into Bangalore was followed by that of Hewlett Packard, DEC and Motorola. By 2000, about eighty multinationals had established software development centres at Bangalore (Singhal and Rogers 2001, 171) and this appears to be on the increase. A crucial link in that process are migrant Indian engineers who have built up a reputation for their industry and initiative. Software companies enjoy a comparatively shorter time lag between entry and becoming operational and that process is facilitated at Bangalore by Electronics City and Software Technology Park. While Bangalore's growth as a software destination is explicable in terms of Porter's industrial cluster or Marshall's industrial districts (Zaheer and Rajan 2003), Kogut (2003) highlights the changes in the city as a spectacular case of a vibrant software sector in one of the world's poor regions. 'To visit Bangalore is to see a strange blend of impressions of traditional India with industrial parks, served by satellite dishes and back-up energy suppliers, including batteries located in the back of rows of Internet capable computers. The strategy of software development led to the creation of silos, or Offshore Development Centres [ODCs], that operated under the internal rules and specifications of the contracting multinational or foreign contractor. There would be the CISCO ODC, GE Capital ODC, the Lucent ODC, sub-divided within the same physical premises, the assigned engineers guarding the intellectual property right agreement but also mingling over lunch, in bars, in each other's homes' (453–54).

The earlier set-ups in Bangalore began as wholly-owned foreign or partially-owned companies but, as their number grew, they moved increasingly towards joint ventures. Joint ventures entered into between IBM and Tata Information Systems Limited and between Microsoft and Tata Consultancy Services bring benefits to both parties and are becoming quite popular. IBM, having departed in 1978 over the issue of sharing equity ownership, has since returned and in June 2006 announced a further investment of US $6 billion, in addition to US $2 billion over the previous three years (*The Age*, 10 June 2006). Addressing the Innovation and Leadership forum organised by IBM, the Chief Minister acknowledged the benefit that Bangalore had derived from the presence of a 'truly global knowledge enterprise' and continued that 'what is good for IBM is good for Bangalore'. Infosys and its mentor N. R. Narayana Murthy came in for praise—'Infosys has done Karnataka and every Kannadiga proud' (*The Hindu*, 7 June 2006). Such strategic alliances between Indian and foreign companies were foreseen by Evans (1995) who predicted that Indian computer policy would move towards midwifery and husbandry deviating from its era of custodian and demiurge.

Like its competitors, Infosys sells customised software along with packaged solutions, such as Enterprise Solutions Practices. Its financial program, Financle, has earned support from banks for its speed when compared to packages offered by its competitors. It was ranked as the fastest growing technological services provider (TSP) in the US in 2006, owing to its use of Global Delivery Model (GDM) for the portfolio of solutions offered to the financial services industry.

Rothermund (2008) regards Infosys as a 'GDM pioneer by identifying the secret of its strategy as global co-sourcing and finding the right partners for it.... Tasks are split into sub modules that are internally cohesive and require as little as possible interface with other modules. One can often concentrate on essential modules and get others from other partners who can produce them more effectively and at lower cost'(107).

Its leadership has brought a new dimension into Indian business through people like Nandan Nilekani who, in his recent book *Imagining India: Ideas for the New Century,* offers ideas about history, politics and education that would put 'most modern Western leaders to shame'. His theory of development rooted in business-speak is spelt out simply: 'When you start thinking about people as human capital you realize that human capital is only developed when you invest in it. Therefore, the Government needs to make health and education top priorities. If you have all this capital, you have to make sure you use it well' (Dan Roberts, 'Optimist will thrive in an even flatter globe', *The Age,* 25 April 2009).

With its international focus, Infosys has been recruiting more non-Indians to work in its operations, with training facilities based at Mysore. The success of this multinational has been attributed to leadership, an optimistic mindset, a willingness to learn from others and a refusal to compromise on the fundamental value of systems rooted in its national culture (*The Hindu,* 13 August 2005). Such an ethic may seem essential with the recent scandal that has engulfed Satyam which, like Wipro, TCS and Infosys, is one of the largest IT operators with a worldwide clientele.

Ventures which blend local engineering skill with multinational initiative and enterprise are proving to be highly productive. TI's Bangalore centre has developed the world's 'first single-chip solution for high speed modems' using analogue and digital circuits. Described by the General Manager of TI Broadband Silicon Technology Centre as 'the biggest challenge', the chip, symbolically christened 'Sangam', the confluence of two rivers, took seventy hardware experts a year to develop. Hundreds of these chips are now fabricated at TI's silicon foundries abroad to the latest 130-nanometre technology, i.e., devices etched on the silicon are about ten millionth of a centimetre apart. Acknowledged to be the most complex project undertaken by the Bangalore centre, the development of Sangam follows that of Ankur (an advanced digital signal processor), Malhar (audio processor) and Zeno (a media chip) (Parthasarathy, *The Hindu,* 30 May 2003).

In 2005, TI announced the successful completion of another project 'putting on the same slab of silicon, two disparate sets of circuits: the digital audio portion that handles the voice capability, and the radio frequency or RF circuits that send the signal, to and fro, as radio waves'. This single chip solution will be built into mobile telephones for the mass markets emerging in Asia. 'While TI does not often identify individual development centres with its products, it will surprise no one if key elements of the single-chip phone work were carried out in India.... Its Bangalore-based development team is a major research hothouse for the Texas-based company' (Anand Parthasarathy, *The Hindu*, 27 January 2005).

Motorola, which followed TI into Bangalore, appears to revel in the local competition, developing new products and achieving quality certification. Its India-based Global Software Group (GSG) has become the first organisation in the world to achieve the most stringent certification in the software business—SEI's CMM Level 5 or the 'continuous representation' model across four disciplines: software, systems engineering, product development and supplier sourcing. Motorola's largest test-bed for Code Division Multiple Access (CDMA) type telephony, based at Bangalore, is already driving the local mobile networks in India. Apparently, the next challenge is 'to provide seamless global connectivity from a single handset, across regions, networks and technologies' (Parthasarathy, *The Hindu*, 19 June 2003).

Quality Engineering and Software Technologies (QUEST), founded in New York by a group of engineers from Hubli (Karnataka), has offices in India, US, UK, Japan and Italy and employs over 520 engineers, of whom 10 per cent have doctorates and 40 per cent are postgraduates. Its main development centre is located at Bangalore employing three hundred engineers. Quest's services include full system and component design, analysis support, field failure investigations and solutions and custom design tool development. Ajay Prabhu, Vice-President of its India office, claimed that Quest had broken the confidence barrier in acquiring a global client base including GE, Pratt and Whitney, GM, Ford, Nissan, Honda, Fujitsu and HAL and was on the verge of further expansion (*The Hindu*, 13 March 2003).

In the pharmaceutical area, Infopro Solutions, a California-based company founded by Vikram Marla in 1995, produced a software suite called 'Clinicopia' for clinical trials of new drugs. Designed largely at its Bangalore Centre, the system enables pharmaceutical companies to ensure that all regulatory requirements of the US Food and Drug Administration are met and that all records of drug trials are maintained. Major companies that have used Clinicopia include Pfizer, Abbott Laboratories, Chiron, and Procter and Gamble. In 2003, the company announced plans to establish a Rs 3.5 crore facility at Whitefield and to double its engineer strength by year-end (*The Hindu,* 31 August 2003).

With the outbreak of the Iraq war, Opto Circuits India Limited, a medical electronics and security system products manufacturer, was flooded with orders from its US distributors for its Blood Warmers used in emergency operations to ensure smooth flow of blood while maintaining its temperature at 37 degrees Celsius. Established in 1990 at Singapore as Elekon Industries Ltd, it moved to India in 1992, and in 2001 acquired Bangalore-based Advanced Micronic Devices Limited, the Critical Cardiac Care equipment manufacturer, giving it access to an extensive marketing network of over 5000 hospitals in India. In June 2002, it acquired the Digital Thermometer division of Hindustan Levers and went further by adding Patient Monitoring Division of Palco Laboratories, a leading US-based company which markets products for diabetes among other disorders. Opto also operates in the optoelectronics area, a subset of the semi-conductor industry, and manufactures baggage scanner equipment, demand for which has increased sharply since the attack on the World Trade Center (Kulkarni, *Deccan Herald Economy & Business,* 7 April 2003). While Bangalore is becoming the sought-after destination for investment in high-tech, the McKinsey Report 2005 wonders if the advantages created at first by clustering will dissipate soon especially 'if the demand for talent overwhelms the supply and if infrastructure investments don't keep up with the same pace' (Farrel et al., *Deccan Herald,* 3 October 2005).

The general perception of Indian software companies has undergone a remarkable change. Known in the 1990s for low-level maintenance jobs, the growth in expertise has resulted in increasing confidence and the willingness to take on new challenges and develop complete products. From developing software applications, the move is now towards outsourced product development. Product development requires close interaction with the client's engineering team and can be both demanding and daunting.

Bangalore's reputation as a strategic base for R&D has encouraged companies such as Cadence, Oracle and SAP of Germany to set up centres, too. 'Since the beginning of 2001, 230 multinationals have piled into the city's industrial parks. Already, some 25,000 engineers work in Bangalore labs. NASSCOM predicts that with an additional investment of $1.5 billion that number will swell to 65,000. When Intel CEO Craig Barrett visited Bangalore in August, he noted that a 'whole ecosystem for IT ... was being built in India' (Kripalani 2002).

The design and development of Intel's dual-core mobile technology platform for laptops was undertaken at its Bangalore development centre. At the launch of the product, Anand Chandrashekar, Senior Vice-President of Intel Corporation, labelled it a major contribution to the world from India. 'We view it as the second major leap forward for the company since the launch of the Pentium Processors in 1993. In the context of mobility, the technology is nothing short of a revolution...' Lavishing praise on the development team at Bangalore, he predicted that by the year 2007, 'almost every laptop being sold would have a component designed by Intel India' (*The Hindu*, 11 January 2006).

As evidence of Bangalore's innovative work culture, Intel showcased its 'Made in India' 6 core processor which was designed and developed at its Bangalore centre. According to Anand Parthasarathy, companies are reluctant to disclose names and claim that their work is a result of 'collaborations across multiple design teams ... it not being company policy to partition credit'. However, he thinks that the policy has more to do with pleasing shareholders back home 'whose parochial minds would rather avoid the truth that 80 per cent of the intellectual property that fuels their fat dividend cheques often originates from places like India' (*The Hindu*, 20 September 2008).

That comment relates to the six-in-one Xeon processor, used to fuel high-end server-type computers. The 7400 series, designed with 1.9 billion transistors on board to drive six separate cores or computing units, uses a chip to deliver one-and- half times more performance and power savings than earlier Xeon processors. 'Having designed the chip from scratch, the Intel India team also carried out "post-silicon validation" making sure the design translates into smooth manufacturing process when it is handed over to the silicon foundry'. At its unveiling, Intel India's president stated that considerable expertise had been achieved during the process of product design wholly done in India. The India centre was also a key partner in 2007 in 'delivering the world's first tera-scale experimental chip capable of one trillion operations per second' (*The Hindu*, 1 September 2008).

An innovation in mobile technology that is helping to reduce the digital divide is mKrishi, a mobile agro advisory system of the Tata Consultancy Services, which allows farmers to send queries to agricultural experts in their local language through a mobile and receive personalised advice or relevant information in that language. Literacy-challenged farmers can send queries and receive advice by 'voice

SMS'. mKrishi was developed through the integration of technologies such as sensors, solar power, CDMA modem and CDMA network, GPS, handset with camera, binary runtime environment for wireless to develop multiple applications on the handset, client software (on mobile phone), expert console software, and an engine to assist in displaying mobile screens in Indian languages. mKrishi has received the Golden Peacock Innovation Award, the Wall Street Journal Technology Award under the wireless category and the NASSCOM Innovation Award and is being implemented in cooperation with Tata Teleservices, M. S. Swaminathan Foundation, etc. (*The Hindu*, 15 May 2009).

A recent arrival on the Bangalore scene is Riya, a software company in artificial intelligence and imaging technology, set up by Manjul Shah and two Stanford colleagues, one from Pakistan and the other from Turkey, which has created software that will identify both texts and faces in a photograph. 'This is the world's first automatic "tagging" technology for faces, and we see this as a huge jump in the computer-driven recognition of human features' claimed Shah at the pre-launch briefing. Even by its 'alpha' or pre-release or testing stage, the company had received $15 million VC (*The Hindu*, 20 January 2006).

Investments from NRIs based in the US represent a 'seamless integration' between Bangalore and the United States (Silicon Valley in particular), marking the emergence of a new generation with a global mindset. A case in point is the move to Bangalore of Silicon Automation Systems (SAS) in 1994 which was originally based in California, embedding software for mobile telephones and Internet applications. Another example is the globally founded Mindtree whose founder directors hail from Wipro, Cambridge Technology Partners and Lucent (Zaheer and Rajan 2003).

An example of movement in the other direction cited by Zaheer and Rajan (2003) is that of Gray Cell/Unimobile. Originally set up in Bangalore as Gray Cell Applied Technologies Limited, it pioneered the use of the Internet in mobile telecommunications and developed the world's first wireless-internet gateway in 1996. Efforts to develop a world-class IT company and the consequent need for large-scale funding led its founder to approach venture capitalists in Silicon Valley. He was encouraged to shift to Silicon Valley where he was funded $2 million by Drapes Int, William Int Investment Group and two Silicon Valley entrepreneurs of Indian origin. The company was eventually acquired by Electronics for Imaging, a US company (EMG), in 2002 (ibid., 215–16).

Kogut sums this up aptly: 'The overall percentage of these "returnees" may not be particularly high relative to the work force, but their impact is important not only in terms of their social contacts and acquired skills, but also in terms of the cultural images transported of successful Indian entrepreneurs, working in the Silicon Valley model. We observe in these patterns the emergence of the global labor market for talent, as well as convergence in cultural expectations' (Kogut 2003, 454). The returning Indians are 'helping to break down old castelike system of social relations and establishing more democratic and egalitarian business and social cultures' (Florida 2005, 109). There is, however, the issue of trust between US and Indian firms. In a study cited by Kogut, US managers worked well with their Indian partners (who belonged to the same firm) if they were brought to the US site and their abilities were rated highly. However, if the Indians worked at the India site, questions as to their abilities rose in the minds of the US managers (2004, 279).

Until recently, most researchers and engineers in R&D centres in India worked on global technology initiatives. However, as MNCs realise the vast opportunities in emerging markets, this outward orientation is gradually changing inwards, towards research on the domestic market (*The Hindu*, 27 December 2005). MNCs are realising the vast opportunities in emerging markets. 'Harnessing these global trends by encouraging MNCs to carry out product innovation for local consumers represents a big challenge facing India today' (Sarin, *The Hindu*, 2 January 2006).

Although lack of entrepreneurship and venture capital was identified as an obstacle, there is evidence that indicates significant progress. Reddy (1997) notes the increasing interest of MNCs in R&D with changes in the global business environment, not only gaining access to personnel but also exploiting the cost differentials. Shortages in personnel in engineering fields relating to electronics have led them to locate some of their strategic R&D in countries like India (1822). With liberalisation of the Indian economy and rationalisation of the operations of MNCs, the primary driving force to relocate R&D to India is the new technology which, unlike conventional technologies that required continuous interaction between design and other functions, is not geographically constrained (ibid.).

Growing economic and political interaction between developing countries and MNCs has led Kogut to ask whether foreign direct investment is good or bad. While the Indian experience, particularly in the pre-Cold War days, was mixed, the experience of the past decade during which 230 MNCs have set up development centres in Bangalore, appears positive for both. Under the leadership of Infosys, the large firms created a Quality Association in the 1990s to share experiences and improve quality. Unusual as this may seem as learning within Indian software industry occurs within the firm and not through interaction with customers and suppliers, this may have encouraged Indian software companies to seek CMM Level quality assurance.

A different view is revealed by Dayasindhu (in Thatchenkery and Stough 2005) in his study of the working of a US-based semi-conductor (SC) company which remains competitive in R&D services domain in the Indian IT industry. To maintain its competitive edge, it manages a network of organisations where resource is inimitable and central to competitive advantage. This is done by the outsourcing of Digital Signal Processing (DSP) software and hardware through a dedicated division (DG) established in the 1990s in Bangalore. Operating in the R&D services domain, DG provides complete solutions using SC's chips and third party organisations in the network. Acknowledging that an SC company's success rests on relationship building and effective communication, the head of the DG in India pointed out the 'dual outlook of the company: the Indian mindset mentoring of third party organisations and the American style of functioning reflected in the contractual rules on fixed cost pricing. This may be a result of the fact that half of the employees of DG are Indian while SC is an American organisation' (133–39).

With the large number of MNC development centres operating in Bangalore which are faced with the problem of keeping expensive teams together between projects, Wipro offers such firms an option by maintaining a big R&D service firm employing 6,500. Engineers are deputed to undertake projects on total product ownership through to global development and maintenance requirements, or other R&D solutions. Elaborate procedures, such as a cooling-off period between clients, have been developed to protect customer intellectual property. Such in-house research teams constitute a third of Wipro's annual revenue of $1 billion (Dahlman and Utz 2005).

Growth in any area has to be fuelled by skilled human power. Recognition of the high quality of India's software engineers brought on by the Y2K crisis and by the Internet boom of the late 1990s (Saxenian 2006) drew attention to the skills of Indian software engineers (291). These changes have had an impact on overseas Indians who are now keen to return to India, a reverse brain drain as it were. 'The passage back is no longer an ordeal, because much has changed in India... Indians who once could choose between only two car models and fly a single airline find they have returned to a profusion of choices, even as the life style gaps between India and the West have narrowed rapidly' (Saritha Rai, *The Hindu*, 27 December 2005). Apart from the desire to enjoy life in familiar surroundings with attractive salaries, other factors are security concerns after 9/11 and the recurring debate on outsourcing. 'The "move to India" initiative taken by i2 Technologies to relocate many of its personnel from the US to its Indian development centre ... has helped the Indian IT industry take crucial steps towards maturity' (*The Hindu*, 3 December 2003). According to the World Investment Report 2005, more and more scientists and engineers are staying or returning to take up R&D work. 'In Bangalore for example nearly 35,000 NRIs have lately returned with training and experience in the US' (Raghu Dayal, 'Prospects of Global Investment', *The Hindu*, 28 March 2006).

Concern in the industry, relating to impending shortages of skilled human resources and declining quality as a result of the plethora of colleges being set up, could be translated into action with some input into training. Bangalore's growth as a hub of technology is due to the growing number of innovative firms, the availability of venture capital and the high quality of design-intensive human resources. While there has been a transformation from production to innovation as seen by the increase in the number of patents, further innovations can only come about with more venture capital and active support from local institutions and government.

8.7 Conclusion

Bangalore's transformation, beginning with electrification in 1902 to its current status as a software capital, is a story of technological progress studded with innovative agricultural, industrial and engineering enterprises and a steadily expanding knowledge base. Industrial unrest in West Bengal and booming real estate prices in Mumbai in the 1970s led to the move of first the engineering industry and then the burgeoning software industry in Bangalore's direction. Economic liberalisation of the 1980s and 1990s and an encouraging state government enabled Indian entrepreneurs to respond to opportunities in IT. A favourable investment climate and an abundance of skills soon attracted the attention of MNCs. Its growing status as a leading centre of IT in the world is attributed to its openness to outsiders who find its cosmopolitan character conducive to creative work. The presence of internationally renowned centres of S&T such as the IISc, major aerospace research and manufacturing institutions and industrial enterprises and its high concentration of scientists and technologists continues to attract multinationals wanting to set up development centres.

However, the unprecedented growth has put great pressure on Bangalore's infrastructure, with increasing traffic congestion and shortage of housing leading to high prices and pressure on essential services like schools, roads and hospitals. It is hoped that initiatives such as the IT corridor, the Metro Rail, the new international airport and the dispersal of software companies to other secondary locations will help to relieve the current congestion and improve living conditions for the average Bangalorean.

9

A Summing-Up

By 2007, India was seen as a knowledge-based economy on the verge of becoming a knowledge superpower. Arising from its diversified science and technology infrastructure, a market economy with developed financial institutions and its skilled human capital, this dramatic turnaround owes its origins to an economy that has grown steadily, a rich cultural base that has generated a wealth of ideas, a vibrant democracy with a free press, free trade unions and a secular state (Dahlman and Utz 2005, *New Scientist,* 19 February 2005). Foreign observers appear to share the popular notion that the entire transformation is due to the 1991 policy of economic liberalisation. Admittedly, India's economic liberalisation opened up the economy by removing restrictive government regulations, but that by itself could not have effected such a transformation. 'The critical thing to understand is not where the seed comes from, but what makes the soil fertile' (Kingdon 1984, 81). In this context, the seed that had come through liberalisation could certainly not have borne the fruit (knowledge economy) without the fertile soil nurtured through several decades. That nurturing process has been discussed in this book. In essence, this study adopts a historical-institutionalist approach and traces the present success to the state's role in building the institutional foundations now acknowledged as the pillars of the knowledge economy: a constitutional democracy, an S&T infrastructure and an industrial economy.

In its journey from scratch in the 1950s to an economic powerhouse early in the twenty-first century, India did not waver from state-directed programmes and policies, adhering more to pragmatic considerations than ideology. Such a practical approach and openness allowed for subtle nuances and adaptations to changing circumstances. An illustration of such pragmatism is the adoption of economic liberalisation in 1991 and rejection of the IMF's insistence on financial deregulation. As it turned out, India and China, the only two countries in Asia which declined to adopt it, survived the Asian financial crisis of 1997. While India's journey has been fraught with obstacles, some domestic, arising from its democratic tradition and its openness, others external, a reaction to its independent position in economic and foreign policy, its IT revolution has come about on the back of a scientific and industrial base laid in the 1950s and 1960s, followed by the green revolution of the 1970s and the white revolution of the 1980s. Those three prior transformations symbolised India's desire for economic self-reliance. In the area of ICT, too, India did assert that sense of independence selectively, illustrated by IBM's exit in 1978.

Even the most ardent supporters of self-reliance cannot overlook the consequences of using bureaucratic machinery to promote state-directed development. The bureaucratic edifice built over the years with elitist traditions inherited from colonial times was entrusted with the task of building an industrial economy. When given the power to decide on investments, it resorted to a range of regulations. That regime of controls and regulations became part of an industrial policy that earmarked areas in which the public and private sectors of the economy could invest. Within the areas earmarked for the private sector, intending investors had to seek licences to apply for scarce foreign exchange and import machinery or raw material not available in the country. Under the 'licence raj', some departments gained undue power; others indulged in bureaucratic infighting, allowing vested interests to thwart the goals of development.

In the context of ICT, one observes an underlying conflict between the AEC and the Defence Production Organisation seeking to establish their respective power over electronics policy making. This battle was temporarily settled when the DOE (1970) and EC (1971) were set up comprised largely of former AEC staff. But then the scene shifted to the ECIL, a public undertaking under a Ministry attached to AEC, and BEL in the matter of defence production. While the ECIL/BEL antagonism remained under the surface, an issue that was of greater importance to EC and DOE was the attitude adopted by IBM vis-à-vis the request of those two institutions to allow greater Indian equity participation in its Indian operations. IBM's refusal to accommodate that request ultimately led to its exit in 1978. What was apparently a business decision for IBM was for DOE a case of asserting India's technological independence. It became a trigger for the indigenous computer industry which utilised this opportunity to extend its operations in India and abroad by competing in the international market successfully (Evans

1995). The exit of IBM was an event of major significance for the Indian computer industry. Not only did it revive the sagging fortunes of ECIL; it provided a great opportunity for Indian programmers who had been working for IBM to be assigned to the newly created CMC that had been set up to undertake maintenance of over two hundred types of imported computers. That experience over different platforms and of diverse legacies proved invaluable in the worldwide computer business. IBM has since returned to India with an employee strength of twenty-five thousand at its various operations and has set up a campus at Bangalore.

While one multinational was unwilling to adapt to local demands, there were others like Burroughs and ICL who had no problems in compliance. In later years, DOE moved from the controlling image associated with Indian bureaucracy to one of flexibility to accommodate TI at Bangalore. This marked the beginning of a new phase in the Indian government's attitude towards investment by MNCs. It is important to acknowledge the influence of the tech-savvy Prime Minister Rajiv Gandhi, who was accessible to DOE technocrats, and the role of Indian expats working in the US, who established official and business links in India. This configuration of forces coincided with rapid technological change in ICT. Further, TI's entry into Bangalore accelerated the process by establishing satellite links with its headquarters in Dallas and allowing other software companies to use them. This communication link to the outside world proved invaluable in energising the slowly evolving Indian telecommunication scene.

Of the expats, Sam Pitroda played a vital role in conjunction with Rajiv Gandhi in modernising communications in India. In persuading the authorities to shift from mechanical to digital switching, he revolutionised Indian communications by making a technological breakthrough suited to local conditions. The use or the attachment of a simple device enabled widespread access even to non-owners of telephones when the setting up of Public Call Offices (PCOs) in towns and villages opened up the communication scene in India. Coinciding with ISRO's development of V-SAT and C-DAC supercomputers, these changes ushered in the age of high-tech culture. The transformation of public undertakings from producers to technological entrepreneurs using the private sector reflected an entirely new attitude. Despite the liberalisation and changes in communication technology, the Department of Telecommunication's (DOT) monopoly control of operations continued to stifle progress. To counteract this, DOE set up the STPI, which offered satellite communication for software exporters. Surging software exports led the industry, with support from STPI, to set up NASSCOM, and together they brought pressure on government to reform DOT. The latter's delayed recognition of the significance of communication to IT certainly had a negative effect. However, the industry has since moved on.

The entry of TI into Bangalore followed by Motorola, Hewlett Packard and Intel was formal recognition of that city's status as India's centre for S&T. With Electronics City, STPI and NASSCOM all working from the same region, the presence of other enabling factors brought in more MNCs, thus establishing the Bangalore-Silicon Valley connection. A climate of academic research, high skills and a network of suppliers enhanced by social capital created a situation aptly visualised by Cooke (2002) as 'all boats ... (being) lifted by a rising tide mentality' (105). Through its S&T institutions, the quality of its human resources, its climate, its cosmopolitan culture of openness (termed 'glocalisation' by Friedman 2004) and its own incentives for investment, Bangalore has succeeded in attracting overseas Indians back to work and to invest, earning for itself the appellation 'Silicon Plateau' (Saxenian 2002, Florida 2005).

The growth of ICT has been phenomenal with rather drastic consequences. Once known for its well laid out roads, gardens and gentle people, Bangalore has failed to cope with the influx from within and abroad resulting in a crumbling infrastructure. BATF, a public-private partnership, which emerged as a 'civic entrepreneur' (Cooke 2002), working closely with state government and local administration to highlight and resolve civic problems, has suffered some setbacks.

The growth of ICT offers wide ranging opportunities for both developed and developing economies although the impact for the latter is uneven because it tends to concentrate in areas where skills are readily available. While this phenomenon of regional advantage is unavoidable, state governments in India are making efforts to use ICT to promote enterprise in rural communities in areas such as fishing, dairying, sugarcane, tobacco and sericulture. Success stories include rural development programmes associated with the M. S. Swamination Foundation with support from the Tatas and ISRO, Karnataka's Bhoomi, Madhya Pradesh's Gyandoot and the ITC supported E-Choupal. Yet for a country of India's size and complexity, there is now greater recognition that the comparative advantage in the new economy will shift to those who have the ability to create, adapt and use knowledge to spur growth and innovation, though access to ICT for all might remain a distant dream. While India is on the verge of becoming a knowledge economy, no one can overlook the immense problems that remain to be tackled or the problems caused by inequalities being aggravated with the success of ICT.

References

Abbott, Jason P. 2004. *The Political Economy of the Internet in Asia and the Pacific: Digital Divides, Economic Competitiveness and Security Challenges.* London: Praeger.

Adiga, Aravind. 2008. *The White Tiger*. London: Atlantic Books.

Balakrishna, R. 1940. *Industrial Development of Mysore*. Bangalore: Bangalore Press.

Balasubramaniam, D. 1996. 'Rid Polio for a Dozen Rupees'. *The Hindu Science and Technology*, 19 December.

Barnes, Trevor and Meric S. Gertler eds. 1999. *The New Industrial Geography: Regions, Regulation and Institution*. New York: Routledge.

Beccatini, Giacomo. 2002. 'Sectors and/or Districts: Some Remarks on the Conceptual Foundations of Industrial Economies' in Edward Goodman and Julia Bamford eds. *Small Firms and Industrial Districts in Italy*. London: Routledge, 123–35.

Bellet, Michel and Corine L'Hermet. 1998. *Industry, Space and Competition: The Contributions of Economists of the Past.* Cheltenham: Edward Elgar.

Berlamaqui, L., Al Castra and H.J. Chang. 2000. *Institutions and the Role of the State*. Cheltenham: Edward Elgar.

Bhagwati, Jagdish. 1988. 'Poverty and Public Policy'. *World Development*, vol. 16, 539–55.

Bhargava, Pushpa Mitra and Chandana Chakrabarti. 2003. *The Saga of Indian Science: In a Nutshell*. Hyderabad: University Press.

Bhatia, Mohan. 1993. 'What Ails Scientific Research'. *The Hindu*, 9 November.

———. 2003. 'What Ails Indian Science?' *Deccan Herald*, 14 May.

Bhatt, V. V. 1980. *Development Perspectives: Problems, Strategy and Policies.* Oxford: Pergamon Press.

Boyer, Robert. 2004. *The Future of Economic Growth: As New Becomes Old.* Cheltenham: Edward Elgar.

Brown, John Seely and Paul Diguid. 2000. 'Mysteries of the Region[illegible] Knowledge [illegible] Silicon Valley' in Chong-Moon Lee et al. eds. *The Silicon Valley Edge: A Habitat for Innovation and Entrepreneurship*. Stanford: Stanford University Press, 16–39.

Brunner, Hans-Peter. 1995. *Closing the Gap: Technological Change in India's Computer Industry*. New Delhi: Sage.

Cadene, Philippe and Mark Holmstrom eds. 1998. *Decentralised Production in India: Industrial Districts, Flexible Specialisation and Employment*. New Delhi: Sage.

Chandrakanth, R. 2005. 'Techno-Managers Propel Growth'. *The Hindu*, 11 July.

Chandrasekhar, N. S. 1940. *Inside Mysore*. Bangalore: Hosali Press.

______. 1981. *Builders of Modern India: Dewan Seshadri Iyer*. New Delhi: Publications Division, Government of India.

Chary, S. N. 2003. 'IITs: The Vision is Gone, Hype Remains'. *Deccan Herald*. 14 March.

Chowdhury, T. H. 2004. 'Liberalisation of India's Telecom: Regulation in the Era of Convergence for Information, Infrastructure and Services' in Kenneth Keniston and Deepak Kumar eds. *Information Technology Experience in India: Bridging the Digital Divide*.

Coenen, Lars and Bjorn Asheim. 2006. 'Constructing Regional Advantage at the Northern Edge' in Cooke and Piccaluga eds. *Regional Development in the Knowledge Economy*, 84–110.

Commander, Simon ed. 2005. *The Software Industry in Emerging Markets*. Cheltenham: Edward Elgar.

Cooke, Philip. 2002. *Knowledge Economies: Clusters, Learning and Cooperative Advantage*. London: Routledge.

Cooke, Phillip and Andrea Piccaluga eds. 2006. *Regional Development in the Knowledge Economy*. London/New York: Routledge.

Dahlman, Carl and Anuja Utz. 2005. *India and the Knowledge Economy: Leveraging Strengths and Opportunities*. Washington, DC: The World Bank.

Das, Aditya Raj. 2000. 'Billing Power Reforms on the Overdrive'. *Deccan Herald*, 11 December.

Das, Gurcharan. 2006. 'The India Model'. *Foreign Affairs*, July/August, 2–16.

Das, Manoj. 2002. 'Kochi Brothers build Country's First Indigenous Airborne Antenna'. *New Indian Express*, 25 April, 7–8.

Davies, Paul. 2004. *What's This India Business? Offshoring, Outsourcing, and Global Services Revolution*. London: Nicholas Brealey International and Association with NIIT Technologies.

D'Costa, Anthony P. and E. Sridharan eds. 2003. *India in the Global Software Industry: Innovation, Firm Strategies and Development*. Basingstoke: Palgrave Macmillan.

Debelle, Penelope. 2007. 'Encounter with Danah Boyd: The Internet Guru'. *The Age (Melbourne)*. 4 August, Insight, 10.

Degnbol-Martinussen, John. 2001. *Policies, Institutions and Development: Coping with Liberalization and International Competition in India*. London/New Delhi: Sage Publications.

Deutsch, Karl. 1971. 'Developmental Change: Some Political Aspects', in J. Paul Leagans and Charles P. Loomis eds. *Behavioural Change in Agriculture: Concepts and Strategies for Influencing Transition*. Ithaca: Cornell University Press, 21–50.

Dore, Ronald. 1989. 'Technology in the World of National Frontiers'. *World Development*, vol. 17, 1666–75.

Dossani, Rafiq and Martin Kenney. 2002. 'Creating an Environment for Venture Capital in India.' *World Development*, vol. 30, 227–53.

Duysters, Gert. 1996. *The Dynamics of Technical Innovation: The Evolution of Information Technology*. Cheltenham: Edward Elgar.

Economist, The. 1987 (9 May), 1995 (21 January). London.

Elkins, Paul and Manfred Max Neef. 1990. *Real Life Economics: Understanding Wealth Creation*. London: Routledge.

Evans, Peter. 1995. *Embedded Autonomy: States and Industrial Transformation*. Princeton: Princeton University Press.

Farrel, Diana et al. 2005. 'Ensuring India's Competitiveness in Offshoring' from The McKinsey Quarterly 2005 in *Deccan Herald*, 3 October 2005.

Florida, Richard. 2005. *The Flight of the Creative Class*. New York: Harper Business.

Foray, Dominique. 2004. *Economics of Knowledge*. Cambridge: MIT Press.

Friedman, John. 2004. 'Glocalisation' in *New York Times*, 11 March.

Gertler, Meric S. 2005. 'Tacit Knowledge, Path Dependency and Local Trajectories of Growth' in Gerald Fuchs and Philip Shapira eds. *Rethinking Regional Innovation and Change: Path Dependency or Regional Breakthrough*. New York: Springer, 23–41.

Gourevitch, Peter, Roger Bohn and David Mckendrick. 2000. 'Globalization of Production: Insights from Hard Disk Drive Industry' *World Development*, vol. 28, 301–17.

Government Sandal Wood Factory. 1960. *Origin of the Sandal Wood Oil Factories in Mysore*. Centenary Celebrations Publication

Granovettor, Mark. 1985. 'Economic Action and Social Structures: the Problem of Embeddeness'. *American Journal of Sociology*, vol. 91, 481–510.

Greenspan, Anna. 2004. *India and the IT Revolution: Networks of Global Culture*. Basingstoke: Palgrave Macmillan.

Greico, Joseph M. 1984. *Between Dependency and Autonomy: India's Experience with International Computer Industry*. Berkeley: University of California Press.

Guha, Ramachandra. 2003. 'The Locality and the Nation'. *The Hindu Magazine*, 31 August.

———. 2004. 'Past and Present: The Mysore Generation'. *The Hindu Magazine*, 25 April.

Hamm, Steve. 2006. *Bangalore Tiger: How Indian Tech Upstart Wipro is Rewriting the Rules of Global Competition*. New Delhi: Tata-McGraw.

Hammish, Murray ed. 1930. *History of Mysore by Lt. Col Mark Wilks*. Bangalore: Mysore Government Press.

Hanlon, Joseph. 1977a. 'India Back to the Villages: Does AT [alternative technology] Walk on Plastic Sandals'. *New Scientist*, 26 May, 467.

______. 1977b. 'India Back to the Villages: AT in the Ivory Tower'. *New Scientist*, 2 June, 536.

Heeks, Richard. 1996. *India's Software Industry: State Policy, Liberalization and Industrial Development*. London/New Delhi: Sage Publications.

______. 2004. 'Facing In Facing Out: Information Technology Production Policy in India from 1960s to 1990s' in Richard Coopey ed. *Information Technology Policy: An International History*. London: Oxford University Press.

Heitzman, James. 2004. *Network City: Planning the Information Society in Bangalore*. New Delhi: Oxford University Press.

Herrigel, Gary. 1996. *Industrial Reconstructions: The Sources of German Industrial Power*. Chicago: University of Chicago Press.

Hinds, Manuel. 2003. *The Triumph of the Flexible Society: The Connectivity Revolution and the Resistance to Change*. London: Praeger.

Hubner, Kurt ed. 2005. *The New Economy in Transatlantic Perspective: Spaces of Innovation*. London: Routledge.

Husain, Dildar. 1960. *An Engineering Wizard of India (1861–1962)*. Hyderabad: Institute of Engineers.

Hveem, Helge. 1983. 'Selective Dissociation in the Technology Sector' in Gerald Ruggie ed. *The Antinomies of Interdependence: National Welfare and the International Division of Labour*. New York: University of Columbia Press.

'India: The Next Knowledge Superpower'. 2005. *The New Scientist*, 19 February, 30–53.

International Institute of Labour Studies. 1997. *Linking Up with the Global Economy: A Case Study of the Bangalore Software Industry*. Rome: ILO.

Ismail, Sir Mirza. 1954. *My Public Life: Recollection of Reflections*. London: Allen & Unwin.

James, Jeffrey. 2003. *Bridging the Global Digital Divide*. Cheltenham: Edward Elgar.

Jayaraman, K.S. 2002. 'India online'. *Nature*, vol. 415, 24 January, 358–59.

Jha, Raghbendra ed. 2003. *Indian Economic Reforms*. London: Palgrave Macmillan.

______. 2005. *Economic Growth, Economic Performance and Welfare in South Asia*. Basingstoke: Palgrave Macmillan.

Joseph, Ammu. 2003. 'Whose Information Is It?' *The Hindu*, 7 December.

Joseph, K. J. 1997. *Industry Under Economic Liberalization: The Case of Indian Electronics*. New Delhi/London: Sage Publications.

______. 2003. 'Perils of Excessive Export Orientation: Case of India's ICT Sector'. Paper presented at a seminar on Indian Development organised jointly by School of Public Policy, George Mason University and the Department of Management Studies, Indian Institute of Science, 3–5 March, Bangalore.

Kalam, Abdul. 2002. *Ignited Minds: Unleashing the Power within India*. New Delhi: Penguin.

Karnik, Kiran. 2003. 'Challenges on the Home Front', *http:/www.nasscom.org/artdisplay.asp?Art_id=2007*.

Katakan, Anupama. 2002. 'Enron: A Sale on Hold' in *Frontline*, 1 May.

Keniston, Kenneth and Deepak Kumar eds. 2004. *Information Technology Experience in India: Bridging the Digital Divide*. New Delhi: Sage.

Kenney, Martin ed. 2000. *Understanding Silicon Valley: The Anatomy of an Entrepreneurial Region*. Palo Alto: Stanford University Press.

Khatkate, Deena R. 1997. India's Economic Growth: A Conundrum' in *World Development*, vol. 25, 1551–57.

Kingdon, John W. 1984. *Agendas, Alternatives and Public Policies*. Boston: Little Brown.

Kogut, Bruce ed. 2003. *The Global Internet Economy*. Cambridge: MIT Press.

______. 2004. 'From Regions and Firms to Multinational Highways: Knowledge and its Diffusion as a Factor in the Globalization of Industries' in Martin Kenney and Richard Florida eds. *Locating Global Advantage: Industry Dynamics in the International Economy*. Stanford: Stanford University Press, 261–81.

Kohli, Atul. 2004. *State-Directed Development: Political Power and Industrialisation in the Global Periphery*. Cambridge: Cambridge University Press.

Kripalani, Manjeet. 2002. 'Bangalore: Multinationals are making it a hub of high-tech research'. *Business Week*/Online, 11 November.

Krueger, Anne O. ed. 2002. *Economic Policy Reforms and the Indian Economy*. Chicago: University of Chicago Press.

Kudaisya, Gyanesh. 2002. 'India's New Mantra: the Internet' in *Current History*, vol. 415, January, 162–69.

Landes, David S. 1998. *The Wealth and Poverty of Nations: Why Some are so Rich and Some so Poor*. New York: W. W. Norton.

Lundgren, Andres. 1995. *Technological Innovation and Network Evolution*. London: Routledge.

McCann, Philip. 2002. *Industrial Location Economics*. Cheltenham: Edward Elgar.

McKendrick, David. 2004. 'Leveraging Locations: Hard-Disk Driven Producers in International Competition' in Martin Kenney and Richard Florida eds. *Locating Global Advantage: Industry Dynamics in the International Economy*. Stanford: Stanford University Press, 142–74.

McKnight, Lee W. et al. 2003. 'Creative Destruction in Emerging Markets: Privatizing Telecoms and the State' in Lorrie Faith Cranor and Steven S. Wildman eds. *Rethinking Rights and Regulations: Institutional Responses to New Communication Technologies*. Cambridge: MIT Press, 367–91.

Maddisson, Angus. 1995. *Explaining the Economic Performance of Nations: Essays in Time and Space*, Cheltenham: Edward Elgar.

Maddox, John and Vera Rich. 1984. 'Science in India: Excellence in the Midst of Poverty'. *Nature*, vol. 308, April, 581–600.

Maitra, Dilip. 2002. 'Delivery in Difficult Times' in *Deccan Herald-Economics & Business*, 15 April.

Mani, Sunil. 1995. 'Technology Import and Skill Development in Microelectronics-Based Industry: The Case of Electronic Switching System' in Amiya Kumar Bagchi ed. *New Technology and Workers' Response: Microelectronics, Labour and Society*. New Delhi: Sage, 98–122.

———. 2003A. *Government Innovation and Technology Policy: an International Comparative Analysis, New Horizons in the Economics of Innovation*. Cheltenham: Edward Elgar, 2–49.

———. 2003B. *Deregulation, Entry of MNCs, Public Technology Procurement and Innovation Capability in India's Telecommunication Equipment Industry*. Maastricht: United Nations University, Institute for New Technologies.

Manor, James. 1977. *Political Change in an Indian State: Mysore, 1917–1950*. New Delhi: Manohar.

Marshall, Alfred. 1919. *Elements of Economics of Industry*. London: Macmillan.

Martin, Max. 2002. 'Building Bridges Across the Digital Divide' in *New Indian Express*, 22 April.

Mascarenhas, Reginald C. 1974. 'A Systems Approach to the Measurement of the Performance of Public Enterprises in India' in *Policy Sciences*, vol. 5, 75–95.

———. 1982. *Technology Transfer and Development: India's Hindustan Machine Tools Company*. Boulder: Westview Press.

———. 1988. *A Strategy for Rural Development: Dairy Cooperatives in India*. New Delhi/London: Sage.

———. 1996. *Government and the Economy in Australia and New Zealand: The Politics of Economic Policy Making*. San Francisco: Austin & Winfield.

———. 1999. *Comparative Political Economy of East and South Asia: A Critique of Development Policy and Management*. Basingstoke: Palgrave Macmillan.

Mascarenhas, Reginald C. 2002. *Comparative Political Economy of Industrial Capitalism*. Basingstoke: Palgrave Macmillan.

______. 2004. 'Sir M. Visvesvaraya: The Grand Engineer Statesman of Mysore' in *Tribute: Bharat Ratna Sir M. Visvesvaraya*. Bangalore: Visvesvaraya National Memorial Trust, 4–9.

______. 2004. 'Institution Building: The Role of Public Entrepreneurs' in P. L. Sanjeev Reddy, Jaideep Singh and R. K. Tiwari eds. *Pursuit of Institutional Excellence: Essays in Honour of V. K. N. Menon*. New Delhi: Indian Institute of Public Administration, 143–64.

Metcalfe, J. S. 2005. 'Equilibrium and Evolutionary Foundations of Competition and Technology Policy: New Perspectives on the Division of Labour and the Innovation Process' in Douglas North, et al. *Wider Perspectives on Global Development*. Basingstoke: Palgrave Macmillan.

Misra, Neelesh. 2001. 'India Begins to see fruits of Information Age' in *San Francisco Chronicle*, 15 January.

Montgomery, John D. 1974. *Technology and Civic Life*, Cambridge: MIT Press.

Moreau, Francois. 2004. 'The Role of the State in Evolutionary Economics' in *Cambridge Journal of Economics*, vol. 28, 847–74.

Murari, Timeri. 2003. 'Sly History' in *The Hindu*, 2 November.

Murphy, Dervlan. 1976. *On a Shoestring to Coorg: An Experience of South India*. London: John Murray.

Murtha, Thomas P. et al. 2001. *Managing New Industry Creation: Global Knowledge Formation and Entrepreneurship in High Technology*. Stanford: Stanford University Press.

Musson, A. E. ed. 1972. *Science, Technology and Economic Growth in the Eighteenth Century*. London: Methuen.

Naidu, B. V. 2003. 'Tracing the History of Indian Information Technology' in Mehroo Jasswalla and Richard D. Taylor eds. *Information Technology Parks of Asia Pacific: Lessons for Regional Digital Divide*. New York: M. E. Scharpe.

______. 2004. *Scientific Technology Parks of India*. Bangalore.

Nair, Janaki. 2005. *The promise of the Metropolis: Bangalore's Twentieth Century*. New Delhi: Oxford University Press.

NASSCOM. 2003. *World Bank Hails India's IT Sector*. 30 July. *http:/www.nasscom.org/artdisplay.asp?Art_id=2007*.

______. 2005. *Indian I T Industry Fact Sheet*.

Nehru, Jawaharlal. 1946. *The Discovery of India*. Oxford University Press. (7th ed. 1988).

Nelson, Richard R. 2005. *The Limits of Market Organisation*. New York: Russel Sage.

Nelson, R. and S. Winter. 1982. *An Evolutionary Theory of Economic Change*. Cambridge: Harvard University Press.

New Scientist Weekly. 2005. *India: The Next Superpower*. Special Edition. 19 February.

Norman, Dorothy. 1965. *Nehru: The First Sixty Years*, vol. II. London: The Bodley Head.

Okada, Aya. 2005. 'Bangalore's Software Cluster' in Kuchiki Akifumi and Masatsugu Tsuji eds. *Industrial Clusters in Asia: Analysis of their Competition and Cooperation*. Basingstoke: Palgrave Macmillan-IDC JETRO, 244–77.

Ojha, Abhey K. and S. Krishnan. 2003. 'Originative Innovation and Entrepreneurship in the Software Industry in India' in D'Costa and Sridharan eds. *India in the Global Software Industry: Innovation, Firm Strategies and Development*. Basingstoke: Palgrave Macmillan.

Panagariya, Arvind. 2008. *India the Emerging Giant*. New York: Oxford University Press.

Parayil, Govindan. ed. 2006. *Political Economy and Information Capitalism in India*. Basingstoke: Palgrave Macmillan.

Parthasarathy, Anand. 2003a. 'Modem on a Chip by an Indian Team' in *The Hindu*, 30 May.

______. 2003b. 'India-based Motorola Team scales New Heights' in *The Hindu*, 19 June.

______. 2004. 'IT for e-Empowerment' in *The Hindu*, 22 January.

Parthasarathy, Ashok. 2003. 'Commentary: A Champion of New Technologies' in *Nature*, vol. 422, 6 March, 17–18.

Parthasarathy, Ashok and Raman Puri. 2008. 'The case to support the indigenous LCA' in *The Hindu*, 9 March.

Patibandla, Murali and Bent Petersen. 2002. 'Role of Transnational Corporations in the Evolution of High-Tech Industry: the Case of India's Software Industry' in *World Development*, vol. 30, 1561–77.

Pavel, Pelikan and Gerhard Wegner. eds. *The Evolutionary Analysis of Economic Policy*. Cheltenham: Edward Elgar, 162–89.

Pedersen, Jorgen. 2000. 'Explaining Economic Liberalization in India' in *World Development*, vol. 28, 265–82.

Piore, Michael J. and Charles F. Sabel. 1984. *The Second Industrial Divide: Possibilities for Prosperity*. New York: Basic Books.

Pitroda, Sam. 1993. 'Development, Democracy and Village Development' in *Harvard Business Review*, Nov.–Dec. 66–79.

Polanyi, Michael. 1958. *Personal Knowledge*. London: Routledge.

Porter, Michael E. 1990. 'The Competitive Advantage of Nations' in *Harvard Business Review*, March–April, 73–93.

Preer, Robert W. 1992. *The Emergence of Technopolis: Knowledge-Intensive Technologies and Regional Development.* New York: Praeger.

Prestowitz, Clyde. 2005. *Three Billion New Capitalists: The Great Shift of Wealth and Power to the East.* New York: Basic Books.

Putnam, Robert D. 1992. *Making Democracy Work.* Princeton: Princeton University Press.

______. 2000. *Bowling Alone: The Collapse and Revival of American Community.* New York: Simon & Schuster.

Raj, K. N. 1973. 'The Politics and Economics of Intermediate Regimes' in *Kale Memorial Lecture.* Pune.

Raja, Adita and T. R. Raghunandan. 2002. 'Pioneer Power Projects' in *Deccan Herald,* 10 December.

Rama Rao, Navarathna. 1965. 'A Prophecy Come True' in *M. Visvesvaraya: By Contemporories and Admirers.* Bangalore: Visvesvaraya Centenary Celebrations.

Rangachar, H. and P. Kodanda Rao. 1965. 'A Brief Life Sketch' in *M. Visvesvaraya: By Contemporaries and Admirers.* Bangalore: Visvesvaraya Centenary Celebrations.

Ram, Susan and N. Ram. 1994. *R.K. Narayan: Early Years, 1906–1945,* vol. I. New Delhi: Vikas.

Ramunajam, T. C. A. 1992. 'Science and Technology for Development' in *The Hindu,* 25 August.

Rao, Hayavadana. ed. 1929. *The Mysore Gazetteer,* vols I–VIII, Compiled by Government. Bangalore: Government Press.

______. 1936. *The Dasara in Mysore: Its Origin and Significance.* Bangalore: The Bangalore Press and Publishing Co.

Rao, Narayana. 1973. *Mokshagundum Visvesvaraya: His Life and Work.* Mysore: Geeta Book House.

Ravi, N. 2005. 'How Human Would the Human Face be?' in *The Hindu,* 25 February.

Ravindran, Nirmala. 2004. 'The Taskless Force' in *India Today,* July 12, 32–33.

Reddy, Manmohan. 2004. 'Wings in Wheels' in *The Hindu,* April, 12.

Reddy, Prasad. 1997. 'New Trends in Globalisation of R&D and Implications for Innovation Capability in Host Countries: A Survey' in *World Development,* vol. 25 (11), 1821–37.

Reid, T. R. 2005. 'Inventor who built tiny foundation for Electronic Age dies' in *The Age,* 23 June.

Rodrik, Dani and Arvind Subramaniam. 2004. 'The Economy's next two Decades' in *The Hindu,* 15 and 17 May.

Roemier, Michael. 1981. 'Dependence and Industrialization' in *World Development,* vol. 9, 429–34.

Rosenberg, David. 2003. 'US Cultural and Economic Hegemony looks like a Case of Send the Clones' in *The Age*, 27 July.

Rothermund, Dietmar. 2008. *India: The Rise of an Asian Giant*. New Haven: Yale University Press.

Rudolph, Lloyd I. and Susan Hoeber Rudolph. 1987. *In Pursuit of Lakshmi: The Political Economy of the Indian State*. Chicago: Chicago University Press.

Ryan, Marie-Laure. ed. 1999. *Cyberspace Textuality: Computer Technology and Literary Theory*. Bloomington: Indiana University Press.

Sachitanand, N. N. 2006. 'Major Obstacles to Metal Sector Growth'. *The Hindu*, 13 March.

Sardan, Ziauddin and Jerome Ravetz. 1996. *Cyberfuture, Culture and Politics in Information Superhighway*. London: Pluto Press.

Satyan, T. S. 2005. *Alive and Clicking: a Memoir*. New Delhi: Penguin.

Saxenian, Anna Lee. 1994. *Regional Advantage: Silicon Valley and Route 128*. Boston: Harvard University Press.

———. 2000. 'The Origins and Dynamic of Production Networks in Silicon Valley' in Martin Kenney ed. *Understanding Silicon Valley: the Anatomy of an Entrepreneurial Region*. Stanford: Stanford University Press, 141–62.

———. 2002a. 'Bangalore: The Silicon Valley of Asia?' in Anne O. Krueger ed. *Economic Policy Reforms in the Indian Economy*. Chicago: University of Chicago Press, 169–211.

———. 2002b. 'Bangalore: The Silicon Valley of Asia' Comments by Narayana Murthy and Sandeep Raju in Krueger ed. *The Economic Policy Reforms*, 160–210.

———. 2003. 'The Silicon Valley Connection: Transnational Networks and Regional Development in Taiwan, China and India' in D'Costa and Sridharan eds. *India in the Global Software Industry*. Basingstoke: Palgrave Macmillan.

———. 2006. *The New Argonauts: Regional Advantage in a Global Economy*. Cambridge: Harvard University Press.

Scherrer, Christopher. 2005. 'Beyond Path Dependence and Competitive Convergence: Institutional Transfer from a Discourse-Analytical Perspective' in Gerald Fuchs and Philip Shapira eds. *Rethinking Regional Innovation and Change: Path Dependence or Regional Breakthrough*. New York: Springer, 1–21.

Schware, Robert. 1987. 'Software Industry Development in the Third World: Policy Guidelines, Institutional Options and Constraints' in *World Development*, vol. 15, 1249–67.

———. 1992. 'Software Industry Entry Strategies For Developing Countries: A "Walking on Two Legs" Proposition' in *World Development*, vol. 20, 143–64.

Scott, Allan J. 1993. *Technopolis: High Technology Industry and Regional Development in Southern California*. Berkeley: University of California Press.

Scott, Allan J. and Michael Storper. 1992. 'Regional Development Reconsidered' in Herb Ernste and Verena Meir eds. *Regional Development and Contemporary Industrial Response: Extending Flexible Specialisation*. London: Belhaven Press.

Sen, Amartya. 1984. *Resources, Values and Development*. London: Basil Blackwell.

______. 2005. *The Argumentative Indian: Writings on Indian History, Culture and Identity*. New Delhi: Penguin.

Sender, Henry. 2000. 'Building the New India' in *Far Eastern Economic Review*, 48–52.

Sharma, Ravi. 2005. 'IAF reluctant to place orders for LCA' in *The Hindu*, 10 July.

Shivkumar, M. T. 2001. 'Compassion Unlimited' in *Deccan Herald*, 5 January.

Singhal, Arvind and Everett M. Rogers. 1989. *India's Information Revolution*. New Delhi: Sage.

______. 2001. *Communication Revolution in India: From Bullock Carts to Cyber Marts*. New Delhi: Sage.

Slater, Gordon. 1926. *Southern India: its Political and Economic Problems*. London: George Allen & Unwin.

Sonnet, Gerhard. 2002. *Ivory Bridges: Connection Science and Society*. Cambridge: MIT Press.

Sorenson, Olav and Toby U. Stuart. 2001. 'Syndication Networks and the Spatial Distribution of Venture Capital Investment' in *American Journal of Sociology*, vol. 106, 1547–86.

Sridharan, Easwaran. 1996. *The Political Economy of Industrial Promotion: Indian, Brazilian and South Korean Electronics in Comparative Perspectives, 1969–1994*. London: Praeger.

Srinivasan, T. N. 2002. 'India's Fiscal Situation: Is a Crisis Ahead?' in Anne O. Krueger ed. *Economic Policy Reforms and the Indian Economy*. Chicago: University of Chicago Press, 47–90.

Stokes, Donald C. 1997. *Pasteur's Quadrant*. Washington: Brookings Institute Press.

Storper, Michael. 1999. 'The Resurgence of Regional Economics: Ten Years Later' in Barnes and Gertler ed. *The New Industrial Geography*, 23–53.

Stuart, Leslie. 2001. 'The Biggest Angel of them All: The Military and the Making of Silicon Valley' in *Understanding Silicon Valley* by Kenney, 48–67.

Subbarayappa, B. 1992. *In Pursuit of Excellence: A History of the Indian Institute of Science*, New Delhi: McGraw-Hill.

Index

Subramaniam, Viswanath. 2000. 'Deliverance Unto Light' in *Deccan Herald,* December.

Sugden, Roger and James R. Wilson. 2003. 'Economic "Prosperity" and "Globalisation": an Agenda and Perspective' in Sugden et al. eds. *Urban and Regional Prosperity in a Globalised New Economy.* Cheltenham: Edward Elgar, 3–29.

Susenathan, I. 2001. 'Message of Peace' in *Deccan Herald,* 5 January.

Swaminathan, M. S. 2004. 'Connecting Rural India' in *The Hindu,* 10 July.

Teece, David. 1981. 'The Market for Know-How and the Efficient International Transfer of Technology', *ANNALS of the American Association of Political and Social Sciences,* 81–96.

Tharoor, Shashi. 2007. *The Elephant, the Tiger and the Cell Phone: Reflections on India, The Emerging 21st Century Power.* New York: Associated Press.

Thatchenkery, Tojo and Roger R. Stough. eds. 2005. *Information Communication Technology and Economic Development: Learning from the Indian Experience.* Cheltenham: Edward Elgar.

Tickner, Ann J. 1987. *Self-Reliance versus Power Politics: The American and Indian Experience in Building Nation States.* New York: Columbia University Press.

Tippoo, Sofia. 2002. 'It's a Digital World Out There' in *Times of India Educational Supplement.* 15 April.

Varshney, Asutosh. 1989. 'Ideas, Interest and Institutions in Policy Change: Transformation of India's Agricultural Strategy in the Mid-1960s' in *Policy Sciences,* vol. 22, 289–333.

Venkatesan, R. and Samuel V. Malvea. 2002. 'Bangalore: IT Cluster in India' in Chia Siow Yue and. James Jerome Lim eds. *Information Technology in Asia: New Development Paradigms.* Singapore: Institute of South East Asian Studies, 295–319.

Visvesvaraya, Sir M. 1934. *A Planned Economy for India.* Bangalore: Bangalore Press.

———. 1943. *Prosperity through Industry: Move Towards Rapid Industrialisation.* Bombay: AIMO.

———. 1951. *Memoirs of My Working Life.* New Delhi: National Book Trust.

———. *Speeches, vols I & II, 1914–1918.* Bangalore: Mysore Government Branch Press.

Wadeyar, Sri Krishnarajendra. 1940. *Speeches by Maharaja of Mysore, vol. I, 1909–1933, vol. II, 1934–1940.* Mysore: Government Branch Press.

Winters, Alan and Shahid Yusuf. eds. 2007. *Dancing with Giants: China and India in a Global Economy.* Singapore: South East Asian Institute.

Wolfe, David. 1999. 'Harnessing the Region: Changing perspectives on Innovation Policy in Ontario' in Barnes and Gertler eds. *The New Industrial Geography.*

World Bank. 2005. *India and the Knowledge Economy: Leveraging Strengths and Opportunities*, Washington, DC.

Xiang, Biao. 2007. *Global 'Body Shopping': An Indian Labor System in the Information Technology Industry*. Princeton: Princeton University Press.

Yue, Chia Siow and Jamus Jerome Lim eds. 2002. *Information Technology in Asia: New Development Paradigms*. Singapore: Institute of South East Asian Studies, 295–319.

Zaheer, Srilata and Radhika Rajan. 2003. 'Creativity Under Constraints: Technological Imprinting and the Migration of Indian Business to the New Economy' in Kogut ed. *The Global Internet Economy*, 191–222.